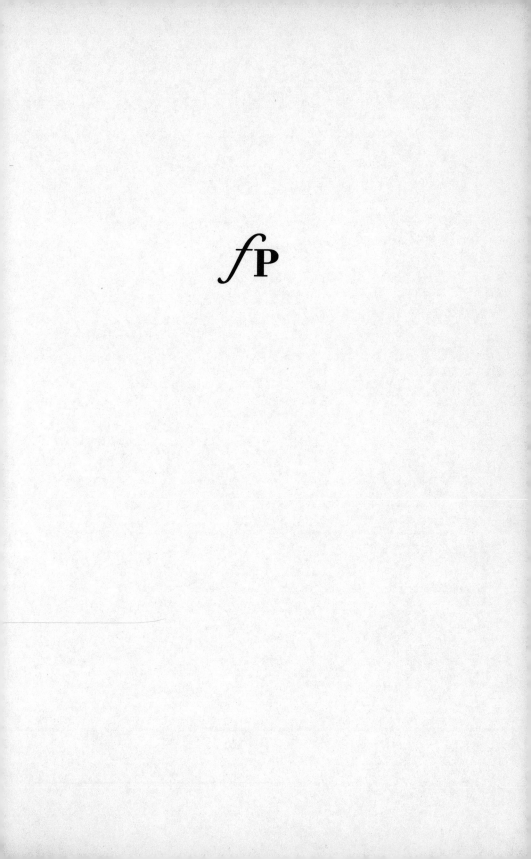

Your Intelligence Makeover

An Easy Way to Learn All You Need to Know

Edward F. Droge, Jr., Ed.D.

Free Press

NEW YORK • LONDON • TORONTO • SYDNEY

*f*P

FREE PRESS
A Division of Simon & Schuster, Inc.
1230 Avenue of the Americas
New York, NY 10020

FREE PRESS and colophon are trademarks of Simon & Schuster, Inc.

For information about special discounts for bulk purchases,
please contact Simon & Schuster Special Sales:
1-800-456-6798 or business@simonandschuster.com

DESIGNED BY PAUL DIPPOLITO

Manufactured in the United States of America

10 9 8 7 6 5 4 3 2 1

Library of Congress Cataloging-in-Publication Data

Droge, Edward F.
    Your intelligence makeover : an easy way to learn all you need
to know / Edward F. Droge, Jr.
        p.   cm.
    Includes bibliographical references.
    1. Intellect. 2. Intelligence tests. I. Title
    BF431.D8155 2005
    153.9—dc22   2005043780

ISBN-13: 978-0-7432-7062-5
ISBN-10:   0-7432-7062-2

For Mary and Abigail

Acknowledgments

While the concept of this book sprang from my endless wandering and browsing (read: getting lost) in the labyrinthine library stacks of Yale and Harvard years ago, its early form developed from more recent conversations with my agent, Marly Rusoff, truly a prescient professional. I am grateful for her enthusiasm and vision, and for her being a beacon of faith and optimism. Leslie Meredith deserves tons of credit for her remarkable editing: she used up a lot of pencils in guiding me to just the right structure and flow. Merci beaucoup. A big thank you to Martha Levin for her support and to Dominick Anfuso for his creativity. They helped me more than they know. Leslie's assistant, Kit Frick, managed all the devilish details with aplomb, and the people behind the scenes at Free Press contributed perfectly. The applause you hear is for all of them.

Many others helped with this project in one way or another. I tip my hat to the following, and ask forgiveness from those I may omit inadvertently: Ralph and Doris Adams merit special mention for their unflagging energy, encouragement, and endorsement. JoAnn and Jim, Pat and Al, and Larry and Marilyn helped with research intangibles, which often meant ad hoc site visits, long taxi runs, and late-night pep rallies. Kim and Ken, Cheryl and Mike, and Chris and Jessica cheered me on, and that was valuable.

My wife and daughter read the manuscript at various stages and contributed enormously. They added much direction and inspiration, and suffered my sequestered hours. Over and over they proved how much smarter they are than I am, and how important it is for me to continue my intelligence makeover just to keep up with them. Even Chloe, our dog, refrained from barking (most of the time) on intense writing days.

To this entire team of all-stars goes much of the credit for this book.

The love of learning, the sequestered nooks,
And all the sweet serenity of books.

— HENRY WADSWORTH LONGFELLOW

Give me where to stand, and I will move the earth.

— ARCHIMEDES

Whatever you can do, or dream you can, begin it;
Boldness has genius, power, and magic in it.

— JOHANN WOLFGANG VON GOETHE

Contents

Your Intelligence Makeover

An Easy Way to Learn . . .

Introduction

AMERICA IS IN THE MIDST of a national makeover. But there's a significant problem. We're making over virtually everything except our minds—our intellects. What sense does it make to paint your car and not put oil in the engine? Restoring your hair while ignoring your brain renders your makeover unfinished. Until we address this oversight, the national makeover cannot be complete—or successful. This book aims to help you increase your knowledge base and tap the limitless power of your intelligence.

It is clear even to the casual observer—from sources including bestselling books and popular television shows—that the country is gripped with reinventing itself. The following examples bear witness:

❖ **Home and garden makeovers** (e.g., popular HGTV shows such as *Before/After, Curb Appeal, Mission Organization, Room by Room, Design on a Dime, Feng Shui, Trading Spaces.*)

❖ **Beauty and fashion makeovers** (e.g., Oprah's makeover shows, *Queer Eye for the Straight Guy, Extreme Makeover,* hair restoration treatments, antiaging creams, skin creams, and cellulite creams.)

❖ **Body makeovers** (e.g., infomercials hawking equipment to improve abs, buns, and thighs, popular programs such as Pilates, yoga, and tai chi, weight loss programs such as the Atkins Diet, the South Beach Diet, and others, popular products such as Botox, antioxidants, and Viagra, and TV shows like *Nip/Tuck, The Swan, Renovate My Family,* and *The Biggest Loser.*)

❖ **Soul makeovers** (e.g., best-selling seminars and books that have dominated the nonfiction and fiction lists such as *The Purpose-Driven Life, The Prayer of Jabez,* and *The Left Behind* series.)

Millions of people around the country want or need to learn but simply are not able to attend to it for one reason or another. Perhaps a family, a job, and other pressures of daily life combine to make it difficult to find time, money, or energy to learn in a formal program, college or otherwise. That's why a swift, sensible, straightforward path to an Intelligence Makeover is so valuable. This book takes you by the hand and leads you every step of the way into learning about intelligence, about yourself, about "super tools" that can take you to new intellectual levels, and about the resources you need for acquiring knowledge in a wide variety of subjects.

Who might want an Intelligence Makeover and why? Let's just look at a sample list:

❖ Accomplished professionals with knowledge gaps.

❖ Busy executives and others who need a refresher.

❖ Businesspeople who seek tools that can raise the bar.

❖ Those seeking self-discovery and improvement.

❖ Those whose early education was lacking and who seek a common knowledge base.

❖ Those who wish to look at information in a new light, with a mind now advantaged by life experience and worldliness.

A solid makeover will recognize your unique nature: your background and experience, level of education, and diverse strengths, weaknesses, learning styles, and interests. Because not everyone is the same, each Makeover Plan presented in this book is designed specifically for the individual who will use it. Just as a beauty makeover aims to reinvent cosmetically, a makeover like this one aims to reinvent intellectually, generating a significant yet quick-and-easy increase in your knowledge and understanding.

You are entering a world in this book that offers change, dramatic improvement, intellectual renewal. Here you can acquire super-fast reading techniques, amazing memory power, incredibly quick math skills, and other high-level talents. You can grow intellectually, obtain steadfast confidence, and gain substantial achievement.

Welcome.

At this point it doesn't really matter who you are and why you're here. You may be a successful professional or a businessperson who wants to be more competitive. Maybe you are a student. Maybe simple curiosity brought you here, or a quest for fun. Or maybe you are just tired of feeling lost or left out of the conversations around the water cooler and want to contribute, break out of the pack, or impress your family, friends, and associates. Who hasn't wished he had paid more attention in school or felt "left out" of a high-minded conversation? Who hasn't discovered rust forming over old skills or dreamed of what it would be like to be even a bit "smarter"?

You've heard that expression, "If I only knew then what I know now." A makeover presents a perfect opportunity to look at information in a different light, engage material anew with a more mature and experienced mind. E. D. Hirsch argued in his book, *Cultural Literacy,* for the importance of possessing a solid base of common knowledge. Not being culturally literate puts you at a serious disadvantage. Whether in banter around the office or in more serious endeavors, an Intelligence Makeover may serve as a great equalizer.

This is an equal opportunity book—it does not discriminate. There are benefits galore for all who pass through here. Your educational background does not matter: Whether you have a Ph.D. or a GED, it makes no difference. Nor does it matter whether you learn quickly or slowly. You might be wealthy or poor, male or female, old or young. It does not matter.

Think of this book as a Fountain of Youth of sorts, a boost for the brain, a magnifier of the mind, an injection of information aimed at regeneration, refreshment, and reinvigoration. This book can change your life.

By the time you finish this book you will have learned—among other things—methods to double or triple your reading speed. You'll complete books and articles in a fraction of the time you now take, and you'll save precious time. In turn, that will permit you the pleasure of more books and articles, or let you take on more projects. You'll have more time for leisure, recreation, fun.

You'll improve your memory power dramatically, and people with good memory skills get noticed and admired. You'll also have the attendant, practical benefits of actually being able to remember names, dates, numbers, and long lists, never forgetting again where your keys are or where your car is parked. In fact, you'll never forget virtually anything again.

You'll perform certain math problems in your head faster than a calculator, develop your writing and speaking skills, and improve your Social Intelligence. On top of that, you'll have at your disposal a treasure chest of Foundational Knowledge in a wide array of subjects—knowledge that provides invaluable background information and closes gaps for you in more than a dozen areas, including History, Literature, Science, English, Math, Sports, Art History, Music, Psychology, Religion, and Nature. Through entertaining, informative essays and noteworthy nuggets of fact, you'll reacquaint yourself with a particular area or introduce yourself to a new subject that has eluded you in the past.

Think of it as a "flash immersion," if you will. Let's say you target Art History. You'll learn about Leonardo da Vinci, Michelangelo, Raphael, and others. The information here will prepare you to strike out on your own. Using the resource guide at the back of that chapter, you'll bring yourself to a new level. You'll learn about the roots of the Renaissance and the place it holds in the history of art. Before long, you'll have firm footing and find that you can be quite conversant in the subject. Not only will you hold your own, but your opinion will be viewed with new respect.

We never take full advantage of the power of our brains. Wouldn't it be nice to be just a little bit smarter, to know more, especially in the subjects that appeal to you, the ones that have escaped you in the past? Wouldn't it be nice also to read faster and remember more? In fact, these are relatively simple functions. Normal brains can do them. The only reason that Joe and Jane Average do not read faster and remember more is that they have not been taught how. They have not been coached to do so. Normal standards of training in the United States and the world fall far short of teaching students to read fast. Heaven knows, this country has trouble teaching students how to read at all. And memory training is foreign to American schools, aside from a sporadic lesson or two anecdotally from an occasional teacher.

The kind of makeover you'll undergo in this book will give you a new persona. It will transform your day-to-day life. You'll wake up in the morning with new energy, new commitment, new joy. You'll have spring in your step, confidence and authority in your voice.

The world will seem a friendlier place. And it will all happen in the space of these pages. You'll make yourself over in a relatively brief period of time.

Let's get you a map of this new world of yours.

In the opening section, you'll learn some exciting theories about intelligence that will help you understand how your mind works. Many of these theories sit under the umbrella-heading of "Social Intelligence." In the following section, you will learn how to use "Super Tools" that help you acquire knowledge—tools such as speed reading, effective memory techniques, and successful writing and speaking methods. With these tools, you will then follow a makeover plan, created especially for you, catering to your unique strengths, weaknesses, learning styles, idiosyncrasies, likes, and dislikes. With that plan in hand, you will pick and choose subjects to explore.

Besides the map of where you're going, you'll also need a guide, and I've been over the terrain you're plunging into many times. I know you can do this because I've done it myself.

The grandson of immigrants, the son of hardworking, blue-collar parents who had to sacrifice their education to provide for their family, I trudged through school—like so many millions of others—with low aspirations and expectations, and, not surprisingly, with little resultant achievement. No one in my clan had ever earned a college degree. Today, I am pleased to be able to say that eventually I came to realize the importance of intellectual maintenance and achievement. I earned a bachelor's degree in English from Yale and both a master's and doctorate in Education from Harvard, and I have enjoyed a 25-year career in Education.

I was nearly 30 years old when I began my intellectual journey. I enrolled in college more than ten years after high school. I had been a police officer in New York City before that, working to support my family. Married when I was 18, I was the father of three children by the time I was 21. I found little time for intellectual pursuits.

In my earlier school days in Brooklyn, I played hooky regularly, preferring to visit amusement parks like Coney Island and racetracks like Aqueduct than to attend classes and do homework. I read the racing newspapers, but steered clear of school books. In fact, I didn't read a book from cover to cover until I was 14, and that was a baseball book. I had no idea what a classic was. I enjoyed working with numbers associated with racing, but treated school math as though it were a contagious disease.

In this book I delve into the pool of knowledge and experience I acquired at Harvard, Yale, and the NYPD, and during more than two decades in Education; distill it; and provide all that you need to get an intellectual boost in a relatively brief period of time—to start, or to restart, an intellectual journey, to reinvent your "self." My experience can help you in your journey. At Yale, for example, I devised methods to improve my reading and memory skills dramatically, tools to help me to acquire knowledge, to help me to sharpen my intelligence. I quadrupled my reading speed and learned how to memorize dates, names, and long lists, which helped me to earn my undergraduate degree *cum laude,* and to earn nothing but A's in my doctoral work. I share these methods with you in this book.

Here are a couple of recommendations for you before you dive into the first chapter.

Keep a Notebook or Two

You will want to have a notebook devoted exclusively to your makeover to keep track of a few items. In it you will record your progress, thoughts, quiz answers, and exercise responses. This notebook will serve as an important resource for you. Use a computer file, if you wish, but devote it exclusively to the makeover, and be sure to keep your laptop handy.

Pay Attention to Your Environment

Without question, our environment influences us. The people around us and the resources at our disposal can have a conspicuous impact. Studies have shown, for example, that reading aloud to children helps them to become better readers. Conversely, children who do not have others reading aloud to them generally find it more difficult to learn how to read. Neuroscientific findings indicate that various intellectual capacities are influenced by neural connections in the brain, and that those neural connections are formed in response to the environment.

If you are intent on an Intelligence Makeover, tend to your environment. Surround yourself with people and resources that can help you.

Be Aware of Your Surroundings—Don't Miss the Obvious

To take advantage of your environment, you need to be aware of it. Sometimes it's all too easy to miss the obvious.

Let's say that you and a friend go camping in the woods. At the end of a long day of hiking, you both enter the tent and go to sleep. In the middle of the night your friend wakes you and asks you to look up and report what you see. You say you see tens of thousands of stars in a pitch-black sky. A breathtaking sight. But your friend rightfully calls you a knucklehead because you missed the obvious: If you can see the sky, the tent is gone.

You and your friend are trying to figure out what happened to the tent when you hear noises coming from the nearby bushes. Behind the bushes you discover a huge bear. The bear sees you, and you and your friend start running, but your friend stops to put on sneakers. You say, "You're nuts. You can't outrun a bear."

"I don't have to outrun the bear," says your friend, reminding you of the obvious. "I only have to outrun you."

Avoid a Negative Environment

A negative environment retards progress or achievement. It could be a person who always takes a pessimistic view and who tries to persuade you to see life in the same way. "That can't possibly work. Why waste your time?" Or it could be a noisy setting that distracts you from your study, a radio in the background, or a television set, or a jack hammer from the construction crew outside your window. Maybe you live near a train track or an airport. Maybe you live downwind from a paper mill or a sewer plant that every once in a while fills the air with a foul odor that assaults your senses.

You want to avoid or change any environment that distracts you from achieving your goals. This does not mean that you have to pack up all your worldly belongings and become a hermit, but you do have to be conscious of distractions, and active in avoiding them. If you have work to do, common sense dictates that you do not attempt to do it in a negative environment. Go to a different room, or to a library, or to a relative's house. Find an environment that will help you, not hinder you.

Seek a Positive Environment

A positive environment encourages you and permits you to succeed. It could be a person who always takes an optimistic view and who tries to persuade you to see life in the same way. "That can work. Try it." It also could be a controlled environment that shuts out distractions: a study carrel in the library stacks, a room in your home in which you can close the doors, windows, and drapes to find peace and quiet, and get away from the noise of the city, the cacophony of the street, the radios, televisions, and telephones of family and neighbors.

A positive environment allows you to think, to advance yourself, and to accomplish the task at hand. In the end, it allows you to stimulate and develop your intellect.

Take Advantage of Resources

Do you live in a city? If so, no doubt you have a treasure trove of resources available to you. Take advantage of them. At the same time, don't let geographical limitations deter you. Maybe the best library is 40 miles away at the university. Go. Arrange your schedule to permit regular visits. Combine visits with other chores and tasks to make the experience a pleasure more than a sacrifice.

Don't ignore or discount local resources. They can be right under your nose: libraries and museums, planetariums and zoos, parks and lakes, theaters and historic sites, newspaper programs and hospital programs, high school campuses and college campuses.

Avoid the Evil Television

A study by The Children's Hospital in Seattle in 2004 found a connection between excessive television watching and the development of Attention Deficit Hyperactivity Disorder in children. Apparently the risk increases significantly for every hour watched. Though the study focused on children, it stands to reason that too much television watching can turn the mind into a vegetable, regardless of the age of the viewer. The term *couch potato* may be more accurate than we realize.

Find the Good Television

Of course, educational programming on channels like Discovery, History, PBS, or any one of dozens of others can be a part of the environment that works for you. Even "good" television, however, should be watched in moderation.

Take a Course, Workshop, or Seminar

Virtually every town has a university or high school that offers adult education courses, workshops, or seminars. Taking a program like this could be an excellent way to close gaps in your knowledge base or to stimulate and enrich your intellectual passions. Some information-rich seminars may be only an hour or so long.

You always wanted to act or sing or dance, but never quite found the time. You always wanted to study the American Revolution or the Russian Revolution or the Beatles' Revolution, but your schedule just wouldn't permit it. You always wanted to learn how to program a computer or how to repair a car engine or how to start your own business, but you could never screw up enough courage and energy to enroll.

If this sounds familiar, stop making excuses.

Book 'Em, Danno

Filling your home with books and magazines can certainly serve as an inspiring backdrop for intellectual growth. A reference library, in particular, can come in handy during your Intelligence Makeover.

The Mozart Effect

In experimenting with college students, researchers at the University of California found that aspects of intelligence were increased after listening to certain music for a determined period of time. (IQ scores improved as much as nine points.) This result has been referred to as "The Mozart Effect." For the past decade many parents have played classical music to their infants in an effort to reproduce this Mozart Effect. Though the results are inconclusive and controversial, many educators steadfastly support the practice, and several successful educationally based corporations feature a quest for the Mozart Effect in their products.

Note that the original study tested college students—adults, not children—yet somehow the application has shifted down to the little ones. If you are seeking an Intelligence Makeover, listen to Mozart's music or to that of other classical composers. If you're a Deadhead or a punk rocker, or you like rap, R&B, Latino, or Sinatra, listen to your favorites. But listen to Mozart, too. No one said you have to like it.

To a large degree you can control your surroundings. Know that an enriched environment can contribute to your intellectual growth.

Quizzes

At several junctures in the book, fun and useful quizzes will help you to see where you stand in subjects covered in depth in later chapters. The quizzes will assist you in determining the extent to which you want to explore those subjects. There are 10 quizzes all together. Be sure to take all of them. The results are private, for your eyes only, and you will review them as you fashion your individualized Makeover Plan. Each question in the quiz corresponds to a particular subject, so you will easily see how you fare in more than a dozen areas. For example, all the questions # 1 concern American History, and all the questions # 6 concern Science, and all the questions # 8 concern Sports. You will want to score each quiz, indicating next to each question whether your response was correct or incorrect, and keep track of your results in the notebook as you go. After the last quiz, you will tally the totals. The answers to all the quizzes are at the back of the book.

IMPORTANT: Designate a specific space in your notebook for your quiz answers—perhaps at the very back. As each quiz is brief, you won't need more than a page or two to accommodate the complete set of 10 quizzes. You will want to have all your responses together for easy reference later.

Before we go any further, here is the first quiz. Have fun with it. If you know some or all of the answers—great! If you know few or none of the answers—no problem.

It's best to write your answers in your notebook, but in case you don't have it handy, record them in the space provided and transfer them to the notebook later. Be sure to score it right away, and indicate which of your answers, if any, were incorrect.

It's all multiple choice for your convenience. Choose the best answers.

1. Where do these words appear? "We hold these Truths to be self-evident, that all Men are created equal . . ."
   a. The U.S. Constitution
   b. The Declaration of Independence
   c. The Ten Commandments
   d. The Articles of Confederation

2. The Ides of March was a bad day for:
   a. Bonnie and Clyde
   b. Abraham Lincoln
   c. Julius Caesar
   d. Napoleon

3. How often does a committee meet that gets together biannually?
   a. once a year
   b. twice a year
   c. three times a year
   d. not a, b, or c

4. Hester Prynne was the creation of which author?
   a. Alistair Cook
   b. Charles Dickens
   c. Stephen Crane
   d. Nathaniel Hawthorne

5. Half of the area of a square with one side of 6 is:
   a. 12
   b. 18
   c. 3
   d. 36

6. "An object at rest tends to stay at rest . . ." describes:
   a. inertia
   b. osmosis
   c. photosynthesis
   d. natural selection

7. Many ballets, including *The Fire Bird,* were composed by:
   a. Mozart
   b. Bach

   c. Stravinsky

   d. Verdi

8. Which coach shares the record for winning the most NBA Championships?
   a. Pat Riley
   b. Vince Lombardi
   c. Phil Jackson
   d. Casey Stengel

9. Trees that lose their leaves are:
   a. deciduous
   b. pine barren
   c. evergreen
   d. fescue

10. Who created *La Joconde*?
    a. Charles De Gaulle
    b. Leonardo da Vinci
    c. The Boeing Aircraft Company
    d. Gustave Eiffel

11. Who is known for theories concerning stages of intellectual development, like the "concrete operational stage"?
    a. Piaget
    b. Freud
    c. Jung
    d. Skinner

12. Of the following, which religion has the largest membership:
    a. Shinto
    b. Sikhism
    c. Buddhism
    d. Judaism

13. "All the world's a stage, And all the men and women merely players" appeared in:
    a. *42nd Street*
    b. *As You Like It*
    c. *Canterbury Tales*
    d. not a, b, or c

YOUR ANSWERS

1. _____

2. _____

3. _____

4. _____

5. _____

6. _____

7. _____

8. _____

9. _____

10. _____

11. _____

12. _____

13. _____

The answers are at the end of the book. Record your results in your notebook.

PART I

UNDERSTANDING INTELLIGENCE

In the past, intelligence and IQ were virtually synonymous. Asking someone "What's your IQ?" was the equivalent of asking "How smart are you?" The term *IQ* stands for Intelligence Quotient, the measured results of a standardized test that focuses on language ability, logical/mathematical prowess, and other capacities, and that takes into account the mental and chronological age of the test taker.

Today, however, many prominent intelligence theorists look beyond IQ to define intelligence. Theorists like Harvard's Howard Gardner, Yale's Robert J. Sternberg, and noted psychologist Daniel Goleman recognize that other abilities have as much validity as language and logical/mathematical capacities. They acknowledge that a person's intelligence may very well have its roots in language and logical/mathematical abilities, but that other capacities warrant consideration as well, such as musical abilities, athletic abilities, and social abilities. They maintain, for example, that Social Intelligence is as valid as any other kind of intelligence. Social Intelligence encompasses a wide range of critically important, frequently underestimated abilities that revolve around how well you know yourself and how well you relate to others.

Today, intelligence cannot be defined simply. The parameters are broader, more inclusive than ever. Even if you are not all that proficient in language or math, you may very well possess a great intelligence, like Social Intelligence. In a complete Intelligence Makeover, therefore, you'll want to understand your own mind better and relate to others more effectively. This will lead you to success.

1. Multiple Intelligences

WHAT DO THE FOLLOWING DESCRIPTIONS have in common?

1. The Completion

The digital clock on the end zone scoreboard counts down the ticks: 8 . . . 7 . . . 6 . . . The quarterback stands over his lineman, surveying the defensive alignment. The opposing players jump around in front of him, switching positions to confuse him, shouting at him in vicious, hard-edged language. The clock counts down: 5 . . . 4 . . . 3 . . . 2 . . .

With the calm of a casual stroller on a Sunday afternoon in the park, the quarterback bends and taps his lineman. The ball snaps up into his hands and both teams lunge toward each other, violently crashing helmet to helmet, slamming all the weight of their armor-clad, tree-trunk bodies into their opponents. The referee's gun pops at the end of the field—time has expired and the game will end at the completion of this play.

The quarterback smoothly drops back from the line of men. His eyes scan the field before him, searching, discerning movements, determining the paths of players, both friend and foe, anticipating changes of direction, all the while keeping a monitoring eye on the charging linemen before him. He knows that this is the last play of the game. His mind whirs: Who is open? Who will be open? His arm rises to his shoulder as his eyes fix on one particular receiver downfield. Swiftly and softly he pulls the ball back behind his head and snaps it forward, releasing it into the air with a smooth and steady rotation, a missile launched at a locked-in target. But he has thrown it toward an empty space in the middle of the field.

The receiver, closely covered by a defender, sees the ball as it is launched. He fakes outside with his head, but breaks toward the middle of the field. He has fooled the defender, whose momentum takes him toward the sidelines. For an instant the receiver is free. From the corner of his eye, however, he can see another defender bearing down on him. The receiver knows that a violent collision is inevitable, but his eyes zero in on the ball, spiraling evenly in an arc toward the space between him and the oncoming defender. He shifts his running angle a bit, striding downfield just slightly more than he had been. The defender adjusts his angle as well. The space between them is closing fast. The collision is a mere second or two away. Abruptly the receiver stretches his arms out in front of him and thrusts his body forward into the empty space. Never taking his eyes from the ball, he lets his fingers grow calculatingly limp, softening his hands to make the reception. Ball and hands meet and the catch is made. Instantly the defender hurtles full-force into his prey. The receiver absorbs the collision, holds on to the ball, and falls forward into the end zone. Completion. Touchdown.

2. The Performance

A handsome grand piano sits alone in the middle of a stage, its polished ebony reflecting the ceiling lights. A woman in a flowing black gown enters from the left and strides toward the piano as the audience welcomes her with enthusiastic applause. She sits and the applause fades and dies. She rests calmly before the keys, gathering herself. There is no sign of nerves or butterflies.

She raises her hands to barely an inch above the black and white ivories, drops them abruptly, and begins to play. Her fingers work slowly at first, then faster as the piece demands, up and down, in and out, hand crossing hand, from one end of the console to the other. She doesn't use sheet music. This piece is planted in the neurons of her brain. She performs what she has composed. The audience does not stir. Magnificent, this music.

And when it ends, she draws her hands into her lap. A thunderous applause ensues.

You may want to take a minute or two to think about the events described above. What is happening in each? How are they similar? What words would you use to describe them? Take some time to review and contemplate. We will return to them in a moment.

One school of thought holds that your level of intelligence is pretty much determined at birth, developed through childhood, and difficult to change as you grow older. Accordingly, IQ tests and other psychometric devices geared to this thinking can determine how "smart" you are.

In the early part of the 20th century, Charles Spearman, one of the first to view intelligence as a single construct, suggested that people have a "general" intelligence, a general mental ability that determines performance. Spearman argued that a person's entire range of abilities is connected, and that an individual's capacity to perform successfully on some tasks indicates a likelihood of being able to perform successfully on others as well. In the 1980s a different way of thinking about intelligence began to take hold, championed by Harvard professor Howard Gardner. This view suggested that there were several different types of intelligence, including but not limited to linguistic and logical/mathematical abilities. Acceptance of this Multiple Intelligences view has grown with each passing decade.

It is important to note that an Intelligence Makeover is as harmonious with a single construct view as it is with a multiple intelligences view. You can achieve an effective makeover—beauty, home, body, or intelligence—simply by highlighting strengths and deemphasizing weaknesses, by taking advantage of the talents and attributes you already have. An increase in knowledge, a shift in behavior, or an emphasis of strengths can help produce a new you, in much the same way that a chic hairstyle, a revamped wardrobe, or innovative applications of makeup creams, powders, liners, gloss, or shadow can produce a new you, without resorting to plastic surgery or other dramatic measures.

According to the theory of multiple intelligences, you already may be smarter than you think. In fact, you may possess intelligence that you never knew you had. You may be entitled to a sense of pride and esteem that has escaped you in the past. Once you know that you have a certain intelligence, you can focus on it, develop it, and use it to your advantage.

The theory challenges the notion that intelligence is static and cannot be improved. According to Gardner, some intelligences simply cannot be measured by psychometric instruments. The gauges for these intelligences may be their value in a cultural context and their ability to solve problems or to create products. Gardner contends that there are at least eight identifiable intelligences: linguistic, logical/mathematical, musical, spatial, bodily kinesthetic, naturalist, intrapersonal, and interpersonal. And there may be even more, as yet undiscovered or unproven.

As you read through the kinds of intelligence, review for yourself the aspects that apply most prominently to you—those that you possess, those that you need. For instance, the actions of the football players and the pianist are examples of bodily-kinesthetic, spatial, and, of course, musical intelligence. Take stock of your strengths and challenges at this point to assist you later as your makeover proceeds.

The Multiple Intelligences

The first two kinds of intelligences are the most familiar: linguistic and logical/mathematical. The others, however, are no less important.

Linguistic Intelligence involves language—reading it, writing it, speaking it, and more. Broadly, it is an ability with words—meanings, interpretations, nuances, translations, syntax, diction, and spelling. Such mastery may show up as an aptitude for clear writing and speaking, an ability to read efficiently, comprehend well, convey thoughts accurately, discern the written or spoken thoughts of others, "hear" the sounds, rhythms, and patterns of words, sense the shades of differences between words, choose the "right" words for the appropriate circumstances, and an ability to use words to describe, to persuade, to explain.

Especially prized in schools and other academic arenas, linguistic intelligence is a gateway to learning, and is beneficial in every arena. The corporate environment, for example, values good speakers and writers, and many of the most effective business leaders possess these skills. Good reading is important in research and development and in medicine, where doctors must read to stay current in their discipline. Technical writers who can translate complex scientific data or computer operations into comprehendible language for the user are worth their weight in gold.

Logical/Mathematical Intelligence involves abilities with numbers and logic. A vast array of operations springs from these abilities, such as observing objects, counting, ordering, calculating, measuring, recognizing and solving problems, formulating rules, understanding and managing abstraction, identifying patterns, working with concepts and relationships of facts, processing chains of reasoning, practicing science, and more.

As with linguistic intelligence, logical/mathematical intelligence is especially prized in the academic world as well as in the corporate world (e.g., banking or accounting), police work (e.g., investigations), science (e.g., research), and computers (e.g., programming).

Musical Intelligence involves an ability to perceive, create, or produce music. It can include capacities that touch upon the following areas: reading music, playing music, composing music, interpreting music, appreciating music, facility with rhythm, tone, pitch, melody, harmony, performance, expression, and more. As with any other intelligence, levels and combinations of characteristics may vary from individual to individual.

Spatial Intelligence is an ability to create spatial images in your mind and use them effectively. The space may be wide or confined, concrete or metaphoric. An astrophysicist plans and calculates successfully in the wide open "outer space" of the universe; the chess master "sees" the space before him and "foresees" variations of that same space in the near future, depending on the moves of his opponent; the choreographer envisions the movements of dancers through a designated space; the school principal sets the calendar for the upcoming academic year; the corporate executive plans sales over a certain time period; the architect considers form and function as she lays out space in a blueprint. Spatial intelligence can also be demonstrated by a composer "hearing" and mapping in her head the notes of a piece she is creating, using two or more intelligences, spatial and musical. A novelist, on the other hand, may combine spatial and linguistic. While all of the described intelligences stand alone, they very well may complement and overlap other intelligences.

Bodily-Kinesthetic Intelligence is the ability to use the body to solve problems or to produce products, as demonstrated by dancers, surgeons, athletes, artists, and others who depend on their bodies to perform or operate. A piano virtuoso uses musical, spatial, and bodily-kinesthetic intelligence; athletes, spatial and bodily-kinesthetic. A recent, record-setting winner on TV's game show *Jeopardy* exhibited not only an impressive knowledge base in defeating more than 100 opponents over the course of many months, but also a sharp bodily-kinesthetic intelligence in consistently being able to "buzz in" with an answer faster than the other contestants.

Naturalist Intelligence is the ability to discriminate in the natural world. Examples include knowing one plant or tree or leaf from another, one mammal, bird, or insect from another, one landscape from another, one cloud formation from another, one sea coast from another. This intelligence serves, among others, environmentalists, park rangers, hikers, gardeners, anthropologists, and, of course, naturalists.

The parameters of the natural world are not limited to jungles, deserts, mountains, or oceans, but reach to the day-to-day lives and locations of the average person. Being able to discriminate or to detect patterns extends even to your life as a consumer, helping you to distinguish one brand from another, one type from another, one function from another.

Personal Intelligences

The remaining two intelligences—intrapersonal and interpersonal intelligence—are concerned with how well we understand and manage ourselves, and how well we understand the dynamics and consequences of our relations with others. These two capacities fall under the umbrella of "Personal Intelligence," or "Social Intelligence."

Before we look at Social Intelligence, however, let's take another quick and fun quiz. When you're finished, be sure to turn to the back of the book to find the answers, and match them to your responses right away. It's important to indicate in your notebook which questions, if any, you did not answer correctly, and to keep the responses for all the quizzes together for easy reference later.

QUIZ #2

1. The U.S. Supreme Court case of 1896, *Plessy v. Ferguson,* held that which kind of laws were constitutional?

2. Which culture is credited with inventing the earliest forms of writing?

3. True or false: there is nothing grammatically wrong with the following sentence. If false, what's wrong? "Since the company made so much money last year, it is donating a portion of it's profits to charity."

4. What was Mark Twain's real name?

5. What is the formula to find the area of a triangle?

6. Whose theory is associated with "survival of the fittest"?

7. Who composed *Für Elise*?

8. What is the second jewel in thoroughbred horse racing's Triple Crown?

9. True or false: "Annuals" are plants that, once rooted, live for about a year, die, then come back, year after year.

10. Which Renaissance painter gave us *The Birth of Venus* and *The Annunciation?*

11. What is Freud's term for an innate, pleasure-driven motivation?

12. With about 2 billion members, this is generally considered the world's largest religion.

13. Confucius said: "Do not use a cannon to kill———."

YOUR ANSWERS

1. _____

2. _____

3. _____

4. _____

5. _____

6. _____

7. _____

8. _____

9. _____

10. _____

11. _____

12. _____

13. _____

Social Intelligence

Our ability to acquire and to apply knowledge can be aided significantly by understanding our own makeup, the inner qualities—both good and bad—that make us who we are and influence our interactions with others. Social Intelligence permits us to know and manage ourselves and to know others well enough to interact successfully with them. The better we know ourselves, the better we can develop, interact, and achieve success, by using our strengths and improving our weaknesses.

It is important not to underestimate the significance of Social Intelligence. In a service-oriented business, for example, dealing successfully with others is of the utmost importance. Some people do it better than others. The corporate world—indeed the entire world—values an ability to manage yourself and to form effective relationships. Sternberg talks about the advantages of "Successful Intelligence"; Goleman talks about the benefits of "Emotional Intelligence"; Gardner talks about the gains to be derived from using "*Intra*personal Intelligence and *Inter*personal Intelligence."

Intrapersonal Intelligence is the ability to know yourself and to use that knowledge productively. It includes the capacity to recognize and understand feelings and idiosyncrasies, strengths and weaknesses, likes and dislikes, needs and desires—virtually every cog in the wheel that makes you tick. Intrapersonal intelligence, for example, would inform you of what makes you laugh and what makes you cry, what makes you motivated and what makes you procrastinate, what makes you afraid and what makes you secure.

An attendant ability permits you to manage, develop, and use the identified information. How, for example, can we use our abilities to reach our goals? How can we improve? How can we make ourselves more productive? How can we use what we know about ourselves to help us in dealing with others?

Interpersonal Intelligence is the ability to know others and to use that knowledge to relate to them productively. It includes the capacity to recognize the feelings and motivations of others, their strengths and weaknesses, likes and dislikes, needs and desires and idiosyncrasies. What you aim to know about yourself, you similarly aim to know about others. Interpersonal intelligence informs you of what makes people laugh and what makes them cry, what makes them motivated and what makes them procrastinate, what makes them afraid and what makes them secure.

It's the ability to act on the information, too: how can you use your knowledge to help others? How can you improve your relationship with them? How can you benefit from your knowledge? How can your relations with others help you in knowing yourself better?

Individuals with interpersonal intelligence can lead, organize, mediate, connect personally, and analyze social situations. In sales, for example, knowing the needs of the customers is a primary requirement. Knowing the apprehension that prevents potential customers from buying can mean the difference between profit and loss, between making the sale and not making the sale. Knowing when customers are satisfied and when they are not is significant. Why are they unhappy? How can I make them satisfied?

Since most career paths involve interaction with others, interpersonal intelligence is vital.

Successful Intelligence concerns itself with the collective abilities that permit you to gain success in life, with you, yourself, defining "success." Yale's Sternberg cites the importance of abilities that are "Analytic," "Creative," and "Practical."

In brief, an "analytic" ability permits you to analyze concepts and solve problems; a "creative" ability permits you to produce innovative ideas; and a "practical" ability permits you to use the analysis and ideas while matching up most advantageously with the environment. A person with Successful Intelligence is able to evaluate a situation, create fresh ideas and goals to improve it, and implement those ideas and goals, all the while remaining aware of the environment and fitting into it well.

Sternberg sees the results of IQ tests and SATs as measurements of "inert" intelligence—that is, intelligence that does not move you toward taking action or reaching goals. While IQ tests and SATs may predict success in school, Sternberg prefers to look for those qualities that will lead to success in life. Consequently, high scores on IQ tests and SATs are not as important as knowing your strengths and weaknesses—using your strengths, taking advantage of them, and shoring up your weaknesses, turning them around. You need not be "book smart" to evince Successful Intelligence. You need only take advantage of your talents to achieve success.

Sternberg sees four primary obstacles to realizing and developing Successful Intelligence: low expectations from others, low self-expectations, a lack of role models, and a limited environment.

Emotional Intelligence

Like Sternberg and Gardner, noted psychologist Daniel Goleman also thinks that there is more to success than high IQ. His notion of "Emotional Intelligence," a theory originally developed by Peter Salovey of Yale and John Mayer of the University of New Hampshire, favors a capacity for self-knowledge, self-management, and social achievement. To Goleman, we have two kinds of minds, a mind that thinks and a mind that feels, and the feeling mind, or emotional mind, evolved first. Attached to the emotional center of the brain is the alarm system, which warns of threats to survival, and which was especially necessary in our prehistoric days, when we had to figure out upon seeing an animal: do *I* eat *it*, or does *it* eat *me*? In our brain's evolution, then, thoughts came after feelings.

In our lives, emotions often overwhelm our thoughts. Sometimes we respond emotionally before our thinking mind has a chance to determine whether it is a wise response or not. Even individuals with the highest IQ or SAT scores have the potential for road rage, which shows us that academic intelligence has minimal connection to emotional occurrences.

In World War I, before he became a renowned statesman, Winston Churchill was a volunteer stationed in France. On the front lines one day he received a message that a certain general wanted to speak with him. In the rain, Churchill walked to a designated meeting place several miles away. He waited and waited until finally a car drove up. A member of the general's staff apologized and said that the timing would no longer permit the general to meet with Churchill.

In the rain, frustrated and angry, Churchill walked back to his post. His mind held nothing but ill thoughts and contempt for the general. But when he discovered that the very location where he had been dug in had been bombed while he was gone, and that the man who had shared the space with him had been killed, he reported that almost immediately his feeling toward the general began to change. While he had been contemptuous of him earlier, now he saw the good spirit that the general had exhibited in sending for him.

Churchill's experience demonstrates the complex interconnection of thoughts and feelings, and how emotions can shift as thoughts and circumstances shift. The physical incident—going from the trenches to the meeting place and back—did not change; only the thoughts surrounding the incident changed, and as the thoughts changed, so too did the emotions.

Emotional Intelligence involves several abilities, not the least of which include capacities for self-motivation, impulse management, persistence, drive, empathy, and sensing and understanding our own feelings and the feelings of others. These concerns differ markedly from those embraced by IQ tests and SAT exams, yet they can prove meaningful in indicating life success.

Goleman breaks down Emotional Intelligence into five primary parts: self-awareness, managing emotions, motivation, empathy, and social skills. Regarding self-awareness, Ralph Waldo Emerson once said that "The primary wisdom is intuition." It is important to know what emotions we are feeling because feelings can be the basis for making sound decisions. It is as valid to listen to "gut" feelings or intuitions as it is to listen to our rational thoughts. Intuition offers valuable information. For example, serious decisions in our life may be aided by gut feelings or intuition, decisions like: "Should I get married?"; "Should I change jobs?"; "Should I purchase this particular house?"; or "Should we try to have another child now?" The emotional center of the brain weighs the question and offers us a gut feeling. (In fact, there actually is a physiological connection from the brain to the intestines.)

Individuals with Emotional Intelligence can control their emotions. The ancient wisdom of Aesop in "The Town Mouse and the Country Mouse" tells us that "A crust eaten in peace is better than a banquet attended by anxiety." Healthy emotions can move us toward our goals, motivate us. In fact, the word *emotion* derives from the Latin "to move." Motivation may be nurtured by optimism and hope. When optimists fail, they believe that the cause can be changed and the outcome improved. When pessimists fail, they believe that they are helpless to change the outcome. Those without hope set lower standards and goals, and lack the motivation for high achievement.

When we are empathetic we also show signs of Emotional Intelligence. Empathy helps us to get along with others—to know how they feel, to identify with their plight, to understand their motives. When we empathize we show that we care about them. We want to help them, if we can. Often we know how someone feels without the person actually telling us. Perhaps it is the expressions the person makes, or the gestures, the tone of voice, the body language. Our sensitivity to others, our capacity to pick up on the cues they exhibit, enables us to know how they feel. Empathy is important in dating, parenting, and marital relations, to name just a few interactions.

There seems to be no connection between empathy and IQ. Empathy is based in the emotional center of the brain, not the thinking center. To illustrate this point, Goleman notes that a serial killer in Santa Cruz, California, had an incredibly high IQ of 160, yet obviously did not care about others.

Good social skills also demonstrate Emotional Intelligence. Social skills involve abilities to manage relationships and the emotions of others. Every time we interact, we have the potential to make others feel better—or worse—than they did when the interaction started, depending on what we do and how we do it. Emotionally intelligent people understand that emotions can be contagious. Haven't you ever "caught" a mood from someone else? Or perhaps you have spread your own emotions to others. Who hasn't been in a situation where a spark of laughter lightens the mood of a whole room? Socially skilled people make others feel good, and who doesn't want to be in the presence of those who make them feel good?

Now that you know more about your own multiple intelligences, the next chapter will help you take a look at your intellectual dreams and goals.

But first, another useful quiz. Put the answers in the quiz section of your notebook, and indicate whether you answered each question correctly or incorrectly.

QUIZ #3

1. Which U.S. Supreme Court case of 1954 declared that segregating blacks was a violation of the 14th Amendment?

2. Son of Philip II of Macedon, he was the prominent empire builder in the fourth century B.C.

3. If anything is incorrect in the following sentence, correct it: While picnicking, I wrote on the stationary.

4. "The Road Not Taken" is a poem written by whom?

5. The sum of the angles of a triangle always equals how many degrees?

6. Fill in the blanks: ——refined——geocentric theory.
   a. Ptolemy, Aristotle's
   b. Aristotle, Ptolemy's
   c. Galileo, Newton's
   d. not a, b, or c

7. This composer wrote *Eroica* and *Moonlight Sonata*. (Sonata No. 14).

8. Which professional basketball star holds the single-season record of averaging over 50 points per game?

9. True or false: A tuber is a fat, underground stem.

10. Who painted the ceiling of the Sistine Chapel?

11. What psychological term describes the use of a socially acceptable form of expression for urges that may be socially unacceptable.

12. Of the following, which is largest?
   a. Islam
   b. Buddhism
   c. Judaism
   d. Jainism

13. Complete: "What does it profit a man if he gains the whole world but loses his——?"

YOUR ANSWERS

1. _____

2. _____

3. _____

4. _____

5. _____

6. _____

7. _____

8. _____

9. _____

10. _____

11. _____

12. _____

13. _____

2. Intellectual Dreams

IN THE FILM GOOD WILL HUNTING, Matt Damon's character, Will, harbors an intellectual dream, but living in his rough-and-tumble, blue-collar Boston neighborhood, he spends his days and nights hanging around in bars, shooting pool, and picking up girls, wasting his incredible mental talents. A genius in math, he knows it, but hides it from his friends. Will wrestles with pursuing his dreams and ultimately realizes how and why to do it.

This chapter will help you define your intellectual dreams.

Self-awareness is a key aspect of Social Intelligence, and so the better we know our intellectual dreams, the smarter we can become in managing ourselves and relating to others.

Of course, it's easy to think that you know yourself. But do you really? Can you answer every important question about yourself without hesitation? Have you actively explored your feelings recently?

My own intellectual dream included a college degree and a career in Education. Along the way, that meant reading and analyzing hundreds of books, writing and rewriting hundreds of papers. It meant turning myself into a thinking person, which was not easy given my background—though it was do-able.

What are your intellectual dreams? Are there books you want to read, disciplines you wish to study, degrees you wish to pursue? Are there relationships you can improve by enriching your intellect? Is there a particular career for which you want to study? Do you want to change jobs in the future and need to prepare for a switch?

Limiting Dreams

I have a friend who talks to his three children regularly about his job at a large retail store. He tells his children that one day they may be able to work at the same store. All seem satisfied with that prospect.

Another friend also talks to his children about his job. He, too, works at a large retail store, but tells his children that one day they may be able to own the store. He has said to me that the reason he takes this approach is that if they fall short, they could still be employees. If they do not fall short, they have achieved at a higher level and receive greater rewards.

As long as you are dreaming, set your sights high. Even if you fall short, you end up better off than if your sights were lower. Limiting dreams is an easy trap to fall into. Instincts or friends may tell you to keep your dreams easy. Overcome that urge or advice.

A Turning Point

As a police officer I worked around the clock in shifts, one week 8 A.M. to 4 P.M., the next week midnight to 8, and the next, 4 to midnight. At one time or another I served in every corner of New York City, from patrolling the streets of Brooklyn's Bedford Stuyvesant in uniform, to working on special details and task forces in each of the boroughs, to cruising midtown Manhattan in plainclothes, locking up drug dealers, pimps, and prostitutes.

When NYPD sent me to detective school, I was very eager to learn. The logistics of the job, however—the shifts, the demands on time, energy, emotion—coupled with the demands of raising a family, presented an insuperable challenge for me. I could have used a book like *Your Intelligence Makeover* back then to help satisfy my growing thirst for knowledge. Some other cops were going to classes part-time, which I tried for a short while in the city's college system, but I found it unsatisfying, unfulfilling, doing homework on the subway, studying in the waiting rooms outside of court. But, frustrations and obstacles aside, at about this time I realized I had turned a corner in what I wanted out of my life.

Against stiff odds, I fulfilled my dreams. Starting late in life, I did eventually earn college degrees, and I have used my training and skills to teach others for 25 years. I am living proof that Intelligence Makeovers work. And it started with an intellectual dream.

Write It Down

Writing helps your mind structure thoughts and remember things. If you do not write down your thoughts, they may fade quickly and you'll lose any potential benefits from them. For example, it is easy to forget dreams you have in your sleep, if you do not record them as soon as you wake up.

Writing down aspirations can help you to focus on them, clarify them, keep them in sight, and work toward fulfilling them. If you transform your dreams into a tangible object, a document, something that you can hold in your hand, you can more easily adjust them, shape them into the form that works best for you, given your strengths and weaknesses, likes and dislikes, needs and wishes, inclinations and idiosyncrasies.

With this in mind, set aside some time to write out your dreams as you see them now. Use your notebook. (Of course, you can do this in a computer file if you prefer. But, as with a notebook, devote it exclusively to your makeover.) Don't worry: there is nothing final about this. You can change them as you move along. But get your notebook now and get something down in writing.

Relax and let your mind lead you to a comfortable place. Dream short term or long term. Think about a new "you," a new "self"—a self with increased confidence, direction, and inner-awareness, with increased knowledge in multiple subject areas, and with fresh, higher-level abilities to acquire new information. Dream. Keep your sights high.

It doesn't have to be long and you can use any style or approach that feels most comfortable. Something along the lines of the description of my intellectual dreams in the paragraphs above would be fine. Or some other form of your own choosing is certainly acceptable as well.

Go off to a quiet place. Close the door. Block out distractions. Turn off the telephone. No radio or television. No music. Turn out the light if possible. Let it be just you and the chair on which you are seated. Shut out the world. And write down your dreams in your notebook.

IMPORTANT: In your notebook, be sure to make a big star—with a red pen, if possible—next to any area that deserves special attention, whenever you write something that you feel ought to stand out, such as a thought that you don't want to miss when you review these notes later.

With notebook in hand, you are ready to begin. Consider the areas below.

Categories

You may want to organize your thoughts about intellectual dreams into categories, like those that connect to "career," or to "relationships," or to "self-esteem," or to just plain old "fun," and so on. One way would be to establish as many categories as you can think of that make sense, and then focus on those categories one at a time. This is just a suggestion. Use whatever approach works best for you.

Some people, particularly those who learn best with visual stimulation, benefit from actually drawing boxes or columns for the categories. Try it. In your notebook, draw a few vertical lines. At the top of each column, write the label for the category, such as "career," "relationships," "self-esteem," "fun," and so on. Draw two horizontal lines across the columns, thus dividing them into thirds. To the side of the top third write "Past," to the side of the middle third write "Present," and to the side of the bottom third write "Future."

Now start filling in the columns with intellectual dreams connected to each category. For example, in the career category you might look back at a past job—let's say "shoe salesman"—and conclude that you had no intellectual dreams then. In the top third of the career column, where it is labeled "Past," write "shoe salesman—none." In the future, however, your intellectual dreams include graduate study at the university to pursue a career in teaching science. In the bottom third of the career column, marked "Future," write "teaching science." Continue like this until you have explored all columns and sections.

As you explore your intellectual dreams and add new subcategories, the chart you draw will expand considerably. In addition, more thoughts inevitably will come to you after a while and each section will become more and more crowded.

As Martha Stewart would say, "This is a good thing." The more you write, the better the indication that you are succeeding in this portion of the self-examination. You are actively engaged in getting to know yourself better, and the more thoughts you have to that end, the better you will understand what makes you tick.

NEOTWY

As we'll explore in the memory section later, acronyms help us keep track of information such as facts or protocols. One such acronym—

NEOTWY—helps journalists remember the areas to cover when reporting a story. The letters in this seemingly silly word stand for the last letters of the questions the journalists should ask themselves: when, where, who, what, how, and why. Of course, the order may be arranged differently. Many would identify more readily with who, what, where, when, why, and how, but that would offer the acronym OTENYW, which is not as easy to pronounce or to remember.

Use NEOTWY to organize your thoughts as the targeted topic of "intellectual dreams" rolls around in your mind. Feel free to change the order as you write, but be sure to include responses to all six questions.

WHEN?

Think in terms of time. Trace your intellectual path as far back as makes sense. In focusing on a particular period, ask yourself: What, if any, intellectual dreams did I have back then, and later, and later, and now, and in the future?

Stages: In thinking about the future, it is helpful to work in stages. For example, where are you now intellectually and where do you want to be next month? And next year? What are your intellectual dreams for five years from now? How about ten years from now? How about at retirement?

WHERE?

As you think about the "where" of it all, you may discover that you can help yourself remember *when* you had certain intellectual dreams by remembering *where* you were in a given period of your life. Dreaming about *where* you will find yourself in the future may overlap with *how* you plan to fulfill a certain dream. My dream to teach at Harvard required my earning degrees first, a bachelor's from Yale, a master's and doctorate from Harvard. The *where* and the *how* overlapped.

The "where" questions may refer to the physical space or the geographic location that you will occupy at any given point. It also may refer to a life situation.

Physical Space or Geographic Location: Perhaps you will want to talk about your intellectual dreams when you were in school or in a particular job or in a particular city. For example, many people who visit the Sistine Chapel in Rome and see Michelangelo's ceiling, or the Louvre in

Paris and see da Vinci's *Mona Lisa,* come away filled with awe and inspiration, which may lead to the generation of fresh and exciting intellectual dreams. In this case, the response to the "where" cue would be Paris or Rome, the cities that ignited the spark. If you generated dreams also fixed on Peoria, Illinois, as, say, the city in the United States to settle into as you fulfilled those dreams, then you would include Peoria in your response.

Life Situation: "Where" are you in life, or what is your mental state, as in, "I don't know where my head is"? Significant events, struggles, or social conditions, such as adolescence, addiction, or developing relationships may exert strong influences on an intellectual dream. In my adolescence, I suppressed intellectual dreams.

WHO?

"Who" is around you at a given time in your life? Your parents may have influenced your intellectual dreams in the past, for example. A teacher might have been the catalyst for other dreams. Or a classic painter of the Renaissance may be moving you to dream intellectually in some way today—perhaps in taking a course of study in painting or art history at the local university. Or maybe you have an opportunity to spend next summer (the "when") on Cape Cod (the "where") in a mentor relation with an author (the "who") or in an apprentice relation with an ironworks craftsman, or in a recording relation with a rock band (the real Who?).

In my intellectual dream about attending Yale, I had a wife and three children and I had to be sure that I could provide for them as I earned my degree. Also involved in the Yale dream was the "who" of the people in the admissions office, who would determine whether I would be admitted. This "who" aspect overlaps with the "how" aspect. You may also want to think about who will help you to fulfill the dream. For example, you may want simply to list here the names of those who will help to bankroll a particular dream—your friends, parents, bankers?—and save the details for the "how" section.

In answering the "who" question, try to get a fix on anyone who has exerted, does exert currently, or will be exerting down the road, any form or amount of influence on your intellectual dreams.

WHAT?

"What" exactly is or was your intellectual dream? In several other sub-categories you may mention the dream briefly, but here you want to expound on it. Take it apart. Examine it.

Take the dream example from your chart, where you made an entry under "career" and "future." Say you planned to study at a university to prepare for a career of teaching science. Here is where you would talk about the specifics: Which university? Which branch of science (e.g., biology, physics, etc.)? At what level do you want to teach it (e.g., K–12, college, graduate school)? What is required? And so on. All of this will help you in making the dream a reality.

HOW?

"How" do you plan to fulfill the dream? What are the means or methods you will use? What resources do you have at your disposal?

If your dream includes reading a number of books over a certain period of time—let's say a dozen books on British literature or on a variety of subjects over the next two years—then you may want to note that your goal would be to read one book every two months, on average. There is no need to get any more detailed at this point.

If preparing to teach, an obvious question that arises is: Who will pay for your education? Do you have wealthy parents or relatives who can loan you money? How about friendly bankers? Are there special programs or scholarships or awards you can draw on?

How about the timing? How will you rearrange your life in order to fulfill this dream? Are you married? Can you go off to college while your spouse stays home? What about the bills? If you are planning to attend full-time and can cover tuition, who will be generating revenue for the household?—someone has to keep the utilities on.

WHY?

Break down the reasoning behind your intellectual dreams. Is the pursuit connected to your career or your relationships? Is it a pursuit of scholarship, personal interest, fun? Just why do you want to stop the world, quit your job, fly to France, and take mime lessons? Remember, you don't have to convince anyone except yourself here. In reverse of the old military slogan, in this section, "Ours is not to do and die. Ours is but to reason why."

Let's say you plan to take a course in Shakespeare. Why? Have you heard that the class is a hot locale for finding other singles? Maybe it is simply a personal thrill you seek—you like to read plays that have a lot of action. Do you plan on auditioning for *Jeopardy*? Do you seek to give yourself a leg up on the Sunday crossword, which invariably offers endless obscure clues about The Bard. Or do you merely want to fill a gap in your knowledge base that has its roots in your having been shut out of the British Lit 101 course in your sophomore year, which has haunted you ever since?

You will want to prioritize your intellectual dreams for the future. Which are more important? Which are more practical? Which can you more easily realize?

Now that you've explored and recorded your intellectual dreams, you can move on to the "Super Tools" section, in which you will learn to separate yourself from the pack with new or strengthened abilities in reading and memory, and in writing and speaking.

But first, it's time for another fun break. How many of the following questions can you answer correctly? Remember to record your answers in the quiz section of your notebook and to score the quiz right after you've finished, indicating clearly next to each question whether or not you got it right.

QUIZ #4

1. Federalism is a philosophy that espouses sharing powers by which two entities?

2. Which ruler issued the Edict of Milan in 313 and called for the Council of Nicaea in 325?

3. Are there any errors in the following sentence? Strawberry shortcake is my favorite desert.

4. *Leaves of Grass* was written by whom?

5. A triangle with an angle of 90 degrees is called what?

6. Hippocrates of Cos is often associated with what professional field?

7. This composer wrote *Haffner, Jupiter,* and *Requiem.*

8. Which thoroughbred horse won racing's Triple Crown in the 1980s?

9. An example of conifer is:
   a. rose
   b. potato
   c. juniper
   d. not a, b, or c

10. Who painted *The Last Supper* and *Mona Lisa*?

11. Identify: Austrian psychologist (1856–1939) known for creating psychoanalysis.

12. Sunni and Shi'ite are branches of which religion?

13. "These are the times that try men's souls." Who said it?

YOUR ANSWERS

1. _____

2. _____

3. _____

4. _____

5. _____

6. _____

7. _____

8. _____

9. _____

10. _____

11. _____

12. _____

13. _____

PART II

SUPER TOOLS: THE THREE-WEEK MASTER PLAN

The chapters in this part will provide you with the "Super Tools" of learning. In three weeks, you will master the skills necessary to double or triple your reading speed, boost your memory, and improve your writing and speaking.

You will learn how to read fast in the first week and continue to practice your reading through the next several weeks as you tackle new areas. The skills are complementary. As you move from learning how to read faster to learning how to improve your memory, you can employ some of the memory techniques as you read, thus helping your comprehension and retention.

In the second week, you will learn a host of memory techniques. And in the third week, you will focus on writing and speaking.

As you begin each chapter, note the day and devote the next full week to learning, practicing, and implementing. Big Brother will not be watching. If you devote more than a week to a chapter, no one will know and you will not self-destruct. As a rule, though, try to put an equal amount of time into each of the chapters. In other words, if you deem it better to spend 10 days with reading, that's fine. But try then to devote 10 days each to memory and writing.

3. Week One—Increasing Reading Speed

I feel the need . . . the need for speed.

—TOM CRUISE AS MAVERICK IN *TOP GUN*

What Is Your Reading Speed?

Most people do not know their reading speed. Have you ever measured yours? Do you know how many words per minute you read? Exactly how fast or slow are you?

Whatever your speed, the chances are very good that you can improve by following the simple steps outlined in this chapter.

PRESENT READING SPEED

First, let's check your reading speed in terms of a words-per-minute rate. Read the following passage at your **normal** reading speed. Do not concern yourself with how fast or slow others read or how fast or slow others think you read. This is not a contest. Do not race through the passage. The object here is to measure your normal reading speed now so that we may get an accurate measurement of your improvement later.

It is important to measure your reading time exactly. Have a pen handy. When you are ready to begin reading, check the seconds of your watch or clock and jot down the **exact** time you begin. You must note the minutes AND seconds. Using the chart provided after the passage, you will convert your reading time into a words-per-minute rate.

Ready?

RECORD THE EXACT CURRENT TIME IN THIS SPACE:

MINUTE _____ SECONDS_____ .

PLEASE READ THE PASSAGE NOW AT YOUR **NORMAL** RATE.

Huck Finn is quite perceptive and uses his perception to the utmost in order to survive in the rough and tough, Southern river country in which he lives. With very little formal education, Huck relies on his senses to carry him through an adventurous life, filled with rafts and riverboats, exaggerations and lies, river-islands and hideouts, strange towns and strange people, con games and con artists, injured men and dead bodies, friendship and slavery, storms and rattlesnakes, Tom Sawyer and The Royal Nonesuch, and more. Huck compensates for a lack of classroom training and information by accumulating an abundance of people-contact and life experience: his senses are his books, the river his classroom, the many people he meets his teachers. Without his keen senses, he would not be able to survive as admirably as he does. Twain permeates the book with instances when Huck "sees" and "hears" and "feels." Huck's senses are the means by which he gains knowledge, and he uses them often and well. He enjoys using his senses, and, when possible, he lies back to absorb all that he can see or hear. Easily enough, his perception enables him to provide detailed descriptions, to "read" the river, to tell time without a watch, to discern revealing characteristics of a footprint, to recognize acquaintances through an ugly mask of tar and feathers, and to judge a person's character or personality with amazing accuracy. Huck is always ready to employ his senses, and relies on them to keep him safe. When his senses are impaired, trouble threatens and he is apt to suffer. When one sense is useless, he switches to another: if he cannot see, he feels or listens, to guard himself from potential harm.

The reader is constantly informed of what Huck sees or does not see, what he hears or cannot hear, what he touches, what he tastes, what he smells. Threatened with being caught holding a bag of money he has taken from the king and duke, Huck shoves it into a coffin and accidentally touches the corpse's hands, which makes him creepy because they're so cold. Sitting down to dinner with Tom Sawyer and his aunt, Huck is pleasantly surprised at the meal in front of him: there was enough food, he says, to feed seven families—and he is impressed that it's all hot and that the meat is not tough, the kind that lies in the cellar for nights at a time, the kind that tastes strange in the morning. Observing the audience of a third-night performance by The Royal Nonesuch, Huck notices that every man has bulging pockets and he smells foul things, like rotten eggs and cabbage, and maybe even dead cats—sixty-four dead cats, he guesses.

Examples such as these of Huck's touching, tasting and smelling can be culled from nearly every chapter. Alone, each may seem insignificant to Huck's character, but collectively they form the core of his existence. And Huck is aware of this. More than once he lets us know the importance of his perception. For example, his perception informs him that people are influenced by the way a person is dressed; his perception enables him to judge the gravity of a situation or seriousness of a person; his perception tells him that there are many ways to view the same thing, that is, interpretations may vary according to the perspective taken. To illustrate, Huck notices the influence of a man's dress when the king changes into his store-bought clothes: Huck says he never realized how clothes could change a person: while earlier, with his old clothes, the king looked like an ornery old timer, now, with his new hat and tie and smile, he looked so different, so noticeably different, like Leviticus, he says.

As for the gravity of a situation, many times Huck is able to sense trouble simply by a person's expression. The duke and king serve as examples when Huck says of them at one point that he can see trouble in their look. And at another point when he is talking with Mary Jane he notes her expression and determines without question that she is dead serious: he notes her spreading nostrils and her snapping eyes. But Huck also knows that he must be flexible: things are not always as simple as they at first may seem. A lot depends on *how* you look, that is, on what perspective you take. For example, Huck sees watermelon being brought to the hut, but figures it is for the dogs. When Tom tells him that the watermelon is more likely for Jim, Huck agrees and thinks about it for a moment. It never occurred to him, he says, that a dog might not eat watermelon. Funny, he thinks, how a person can see something but not really see it for what it is.

That Huck's senses are keen is evinced by, among other things, his very detailed descriptions, his ability to read the river and footprints, and his ability to discern even in the most trying circumstances.

When Huck describes a person or place, the reader is given a very detailed account. Of the Grangerford home, for example, he tells us that it has brass doorknobs, a big, clean, bricked fireplace with brass dog-irons, a clock with an intricate picture painted on it, a gaudy chalk parrot on each side of the clock, a crockery dog and cat that squeaked when you pressed them but did not do anything else that made them remarkable in any way, a couple of fans made of wild turkey wings, and on and on and on. Of Colonel Grangerford himself, Huck reports that he is tall, very slim, clean-shaven, thin-lipped, with a high nose, thin nostrils, heavy eyebrows, high forehead, blackish eyes, straight black hair that hung to his shoulders, long, thin hands, and so on. The point is, of course, that not very much escapes Huck's perception of people or places, not very much at all.

CHECK YOUR CLOCK OR WATCH AND RECORD THE EXACT CURRENT TIME HERE:

MINUTE _____ SECONDS _____ .

DETERMINE THE NUMBER OF MINUTES AND SECONDS IT TOOK TO READ THE PASSAGE. (SUBTRACT START FROM FINISH.)

RECORD YOUR TOTAL READING TIME:

_____ MINUTES _____ SECONDS.

NOW CHECK THE CONVERSION CHART BELOW TO DETERMINE YOUR WORDS-PER-MINUTE RATE.

CONVERSION CHART (Find the time closest to your Total Reading Time)

MINUTES/SECONDS = WORDS-PER-MINUTE					
9min/50secs = 102;	9/40 = 103;	9/30 = 105;	9/20 = 107;	9/10 = 109;	9/00 = 111;
8/50 = 113;	8/40 = 115;	8/30 = 118;	8/20 = 120;	8/10 = 123;	8/00 = 125;
7/50 = 128;	7/40 = 130;	7/30 = 133;	7/20 = 136;	7/10 = 140;	7/00 = 143;
6/50 = 146;	6/40 = 150;	6/30 = 154;	6/20 = 158;	6/10 = 162;	6/00 = 167;
5/50 = 171;	5/40 = 176;	5/30 = 182;	5/20 = 188;	5/10 = 194;	5/00 = 200;
4/50 = 207;	4/40 = 214;	4/30 = 222;	4/20 = 231;	4/10 = 240;	4/00 = 250;
3/50 = 261;	3/40 = 273;	3/30 = 286;	3/20 = 300;	3/10 = 316;	3/00 = 333;

2/50 = 353;	2/40 = 375;	2/30 = 400;	2/20 = 429;	2/10 = 462;	2/00 = 500;
1/50 = 545;	1/40 = 600;	1/30 = 667;	1/20 = 750;	1/10 = 857;	1/00 = 1000

RECORD YOUR WPM RATE HERE _____ .

This may be the first time you have ever measured your reading speed, but it should not be the last. Following the simple steps below will improve your rate, perhaps dramatically. You can improve your reading if you try.

For most people, reading occupies hours and hours each week and plays an important role in our lives: students read for school, sunbathers read leisurely on the beach, commuters read on the subway or the bus. Whether it's a novel, a magazine, the daily newspaper, or a business report, there always seems to be something nearby that beckons to be read. For many, however, reading takes up much more time than it should. Some people, in fact, view the act of reading as a chore, intimidating, anything but enjoyable: "The book looks too thick." "The subject matter is unattractive." "I *have* to read it, but I don't *want* to read it."

NOT AN OBSTACLE BUT AN OPPORTUNITY

Whether you like to read or not, and whether you are intimidated by a thick book or attracted to it, you can read faster if you try. Perhaps you have piles of unread magazines in your living room, a back-up of reading. Perhaps you have several books or articles or reports to read for work. You may even have so much reading lined up that you can hardly consider doing much of anything else until you get it finished.

Think of your reading piles as an opportunity. You will want to practice your new method every chance you get. And with your new skill, just think of how fast you will be able to plow through those piles. You will be learning, increasing the body of knowledge over which you have command. You will be performing at a high level for work or for school. You will be reinventing yourself.

PRACTICAL GOALS

The purpose of this reading method is not to increase your reading speed to a phenomenal 2,000 or 3,000 words-per-minute rate. If that happens, great. But don't make that your primary aim. The object is to read faster than you presently do. Much faster. No specific number goal is necessary.

"Speed" reading is just not practical at times. Technical material can be difficult to negotiate. A science textbook, for example, is not ideal for practicing your speed-reading. In general, the speed at which you choose to read should depend on the difficulty of the material you are reading, in the same way that the use of low gear and high gear on a bicycle or car depends on whether the vehicle is going up the hill or down.

Reading should be fun, and reading at a leisurely pace is always an option. But you should also have the option to read quickly if you want to, or need to. Once you learn—like learning to ride a bicycle—you'll never forget.

Before moving on, it's time for another quick quiz. Choose the best answers and then check the key at the back of the book. Score each of your responses in the quiz section of your notebook.

QUIZ #5

1. The term "Carpetbagger" was heard often after which major period in the nation's history?

2. Who was crowned the first Holy Roman Emperor in 800?

3. If anything is incorrect in the following sentence, correct it: Yesterday the tour guide lead the group through the catacombs.

4. Who was the Belle of Amherst?

5. The longest side of a right triangle is called what?

6. Who discovered gravity?

7. What are the lines on a G Staff and what are the spaces on a G Staff?

8. Which NHL hockey player scored 200 or more points in a season four times?

9. Zoysia and fescue are types of what?

10. Identify: Dutch painter (1853–1890), painted *Sunflowers* series.

11. What is Piaget's fourth stage of intellectual development?

12. The largest Hindu population is in which country?

13. "The reports of my death are greatly exaggerated." Who said it?

YOUR ANSWERS

1. _____

2. _____

3. _____

4. _____

5. _____

6. _____

7. _____

8. _____

9. _____

10. _____

11. _____

12. _____

13. _____

Seven Days, Simple Steps

Here we go. From start to finish, it will take seven days for you to learn the steps presented below. Continue to practice each step for however long it takes you to feel completely comfortable with it. There is no deadline. Proceed at your own practical pace.

Your speed will rise in a week, but you should continue to practice the method longer than that. This is not a race to see how quickly you can learn how to read faster. Everyone who follows the plan will be able to improve by the end of the week, but while you may improve by "X" number of words per minute, someone else may improve by "Y" words per minute. That's okay. Everyone is different.

Day 1, Step 1. Flex Day, Flex Step. Stock Up

This day assigns a task that is "flexible"—you can fulfill it at any time. It is designated a "flex" day and a "flex" step. "Flex" does not imply that you have a choice of doing it or not doing it. You are expected to do it. In fact, sooner is better than later.

First, you need to make some lists, starting with "Books I Feel I Must Read," for whatever reason you deem. Then you need to acquire, by any means possible—via the library, via purchase, via friends or family—the top five books on this list. Perhaps these are classics, or current bestsellers, or books that your friends have been urging you to read, or books that you feel you must read before you die.

Also, you need to acquire the top five books on your list of "Books I Absolutely Want to Read More than Any Other Books." No strings attached here. Whatever books you want to read are fine.

Also, acquire the top five books on your list of "Books on Topics I Am Most Interested in Exploring Now." Maybe you have been yearning to explore American history, or English literature, or quantum physics, or economics. Or maybe you have a craving to find out about the pyramids of Egypt, or the latest UFO theories, or the hippest fashions, or the richest celebrities, or the newest diet craze. Or maybe you just want to read some novels on interesting topics. Fiction or nonfiction is acceptable here.

In a related quest, acquire five magazines that include at least one article of 4,000 words or more on "Topics I Am Most Interested in Exploring Now." A news magazine with several interesting topics that interest you would be fine, as long as the articles are 4,000 words or longer.

That's it. To satisfy this first assignment, you will acquire by any means possible 15 different books and five different magazines.

As "flex" would indicate, you need not complete this assignment today, but you should at least start it today or tomorrow, and tend to it regularly until you complete it. Getting a few books or magazines today, and a few tomorrow, and a few the next day would be acceptable.

Please do not discount this step. You will be using these books and magazines to practice your reading skills, and you will want to have them on hand soon. As long as you are going to be reading, you might as well read books and articles that you deem worthwhile and that you suspect will interest you. Unless otherwise noted, use these books to fulfill assignments in the other steps.

In Summary (Step 1)

Stock up by:

❖ Acquiring five books: "Books I Feel I Must Read."

❖ Acquiring five books: "Books I Absolutely Want to Read More than Any Other Books."

❖ Acquiring five books: "Books on Topics I Am Most Interested in Exploring Now."

❖ Acquiring five magazines: each with at least one article of 4,000 words on "Topics I Am Most Interested in Exploring Now."

Day 2, Step 2. Preview the Reading

Before you begin reading any text at length, get a general idea of its content. This will permit you to understand the subject matter a bit more when actually reading, and will help you to be more receptive to the material. If, for example, you are about to read an article or a report, begin by reading the first and last sentence of each paragraph. If for some reason this is not practical (maybe the article or report is very long and you do not have much time), at least read the first sentence of each paragraph. Generally, the first sentence of each paragraph is loaded with information about what is to follow. It may be the topic sentence or the thesis sentence. By reading the first sentence, you will acquire a general knowledge of the piece. **This will improve your comprehension** when you read the entire piece, since you will be prepared a bit for what the writer wants to tell you.

KEY WORDS AND PHRASES

Skim the article for key words and phrases like: **most important; in conclusion; in summary; never; always;** and so on. If you read a paragraph that begins "In summary," you will, of course, have a very good idea about the content of the piece. **This will improve your comprehension.**

In addition, skim the article for words, phrases, and sentences that are **underlined** or in **quotation marks or bold print. This will improve your comprehension.** The writer often uses underlining or bold print for emphasis or to draw your attention to something that is important. Quotations are worth noting and may reveal memorable opinions.

SURVEY

If you are about to read a book, first **survey** the title page, the copyright date, the contents page, the dust jacket, the preface, and whatever else might give you a general idea of what the author wants you to know. **This will improve your comprehension.** You can find out a lot about a book even before you read it.

Can you think of other ways to preview the reading? If so, do not hesitate to use them. Don't underestimate the importance of previewing; it will make you a better reader.

In Summary (Step 2)

Preview the reading by:

❖ Reading the first sentence of each paragraph.

❖ Skimming the piece for key words and phrases.

❖ Looking for quotation marks, underlines, bold print.

❖ Surveying the book.

❖ Using other methods of your own.

Day 3, Step 3. See More

You are capable of seeing more than you presently see when you read. The eye is an amazing instrument, and we usually underuse it.

When you first learned how to read, your teacher marked your progress by listening to you "read aloud." But when you do read aloud, you can *say* only one word at a time, and, therefore, you *look at* only one word at a time. **Your reading speed is slowed up considerably by seeing only one word at a time.**

TRY THIS

Hold up two fingers. Look at the finger on the right. While looking at the finger on the right, you can still see the finger on the left. Move the finger on the left. You saw it move, didn't you?

When you look at a car driving by, you see the whole car. When you are at the zoo, looking at an elephant, you see the whole elephant. Of course you can see more than one little word at a time. You simply need to retrain yourself to do so. Now look at the following pairs of words:

the book

good luck

my tie

thanks, pal

main event

Look at the word on the right. When you look at *book,* you notice that there is another word to the left, though you may not be able to see clearly that it is the word *the.* The same is true with each pair: When looking at the word on the right, you can see that there is a word to the left, though you may not be able to see it clearly.

Now **draw back your focus** when you look at each pair of words. Instead of looking directly at the word on the right, look **between** the two words. Focus your eyes so that you can see and **understand** both words. This may take some practice at first. Keep trying until you master it.

Your focus does not have to be exactly between the two words. Where you have to focus in order to see both words clearly may be different from where someone else has to focus. Your personal focal point, the one that is comfortable for you, is what you should look for now.

You can do it, no matter how old you are or how long you have been underusing your eyes. It may take some people a little bit more practice than others, but you know you can do it—remember that you saw **both** of your fingers before. Now you must see more on the written page.

Practice looking at the above pairs of words and any other pairs of words until you can see clearly **both** words at the same time. **When you can see more, your reading speed will improve.**

HOW MANY STOPS?

If there are 12 words on a line and you focus on only one word at a time, your eyes will stop 12 times on that line. **Unnecessary "eye stops" waste precious time.**

You have been instructed to see two words at a time, just as you saw both your fingers and both words in the given pairs. Now if there are 12 words on a line and you see <u>2 at a time</u>, your eyes will stop only 6 times on that line. You will have gone from 12 stops to 6 stops. In effect, you have the tools necessary to double your reading speed already, since, with practice, it will take you only half the amount of time it did previously to read that line.

Take the "refocusing" method and develop the theory one step further: see 3 words at a time. A line with 12 words would require only 4 stops. **<u>Theoretically, if you master this, you will have tripled your reading speed!</u>**

This "refocus" is not a very difficult process, but it takes practice. Don't forget, you have been reading as you now read for many years. **<u>You must retrain yourself to break an old habit.</u> <u>But you can do it.</u>**

AN IMPORTANT NOTE

Your goal now should be to master the technique of refocusing to see more, and it would not be unusual at first if you had to read slower than you presently do in order to accomplish this goal. Don't worry: the speed will come. But you must become comfortable with the technique first. And you have to practice. Once you have mastered the technique, you will read faster and comprehend better. But, for now, read only as fast (or as slowly) as you have to, in order to feel that you see more.

VERY IMPORTANT—SEE PHRASES OR BLOCKS

You must keep something in mind as you practice this "refocus." It is better if you train yourself right from the start to see phrases or blocks of words, rather than merely seeing every 2 or 3 words. Be practical whenever you can.

For example, suppose you are practicing, and you want to see 2 words at a time, and you come to a line that contains the following: ". . . Jack sat in the chair . . ."

Seeing "Jack sat" in one stop of the eyes certainly would be fine. But, if in the next stop you saw only "in the," then you might be making the process more difficult than it should be.

Try to see the whole phrase, "in the chair." Your mind will accept the whole phrase quite readily. By seeing phrases or commonly related blocks of words, rather than strictly 2 words per stop, you will save yourself an unnecessary, awkward step.

In the beginning, you may have difficulty understanding what you are reading while you are retraining your eyes—**this is to be expected and will be temporary only**. Once you master the skill, you will comprehend better.

Give yourself all the opportunities that you can. If you can understand "of the house" more easily than "of the" and "house," then you should <u>see</u> or <u>focus on</u> the whole phrase, "of the house." **See phrases or blocks of words whenever practical.**

EXERCISE

Find a long article in a magazine or newspaper, or turn to any page of a book, preferably a novel. **With the intention of seeing 2 or 3 words at a time**, take a pencil and circle the word, words, phrases, or blocks of words that you can see at each eye stop. Don't worry at all about comprehension for this exercise.

Read slowly while practicing your new method of focusing. Be honest with yourself when circling the words.

Do not read on in this section until you have finished this exercise.

If you have completed the exercise, please continue.

YOU CAN DO IT

You should not be surprised if your circles got bigger and bigger as you went along. You saw more and more as you progressed. Your eyes are already responding to the task. They are quite capable of "seeing more" than you have asked them to see in the past. You've started retraining yourself. Don't be surprised if your comprehension was low with this exercise. It will improve.

If your circles did not get bigger, and if you did not see more as you progressed, do not despair. All this means is that you need a little more practice. You'll get it. Think "positive." Do not be discouraged if you do not master immediately any suggestions in this system. With practice, your reading will improve. The key to success is: Don't give up.

In Summary (Step 3)

See more:

❖ Refocus to see more than one word per stop.

❖ Retrain yourself to break an old habit.

❖ Master the technique, even if you must read slower to do so—it is only temporary.

❖ Be practical: see phrases or blocks of words.

❖ Don't worry about low comprehension now; good comprehension comes when you master the technique.

❖ Be confident that you can do it.

❖ Practice, practice, practice.

ASSIGNMENT

Read as much as you can. Practice seeing more than one word per stop. Master Step 3 before moving to Step 4.

FORMULA FOR MEASURING

If you wish to monitor your progress by measuring your reading speed regularly, here is a simple formula that will help: To measure your words-per-minute rate, you will need to know how many words you have read in the passage, and exactly how many seconds it took to read. Once you know these figures, calculate your words-per-minute rate as follows: **(Total Words in Passage x 60) divided by (Number of Seconds) = Words-per-minute.**

(You can estimate the number of words in a passage by determining the average number of words per line and multiplying that by the number of lines. Of course, if the text is laid out unevenly, the average number of words per line may be difficult to determine.)

If you are estimating the number of words in a passage or the time it took to read, the words-per-minute rate is not particularly reliable. Estimating is fine occasionally, but try to be as exact as you can as often as you can.

Of course, if you are reading on a computer, you should be able to determine the number of words easily. Most word processing programs contain a feature that counts the words for you in a given passage. In Microsoft Word, for example, simply highlight the passage to be counted (no highlighting necessary if it consists of the entire document), click on TOOLS on the tool bar, then click on WORD COUNT. A box will pop up that shows not only the number of words highlighted but also the number of pages, characters, paragraphs, and lines.

Day 4, Step 4. 3 Stops per Line

Congratulations! Since you now see more than one word per eye stop, your reading speed has improved. You are ready to advance even further.

The next step is logical. Since you have retrained yourself to see more than one word each time you focus within a line of print, you must put that skill to work by forcing yourself to make **a maximum of 3 stops per line.**

EXERCISE

Below you will see a series of blocks of x's, three blocks per line. As you look at each line, **focus on each whole block only as long as it takes you to see it all clearly**, then move your eyes to the next block, focus, then move to the third and last block on the line and focus. After a clear focus on the third block, move your eyes to the beginning of the next line and focus on its first block. Repeat the process.

This exercise is designed to train your eyes to make **only 3 distinct stops per line.** Now, of course, you will be focusing on blocks of x's, but soon you will substitute words. Your eyes must get used to, and be comfortable with, 3 stops per line. **Practice until you feel you have mastered the skill.**

xxxxxxxxx	xxxxxxxxx	xxxxxxxxx
xxxxxxxxx	xxxxxxxxx	xxxxxxxxx
xxxxxxxxx	xxxxxxxxx	xxxxxxxxx
xxxxxxxxx	xxxxxxxxx	xxxxxxxxx
xxxxxxxxx	xxxxxxxxx	xxxxxxxxx

GRADUATION

You are ready to graduate from blocks of x's to words. In the same way that you trained your eyes to make only 3 stops per line with the blocks, focusing on each whole block with each stop, now you will train your eyes to make only 3 stops per line with printed words.

NOTE WELL

When you begin to practice, you will notice that different magazines, newspapers, books, and other reading materials have lines of print that vary in size and length. Even within the same magazine or newspaper, the lines vary in length.

For example, in *The New York Times* on any Sunday, there are several sections. In the news section, each column of print may have only 6 or 7 words per line. But in "The Book Review," each column of print may have as many as 15 words per line. This is not an obstacle but an opportunity. **You can use varying lengths of printed lines to your benefit.**

STRATEGY

Since you are going to make only 3 stops per line, each stop or focus should take in approximately one-third of the line (allowing, of course, for being practical—that is, if a phrase or group of commonly related words, like "in the house," causes you to take in more than one-third, this is perfectly acceptable; in fact, it is encouraged).

The best path for you in your training is a **gradual progression**. Therefore, read the shorter length lines in the beginning, and work your way up to the longer lengths. For example, if a column of newsprint has about 6 words per line, and you are to make 3 stops per line, then with each stop you should take in, or focus on, 2 words (one-third of the line). If there are 15 words in the line, you will be asking your eyes to take in 5 words with each stop. It would be best for you to make a gradual progression, from 2 words per stop to 5 words per stop.

Begin practicing with narrow columns of newspapers or magazines, making only 3 stops per line. When you feel you are ready to advance, practice with reading materials that contain more words per line. I don't encourage you to begin with books, since usually there are too many words per line.

HELPFUL HINT

You may find it easier in the beginning to guide yourself into making only 3 stops per line by putting 3 pencil dots (placed in line with where you intend to make your eye stops) on the very top and very bottom of what you intend to read. You may want to think of an **imaginary line** connecting the dots, if it makes it easier for you to stop in about the same spot on each line. (See illustration A.)

Illustration A

•   •   •

Huck's senses are the means by which he

gains knowledge, and he uses them often

and well. He enjoys using his senses, and,

when possible, he lies back to absorb all

that he can see or hear. Easily enough,

his perception enables him to provide

detailed descriptions, to "read" the river,

and to tell time without a watch.

•   •   •

GUIDE YOURSELF

In the beginning it might also help if you used a pen or pencil, or even your finger, to guide you in your 3 stops. On each line, make 3 distinct stops with your pen, pencil, or finger, following along with your focus, spacing the stops so that your eyes can take in one-third of the line.

You may even wish to use the dots and your finger to guide yourself. Line up your finger stops with the dots. Whatever method you use, it is acceptable as long as it strives to make you feel comfortable while it helps you to master the skill quickly and easily.

If, while you are practicing, you come to lines that need only 2 stops, you are encouraged to make only 2 stops. Perhaps, for example, you come to a line with only 2 lengthy words taking up the whole line. Three stops in this case would be counterproductive, especially if you can take in each whole word with one eye stop. So, if you can read a line with only 2 stops, don't fight it; do it.

Find something to read and practice this technique of 3 stops per line. Pace your speed to maintain comprehension, but know that both high speed and high comprehension will come with practice. **The more you practice, the quicker you will master the skill.**

In Summary (Step 4)

Make only 3 stops per line:

❖ Practice with the blocks of x's until your eyes get used to 3 distinct stops.

❖ When you are ready to practice with words, make a gradual progression; in the beginning, the fewer words per line, the better.

❖ Remember always to be practical, taking in phrases and groups of commonly related words whenever possible.

❖ Use dots and/or your finger to guide you.

❖ Low comprehension and slow reading in the beginning are to be expected; do not be discouraged.

❖ The more you practice, the quicker you will master the skill.

ASSIGNMENT

Your assignment is to read as much as you can before moving on. Practice making only 3 stops per line. Follow the guidelines for a gradual progression.

Day 5, Step 5. 2 Stops per Line

Congratulations are in order again. You are well on your way to the goal you have set for yourself. And the next step follows naturally.

Instead of 3 stops per line, now you will make only 2 stops per line. The theory is the same: Take in more with each focus. Now, however, you will train your eyes to take in one-half of the line with each eye stop.

GRADUAL PROGRESSION AGAIN

As with the 3 stops per line, you should aim for a gradual progression to 2 stops per line. First, get comfortable with 2 stops. Use the blocks of x's below in the same way that you used them before: practice focusing, moving on, focusing, and so on.

Again, you should use varying lengths of printed lines to your benefit. Start with narrow columns in newspapers and magazines, and work your way up to books.

Below, see each **whole** block of x's before moving on.

xxxxxxxxxx	xxxxxxxxxx
xxxxxxxxxx	xxxxxxxxxx
xxxxxxxxxx	xxxxxxxxxx

HINTS

When you move from the blocks of x's to actual reading, don't forget to be practical—take in phrases and groups of commonly related words whenever possible. Use the dots again, except now only 2 dots, making sure they are properly spaced. And use your finger, pen, or pencil to guide yourself, if that helps. Low speed and comprehension may be expected in the beginning.

You need not worry that each stop takes in <u>exactly</u> one-half of the line. You need to keep in mind only that you are to make a maximum of 2 stops per line. One-half of the line per stop is merely a guide.

In Summary (Step 5)

Make only 2 stops per line:

❖ Practice with the blocks of x's until your eyes get used to 2 distinct stops.

❖ When you are ready to practice with words, make a natural progression—narrow newspaper columns to books.

❖ Always be practical, seeing whole phrases when possible.

❖ Use dots and your finger to guide you.

❖ Low speed and comprehension may be expected in the beginning; do not be discouraged.

❖ Practice, practice, practice.

ASSIGNMENT

Read as much as you can—as much as it takes—to master the skill.

MEASURE YOUR PRESENT READING SPEED

Let's find out how fast you read now. If you have mastered the skills, you should be able to see much more with each eye stop.

Do not preview here. The next step—Step 6—concerns comprehension, so, for now, do not be too concerned with how well you comprehend. But, at the same time, **do not be surprised if you feel your comprehension is improving**, even if you are making no conscious effort to understand or retain more. You will learn why this happens in the next step.

For now, just be concerned with your present reading speed. Have a pen handy. Check your watch or clock and read the following passage.

RECORD THE EXACT CURRENT TIME IN THIS SPACE:

MINUTES _____ SECONDS _____ .

_____

The keenness of Huck's senses permits him to interpret the river as a person who lives on it must. Often he maneuvers up and down and across the river, paddling or floating from shore to shore, sojourning on river-islands of tangled wood, avoiding debris and sand bars, ever on the lookout for riverboats, the shore line, the signs of land. No city boy could perceive the river the way Huck does. One particular time, for example, he tells us about seeing a streak in the water, which, he knows, signifies that there is a certain snag in the current which makes the streak look that certain way. He knows, therefore, how swift the current is.

Huck's keenness of perception is also exhibited by his discerning eye. When he sees footprints in the snow outside his aunt's house, he is curious, and upon closer examination he notes that there is a certain cross in one of the heels made by two nails of the boot. He knows immediately that it is his father's footprint. More dramatically, he sees a riotous gang carrying two tarred and feathered people out of town on a rail, and knows immediately who they are: he knew it was the king and duke, he says, even though they had tar and feathers from head to toe, making them look hardly human, let alone recognizable. He just knew.

Adding to the effectiveness of his perception, Huck is always on guard with his senses. At one point in the beginning of the book, Huck escapes his father and rushes through the woods. Repeatedly he tells us how he listens and watches, listens and watches: his strategy is to stay in the thick of the woods where the ground is deeply covered with leaves, and every once in a while he stops to listen and look. Surely he will hear or see anyone in the vicinity. At another point the reader cannot help thinking that Twain is overtly emphasizing Huck's reliance on perception. Jim and Huck are camped on an island, passing the time with conversation, when Huck interrupts, asking the others if they hear a noise. They investigate and find that it was only the paddle of a far off steamboat, so they relax and resume their conversation. There is little or no reason for this interruption other than the author's wish to stress the importance or quality of Huck's perception. That Huck does rely on his perception to keep him safe is obvious.

But Huck does not use his senses only to guard against danger; rather, he uses them whenever he can. He enjoys lying down and sucking in everything his senses will record. On one occasion he tells us that he grew a bit lonely and so he went to the bank of the river so that he could simply listen to the water as it rushed by and so that he could count the stars and the driftwood and the rafts as they passed. There is no better way, he says, to counteract the feeling you get when you are lonely. On another occasion he tells us about how he is inclined to lie down in his canoe and let it float among the driftwood on the river, resting, smoking his pipe, scanning the sky and noting that nary a cloud is to be seen. He marvels at how vast the sky is and how far a person can see at night on the water in the light of the moon. And on yet another occasion Huck reports that, even though it is dark at night on the river, a spark from a passing raft, or a fiddler's song, would alert you to the traffic passing by. What could be better, he wonders, than to lie on your back on a raft, watching the stars and listening to the river all around you? Twain gives us a character who has keen perception, who uses it, and who enjoys it.

But often Huck's senses are impaired, and when this happens he must be ever careful of impending trouble. A constant nemesis on the river is fog, and the fogs Huck encounters are thick and difficult to negotiate: he penetrates a fog once, he tells us, and he loses all idea of direction. Without sight to help him, he switches to hearing. He and Jim have become separated in the fog and Huck decides to yell, hoping Jim will answer. His spirits are buoyed when he hears a faint yell in response. He heads toward it, all the time listening, listening, listening. But he soon discovers that his hopes of locating Jim had been premature: when he hears the faint yell again, it is behind him this time and each time it comes it seems to be coming from a different place. He is frustrated and he acknowledges just how confusing a fog can be. Nothing looks or sounds normal in a fog, he says. He echoes the same thoughts when caught in another fog later in the book. A scow or raft passes Huck's raft so closely that voices could be heard, though people could not be seen: he tells us that he can hear them clearly though he cannot see them at all; it spooks him and makes him think of ghostly things. But Huck knows that his senses will get him through the fog eventually, and he never gives up. He knows that as long as he can sit still, keep quiet and listen, he will be fine. More than this, though, he knows that even if his vision or hearing are impaired by the fog, his sixth sense will pull him through, his sense of "feeling." This is not to be confused with the sense of touching. Feeling is best described as a judgment based on intuition. Huck has feelings throughout the novel, and is alert enough to know that sometimes they may be deceptive. He is very grateful, nevertheless, for yet another sense.

CHECK YOUR CLOCK OR WATCH AND RECORD THE EXACT CURRENT TIME HERE:

MINUTES _____   SECONDS _____ .

DETERMINE THE NUMBER OF MINUTES AND SECONDS IT TOOK TO READ THE PASSAGE. (SUBTRACT START FROM FINISH.)

RECORD YOUR TOTAL READING TIME:

_____ MINUTES _____ SECONDS.

NOW GO BACK TO THE CONVERSION CHART TO DETERMINE YOUR WORDS-PER-MINUTE RATE.

RECORD YOUR NEW WPM RATE HERE:_____.

COMPARE

Compare your present words-per-minute rate with the rate at which you were reading when you started this system. You should see an improvement. Congratulations. If you would like to improve even more, you must practice more.

Now that your speed is improving, turn to Step 6 to concentrate on better comprehension.

Day 6, Step 6. Better Comprehension

Do you ever get to the end of a paragraph and realize that you don't know what you just read? The reason: your mind wanders. Perhaps you were thinking of the people who live next door, or the test you will take tomorrow, or all the work you have to do—so many things can crowd your mind and force you to lose your concentration.

Many people believe that the slower you read, the better you comprehend. No research supports this myth. As a matter of fact, just the opposite is true—the slower you read, the less you comprehend. The reason is that your mind wanders. One thing is certain: Good comprehension comes from reading at a **proper** speed, not a slow speed. Again, proper speed varies from individual to individual.

WHAT YOU CAN DO

Reading at the proper speed will combat mind-wandering. The principle is very simple: If you are concentrating on the proper speed, you will not be able to concentrate on anything else that interferes with the reading. Your mind will not be permitted to wander.

What is the proper speed for you? **Only you know.** Not too fast, not too slow—each person's proper speed is a personal decision. You must feel comfortable with your reading. You will not feel optimum comfort if you read at a speed that someone else chooses for you.

Find your proper speed and concentrate on it while you are reading. Do not let your mind wander.

OTHER CONSIDERATIONS

Give your concentration a chance. Even if you think that the television or stereo is not bothering you while you are reading, you are not giving your mind the isolation it deserves when attempting to concentrate. If it is loud enough to hear, a television or stereo—even in the next room—can be harmful to your comprehension. You can't close out the world, but you can try to create optimum conditions.

Find a quiet place to read. Close the door, if possible. Be sure the lighting is good, and don't get *too* comfortable in your chair unless you seek to go to sleep.

REREAD

Unfortunately, by the time the reading instruction stops in school—often in the 5th or 6th grade—we have never been told that it is okay to reread the material. To many people, rereading indicates that the material has not been understood, which implies that the reader has failed somehow. In some circles, rereading is not acceptable under any circumstances. Do not buy into this. Some rereading is bad, and some is good.

Certain types of rereading can hinder progress. For example, it can be counterproductive to habitually reread a sentence or a paragraph because your mind is wandering. This rereading, known as regression, is a major impediment to speed. It becomes a crutch for many readers, a way to help comprehension temporarily. A better way to help comprehension is to read at the proper pace. Regression is a bad habit, but rereading material with specific purposes in mind, like preparing for a presentation or an exam, is perfectly acceptable.

Have you ever seen a movie more than once? Have you ever felt as though during the second or third viewing something surfaced that you never noticed before? Maybe you picked up on a subtle point made by one of the characters. Or maybe you understood a line or two of dialogue that you misheard or misinterpreted the first time around.

In the end, after the second or third viewing, you felt as if you knew the film better.

Rereading may have the same effect, and it can help comprehension. If you are studying the material, you may want to reread it one or more times to reinforce ideas and concepts. In addition, the second or third reading may yield subtle points that you did not pick up previously, and may help you to remember more.

READ WITH PURPOSE

Define for yourself the purpose of the reading, and read accordingly at the proper pace. Not all material is meant to be read the same way. You may want to take your time with a novel. You may want to read and reread material before taking a test.

CHECKS IN THE MARGINS

As you read, put a check in the margin each time you get to a part that you think is important. Checks in the margins offer advantages over underlining, since checks do not take as much time, and, after a while, can be done rather mechanically without breaking your concentration.

When you have finished your reading, go back to the checks and reread those sections. This will reinforce your reading and help you to retain the material. You will have invoked a simple principle that helps your memory.

REVIEW—ESPECIALLY FOR SCHOOL OR BUSINESS

Your retention should be very high if, after going back to the checks immediately after reading, you go back to them again **just before** a class or a meeting. You will welcome a test on the material.

In Summary (Step 6)

Improve your comprehension by:

❖ Reading at the proper speed.

❖ Reading in the proper environment.

❖ Rereading when necessary.

❖ Reading with purpose.

❖ Putting checks in the margins as you read.

❖ Reviewing before a class or meeting.

Day 7, Step 7. Practice, Practice, Practice

Spend a full day practicing, using the following exercises:

EXERCISE 1

Practice the reading method to improve your speed.

Using a timer, read for three minutes in a chapter of a book. When the timer signals you, stop reading and mark your place by writing in the margin the word "fast."

Now reread the same material for three minutes, trying to go a bit farther in the text. Since you are reading material that you have read before, it should go smoother and faster. Do not stop for any reason until the timer sounds. Do not go back to reread a sentence. When the timer signals you, stop reading and mark your place by writing in the margin the word "faster."

Yet again reread the same material for three minutes, trying to go even farther in the text. Do not stop for any reason until the timer sounds. When the timer signals you, stop reading and mark your place by writing in the margin the word "fastest."

Reread the same material for three minutes, again trying to go a bit farther in the text. Do not stop for any reason until the timer sounds. When the timer signals you, stop reading and mark your place by writing in the margin the word "better."

One final time, reread the same material for three minutes, trying to go a bit farther in the text. Do not stop for any reason until the timer sounds. When the timer signals you, stop reading and mark your place by writing in the margin the word "best."

Now, with the word "best" as your guide, count the total number of words you were able to read in three minutes. Divide that total number by 3 to find out how many words per minute you were able to read.

RECORD YOUR WORDS-PER-MINUTE RATE HERE: _____.

As you will note, it is possible to increase your speed. This practice exercise will sharpen your skills. Your eyes, your finger, and your mind need to be trained for the new method. The more practice you afford yourself, the better you will get.

Be sure to give yourself plenty of breaks between exercises during the day.

EXERCISE 2

Practice your new reading method. Note that this time you will not be rereading material. You will be selecting new material each time, and you will be recording your words-per-minute rate. The focus here is speed.

❖ Using a timer, read for three minutes in a chapter of a book or in a magazine article with more than 4,000 words. Do not stop for any reason until the timer sounds. Do not go back to reread a sentence. When the timer signals you, stop reading and mark your place by writing in the margin the word "fast." Determine how many words per minute you read. Record the date, the time, and your rate in your notebook.

❖ Using a timer, and selecting a different book or magazine, read for three minutes in a chapter of a book or in a magazine article with more than 4,000 words. Do not stop for any reason until the timer sounds. Do not go back to reread a sentence. When the timer signals you, stop reading and mark your place by writing in the margin the word "faster." Determine how many words per minute you read. Record the date, the time, and your rate in your notebook.

❖ Using a timer, and selecting a different book or magazine, read for three minutes in a chapter of a book or in a magazine article with more than 4,000 words. Do not stop for any reason until the timer sounds. Do not go back to reread a sentence. When the timer signals you, stop reading and mark your place by writing in the margin the word "fastest." Determine how many words per minute you read. Record the date, the time, and your rate in your notebook.

❖ Using a timer, and selecting a different book or magazine, read for three minutes in a chapter of a book or in a magazine article with more than 4,000 words. Do not stop for any reason until the timer sounds. Do not go back to reread a sentence. When the timer signals you, stop reading and mark your place by writing in the margin the word "better." Determine how many words per minute you read. Record the date, the time, and your rate in your notebook.

❖ Using a timer, and selecting a different book or magazine, read for three minutes in a chapter of a book or in a magazine article with more than 4,000 words. Do not stop for any reason until the timer sounds. Do not go back to reread a sentence. When the timer signals you, stop reading and mark your place by writing in the margin the word "best." Determine how many words per minute you read. Record the date, the time, and your rate in your notebook.

RECORD THE HIGHEST WORDS-PER-MINUTE RATE HERE: _____ .

This practice exercise is meant to give you speed. Your times should reflect your improvement.

Get ready for a nice surprise. Note the quickest time above. Now go back to the beginning of the chapter where you recorded your words-per-minute rate for the very first time. Though you may not have absorbed the new method completely yet, and though you have practice sessions ahead of you, it should give you a sense of satisfaction and achievement to note that your rate is now higher than when you started. In fact, it may be a lot higher.

Have you doubled your speed? Better than that? Write yourself a note in your notebook, describing your improvement. Put a star next to it so that you can find it easily.

Also, please drop me a line to let me know how you are progressing. Write to me at DrEDroge@aol.com. Put "Reading Improvement" in the subject line.

EXERCISE 3

Practice the reading method described in the previous sections. The focus here is speed and comprehension.

❖ Using a timer, read for four minutes in a chapter of a book or in a magazine article with more than 4,000 words. When the timer signals you, stop reading and mark your place by writing in the margin the word "fast." On a sheet of paper, briefly write single facts garnered from the material. Write in as few words as possible—two or three words are fine—and no matter what, do not use more than one line per fact.

❖ Reread the material for four minutes. When the timer signals you, stop reading and mark your place by writing in the margin the word "faster." On the sheet of paper previously used, add as many new facts as possible. Again, be brief, no more than one line per fact.

❖ Reread the material for four minutes. When the timer signals you, stop reading and mark your place by writing in the margin the word "fastest." On the sheet of paper previously used, add as many new facts as possible. Again, be brief, no more than one line per fact.

❖ Reread the material for four minutes. When the timer signals you, stop reading and mark your place by writing in the margin the word "better." On the sheet of paper previously used, add as many new facts as possible. Again, be brief—no more than one line per fact.

❖ Reread the material for four minutes. When the timer signals you, stop reading and mark your place by writing in the margin the word "best." On the sheet of paper previously used, add as many new facts as possible. Again, be brief, no more than one line per fact.

You may find that the more times you read the material, the fewer facts you have to add. This is understandable because there are only so many facts to be culled, and in the previous readings you extracted the more conspicuous ones. In the later readings you may be finding subtle facts or peripheral facts that are not connected to the main point of the piece quite as much as the previously collected facts.

You should discover, however, that indeed you are able to read fast and comprehend well. The more you practice, the better you will get. Eventually—and the time it takes for this will vary from individual to individual—you will train yourself to read fast and cull the primary points of the material each and every time you read. Rereading will not be necessary, unless, of course, you wish to employ it as a strategy, as for a test for example.

EXERCISE 4

Practice your new reading method. The focus here is speed and comprehension.

❖ Using a timer, read for four minutes in a chapter of a book or in a magazine article with more than 4,000 words. When the timer signals you, stop reading and mark your place by writing in the margin the word "one." On a sheet of paper, briefly summarize the material.

❖ Using a timer, and selecting a different book or magazine, read for four minutes in a chapter of a book or in a magazine article with more than 4,000 words. When the timer signals you, stop reading and mark your place by writing in the margin the word "two." On a sheet of paper, briefly summarize the material.

❖ Using a timer, and selecting a different book or magazine, read for four minutes in a chapter of a book or in a magazine article with more than 4,000 words. When the timer signals you, stop reading and mark your place by writing in the margin the word "three." On a sheet of paper, briefly summarize the material.

❖ Using a timer, and selecting a different book or magazine, read for four minutes in a chapter of a book or in a magazine article with more than 4,000 words. When the timer signals you, stop reading and mark your place by writing in the margin the word "four." On a sheet of paper, briefly summarize the material.

❖ Using a timer, and selecting a different book or magazine, read for four minutes in a chapter of a book or in a magazine article with more than 4,000 words. When the timer signals you, stop reading and mark your place by writing in the margin the word "five." On a sheet of paper, briefly summarize the material.

This practice exercise permits you to judge the consistency of your comprehension. Are you able to summarize the material comfortably? If not, keep practicing until you can.

If you are approaching a piece knowing that you will have to summarize it afterward, you will gear your mind to read it alertly. It is a good habit to form, summarizing the material for yourself, even when there is no ostensible need to do so. It will keep you reading alertly and it will maintain or improve your comprehension.

AFTERWORD

Your reading has improved and you should be proud of yourself. Keep up the words-per-minute rate you now have, or keep trying to improve.

You may get rusty if you do not maintain your newly mastered reading skills. But rest assured that you will always have the skills, and whenever you choose to sharpen them, you need only review the underlinings, bold print, and summary sections of this chapter.

Before moving on, it's time to complete another fun quiz. After you've finished it, and checked the answer key, put an indication of correct or incorrect next to each of your responses. Remember to keep quiz responses together in a designated section of your notebook for easy reference later.

QUIZ #6

1. The Great Depression may be traced back to the major stock market crash of what year?

2. What term is used for the Middle Ages practice of landowners granting land use in return for services and loyalty?

3. A symbiotic relation is:
    a. harmful to both
    b. mutually beneficial
    c. short-lived
    d. not a, b, or c

4. Who wrote *Pride and Prejudice*?

5. What is an isosceles triangle?

6. Jonas Salk is known for developing a vaccine for what illness?

7. This composer wrote *Emperor.* (Piano Concerto No. 5).

8. This NFL quarterback won MVP Awards back-to-back-to-back in 1995, '96, and '97.

9. What do the letters N-P-K on fertilizer packages stand for?

10. Identify: French artist (1841–1919), *The Umbrellas, Girl With a Watering Can.*

11. Who originated the concept of the "collective unconscious"?

12. The largest Buddhist population is in which country?

13. "I have nothing to offer but blood, toil, tears, and sweat." Who said it?

YOUR ANSWERS

1. _____

2. _____

3. _____

4. _____

5. _____

6. _____

7. _____

8. _____

9. _____

10. _____

11. _____

12. _____

13. _____

4. Week Two—Boosting Memory with Powerful Techniques

Memory is the mother of all wisdom.

—AESCHYLUS, *PROMETHEUS BOUND*

A FAN FAVORITE IN PROFESSIONAL FOOTBALL, Big Daddy Lipscomb weighed about 300 pounds soaking wet. A defensive lineman for the Colts, back when they were in Baltimore, he was asked by a reporter one day how he approached his task of tackling the back with the ball when he was surrounded by numerous runners. How could he know who had the ball? Big Daddy smiled with a mouth full of white teeth and said simply, "I grabs 'em all, baby. I grabs 'em all."

Big Daddy did whatever he had to do to get the job done. He didn't let anything prevent him. He had a problem and he solved it with his own personal style. He didn't have to know specifically who had the ball as long as he tackled all those around him. One was likely to be the ball carrier. It's important to be practical in our efforts to be successful. Big Daddy was practical and successful.

When I got to college, I had to be practical. I had to figure out how I was going to spread my arms like Big Daddy and embrace the problem of learning a huge volume of material in a short time. Partly from inspiration and partly from desperation, I developed a memory system that helped me to remember names, dates, numbers—virtually everything. Combining my own inventions with tried-and-true techniques, some of which had been used for centuries, dating back as far as the ancient Greeks, I created a personal repertoire of mnemonic devices that could work for me in diverse settings. I tweaked them to fit my various needs, and I rehearsed them unendingly, until it got to a point where I could memorize a list of numerous items and recite them forward and backward, and from the middle out. I now had a system that could help me never to forget again.

In this chapter, I'll teach you the same memory techniques that I depended on to satisfy rigorous academic demands. They remain extremely useful to me today. These techniques work, and I have taught them to many others who have also benefited from them.

Over the next week, read this chapter thoroughly and practice the techniques intensely. Beyond the week, continue to practice them until they become ensconced in your brain and habitual aids in your daily life.

Despite the fact that we are required to remember things from the time we are tykes, our education generally does not include formal training in memory techniques. When we are in kindergarten we must remember our name and address and telephone number. When we are in high school and college we must remember dates, facts, theorems, and much more. In our adult life we must remember names and numbers, grocery lists and to-do lists. The challenge is significant.

As a headmaster I have introduced schools to programs aimed at improving memory. One year, for example, I taught a minicourse that presented a core of helpful memory techniques to students in various grades.

When a reporter from the local newspaper came to the school to do a story on the course, the children had an opportunity to demonstrate the power of the lessons. Early in the day the reporter and I spoke about some of the things the students had been asked to remember in the course. I mentioned a sampling of items, from names and dates to grocery items and a list of random numbers. Later in the day, at an assembly of the students in the course, the reporter selected a girl and asked her if she could repeat the list of random numbers given to the class several months earlier. This was a list that had been given to the students only once, in an isolated exercise more than eight weeks prior to the reporter's visit. The children did not even know that a newspaper story was going to be written, and had had no review or preparation for the reporter's questions. But without hesitation, the little girl spouted out the list of ten numbers, and the reporter's mouth dropped a foot. The reporter told me afterward that it was the most astonishing display of intelligence she had witnessed in her life. Quite a few of the other students would have been able to recite that list of numbers, so powerful was the brief training that they had received. You, too, could have done it, if you had known the techniques in this chapter.

When I gave memory training to students in various grades, I tested them before and after teacher intervention. A sampling of the results follows:

❖ Scores increased in each grade, ranging from 32 percent to 128 percent.

❖ Some students more than doubled their scores, and at times improved as much as nine times.

❖ In one of the tests, 100 percent improved or stayed the same, and in another, 63 percent of those improving had perfect scores.

Clearly, this is powerful stuff. The examples above serve as due witness to the potential of memory training.

In this chapter you will learn:

❖ What a powerful tool memory can be.

❖ How memory works.

❖ How to "CURE" your memory problems.

❖ How to visualize and zoom to solve significant memory challenges.

❖ How to remember lists.

❖ How to use "mnemonics"—easy-to-apply memory helpers.

❖ How to use acronyms to remember.

❖ How to use the amazing "Loci" method of the ancient Greeks.

❖ How to use body zones to remember.

❖ How to use written notes to remember.

❖ How to use motivation and an active mind to insure success.

❖ How to use patterns to remember.

❖ How to remember state capitals.

❖ How to remember names—never forget a name again.

❖ How to remember numbers and dates.

❖ How to remember speeches.

❖ How to use rhyme and repetition to remember.

❖ How to use review, links, and structure to remember.

❖ How never to misplace keys or car again.

❖ How to insure high grades on tests.

ASSIGNMENT

Read and reread this chapter every day for the next week. Repetition is an effective method for absorbing and remembering material. If you finish reading the chapter on the second day of the week, begin to reread it on the third day. If you finish rereading it on the fourth day, begin to reread it again on the fifth day. And so on. Work at your own pace, but reread the chapter as many times as possible during the week you have devoted to improving your memory.

Memory Can Be a Powerful, Transferable Tool

Memory skills are transferable. For example, if you learn how to remember grocery lists, you can use the same principles for remembering names, numbers, and speeches. When trying to remember facts that span numerous subject areas, you can use several different techniques, because they complement each other.

How Does Memory Work?

Simply put, the memory process involves three primary steps: recording information, storing it, and retrieving it. Most often the problem arises when we try to retrieve something that has been recorded and stored.

Learn the first powerful memory technique right after the quiz below. After you've finished it, check the answer key at the back of the book, and in your notebook indicate "correct" or "incorrect" for each question.

QUIZ #7

1. These words begin what document? "We the people of the United States, in order to form a more perfect union . . ."

2. What was the name of the 3rd century B.C. Carthaginian commander with elephants in his army?

3. "Antebellum" refers to a period
    a. after the war
    b. against the war
    c. before the war
    d. not a, b, or c

4. *The Canterbury Tales* is set in:
    a. the 3rd century B.C.
    b. the 1300s
    c. the 1800s
    d. the 2nd century A.D.

5. What is a scalene triangle?

6. In science, what is the heliocentric theory?

7. This composer wrote *Swan Lake* and *Sleeping Beauty*.

8. The all-time career pitching strikeout leader in Major League Baseball is who?

9. Perennial plants usually last:
    a. less than a year
    b. a year
    c. more than a year
    d. 17 years

10. Identify: Norwegian painter (1863–1944), *The Scream.*

11. What is the psychological term for "one who tends to direct attention inward"?

12. Punjab, India, is home to about 80 percent of the world's population of which religion?

13. "Not everything that can be counted counts, and not everything that counts can be counted." Who said it?

YOUR ANSWERS

1. _____
2. _____
3. _____
4. _____
5. _____
6. _____
7. _____
8. _____
9. _____
10. _____
11. _____
12. _____
13. _____

Memory Challenge?—Cure It

CURE (Connections: Unlikely, Ridiculous, Extraordinary)

Connections, connections, connections. Make connections between the items you want to remember. But not just any connections: make **unlikely**, **ridiculous**, **extraordinary** connections. This is the key to great memory. Most often we forget things because we have not actively and aggressively made them stand out in our minds. You need to record a **trigger** with the rest of the information. The brain stores virtually everything you see, and hear, and think. The information does not disappear from the brain; it is not erased. It is waiting to be retrieved. But, as with information stored on the hard disk of a computer, unless you know how to get at it—which keys to push on the keypad or icons to click on the screen—you can't retrieve it.

All you need is a trigger, some device that will bring the information to the surface. **An unlikely, ridiculous, or extraordinary connection** is exactly the device that will trigger the information virtually every time.

If you have a memory problem: CURE it.

Here is what to do:

When remembering a list, connect each item you want to remember to the next item in the sequence, but connect it in an unlikely, ridiculous, or extraordinary manner. For example, let's say that you want to remember the following five items: **mouse, baseball, false eyelashes, beer, skirt**. CURE each item with the next.

Connect in pairs. Pairing reduces the number of items to remember to only one. Remembering that item will trigger the one with which it is paired.

Most important is that *you* make the connections that work for *you*, since you need the information to stand out in your mind, not mine or anyone else's. I will offer my connections as examples, but *your* connections will work best for *you*.

VISUALIZE

Whenever possible, use mental pictures to help your memory. The mind remembers pictures very well. Visualizing—making mental pictures—adds another dimension to your memory. Visualize when you CURE.

Make the mental picture as vivid and as detailed as possible. Visualize by using camera techniques, such as ZOOMING IN or OUT. And whenever you can, bring other senses into play. If you're trying to remember "lemon," for example, imagine biting into a lemon and feel the sensation in your mouth. Or if you're trying to remember "pot roast," smell the aroma as it cooks. If you're trying to remember "blanket," touch it in your mind, feel how soft and warm it is.

BACK TO THE LIST

Okay, you have to remember the five items above. CURE in pairs. One way to connect mouse to baseball would be to make a mental picture of a mouse with a baseball on its head. Or a mouse with a baseball in its mouth. The idea is to make the connection as unlikely or ridiculous or extraordinary as you can—*a connection that will stand out in your mind.* You are not likely to forget an image of a mouse with a baseball on its head, are you?

Now that you have mouse CUREd with baseball, you must CURE baseball with false eyelashes. Imagine, for example, a baseball with a face that has a prominent feature—false eyelashes. Or picture a woman's face with false eyelashes and balanced on each eyelash is a baseball. Ridiculous? Right. And that is exactly what we want.

Now CURE false eyelashes to beer. Let's conjure up the mental picture of false eyelashes floating in a mug of beer. Or a bottle of beer wearing false eyelashes. (Use mental images—visualize.)

Now CURE beer to skirt. Let's picture a skirt with a pattern of little cans of beer on it. Or, perhaps, a bartender pulling the spigot to draw a frothy beer, but instead, out comes a steady stream of tiny skirts.

Get the idea? Unlikely, ridiculous, extraordinary connections. In pairs. It does not matter how many items you need to remember, since you will remember them only two at a time, and you will always be able to remember all the items by simply recalling each pair at a time.

Take just a minute to review the CUREs above. You will amaze yourself at how well you will remember the items.

Try it. If I write "mouse," now what do you think of? Baseball, right? And did that baseball have a face with something prominent? Right: false eyelashes.

This method also permits you to remember items in reverse order. For example, if I say "skirt," what do you think of? Beer, right?

Another Option—Stories

If you have the kind of a mind that likes to create stories, an imaginative side that stands ready for service, then you can take this CURE method a step further. Connect in pairs, and weave the pairs into a story.

For example, another way to make the connections of the five items to be remembered may be:

A **mouse** is up at bat in a baseball game. He hits the **baseball**.

This is ridiculous, but that is the point. Picture a mouse in a baseball uniform. In fact, this is a baseball game being played by two teams of mice. The pitcher mouse throws the baseball and the hitter mouse hits it. I have connected **mouse** and **baseball** in a way that I am unlikely to forget BECAUSE IT IS SO RIDICULOUS.

Now connect baseball and false eyelashes. My mind ZOOMS IN on the **baseball** as it is flying through the air, and, as in a TV cartoon, the baseball has a face on it, and the most prominent feature: **false eyelashes**.

Now the **false eyelashes** are floating in **beer**, since the ball went flying into the stands and landed in some guy's cup of beer.

Can you picture a baseball with a face on it with false eyelashes and the false eyelashes are floating in the beer? Are you likely to forget an image as weird as that? I doubt it. You are not likely to forget the two items, either: false eyelashes and beer. The spectator with the beer is a burly man, but he is wearing a skirt. The impact of the ball into his beer has spilled some **beer** on the **skirt**.

In seconds, in my mind I have made a series of unlikely, ridiculous, extraordinary connections, two at a time, and I have connected the five items together: a **mouse** is up at bat in a baseball game. He hits the **baseball**. The **baseball** has a face on it, and the face has **false eyelashes**. The **baseball with false eyelashes** flies into the stands and lands in the **beer** of a burly male spectator, and the **false eyelashes** are now floating in the **beer**. The **beer** spills all over the **skirt** the man is wearing.

I have made the ridiculous connections necessary to trigger those five items for me at any time I need them. Moreover, I now can remember them in reverse order, if I wish, since I have connected them two at a time. Even if I remembered only one of the five items, and if it were somewhere in the middle of the sequence, I would still be able to remember all five items by remembering the connections on each side. See for yourself: Think of the **false eyelashes**. What are the items on each side?

Close your eyes and try to remember all five items again.

It's simple, isn't it? And so powerful.

You do not need to make a story out of the items, but it is one more option. To CURE in pairs is most important; you don't need a story unless that helps *your* memory.

Now that you have the idea of how to CURE, let's try a list of 10.

Remembering Lists

Never forget another item at the grocery store, or in an assignment, or in any list at all: CURE the list. You have already CUREd a list of five items; you can CURE a list of 10 items in the same way. Let's use groceries as an example, but remember that this method is just as useful for a list of facts. It also can help you to absorb the information in this book.

Okay, here are the 10 items you want to buy: **bread, shampoo, cereal, diapers, lettuce, bacon, milk, batteries, cookies, magazine**.

Remember, *your* CUREs are what will make *you* remember this grocery list, but for the purposes of demonstration, I will offer mine. Please try to make your own CUREs as we move along, to embrace the process more intimately.

Bread and shampoo. Imagine a loaf of bread with one end of it frothy and bubbly, as if it were in the shower.

Shampoo and cereal. A bowl of shampoo bottles. I have opened the box of cereal and poured out little bottles of shampoo into the bowl.

Cereal and diapers. The box of cereal is standing straight up. Your baby, in her diapers, is balancing herself upside down on top of the box of cereal.

Diapers and lettuce. There is lettuce sprouting from your baby's diaper.

Lettuce and bacon. Picture a pig—its head is not that of an ordinary pig, however, but instead it has a head of lettuce.

Bacon and milk. You are frying bacon and into the frying pan you pour milk. (Yuk.) The milk bubbles and the bacon floats.

Milk and batteries. You are milking a cow and out of the udders come batteries.

Batteries and cookies. Chocolate chip batteries. You take the box of cookies from the shelf and see that in the box are not cookies but batteries instead—chocolate chip batteries.

Cookies and magazine. You know how annoying it is when you leaf through a magazine and those subscription cards fall out on to your lap. Imagine that you are leafing through a magazine and cookies keep falling out of it on to your lap.

There you have it, a list of 10 grocery items. Do you know it? Let's see.

Think of one item that you know you would need. Let's say milk. Okay, what else do you think of?

Immediately I think of milking a cow and batteries coming out of the udders. Aha! Batteries.

But I know that milk is somewhere in the middle of the list, which means that there is another CURE. Yes. Bubbling milk in a frying pan, with bacon floating in it. That's it—bacon.

From there I can proceed in both directions to remember my CUREs and cover the entire 10 items. Of course, if I simply remember the first item—in this case, bread—I can proceed in the order I CUREd. **Bread** with bubbling **shampoo** on one end; a bowl of shampoo bottles that came from a box of **cereal**; a box of cereal with a baby in **diapers** balanced on top; **lettuce** is sprouting from the diapers; a head of lettuce sits on a pig's body (**bacon**); bacon floating in a frying pan of **milk**; milking a cow and **batteries** coming from the udders; chocolate chip batteries—aha! **cookies**; cookies keep falling from the **magazine** onto my lap.

Master this method and never forget another item at the grocery store.

Be Practical—Daily Curing

Be practical with this memory method. You can use it routinely to remember what you have to do each day.

Say that today, in particular, you have an unusually busy schedule—lots of errands to run, people to see, things to do. You have to remember to buy light bulbs and cereal. You want to stop at the boat show so you can see that boat you're always dreaming of owning some day. You have to confirm airline reservations for your vacation trip. When you get home you have to glue the dish that you broke. And you have to do the income tax report.

Light bulb, cereal, motorboat, airplane, glue, taxes. Six items to remember. You already know that you can remember at least 10 items, and so six should be a snap.

You see a light bulb eating cereal from a bowl. ZOOM in on the bowl. The cereal is in the shape of motorboats and they are zipping through the milk. One of them zips right out of the bowl into the air and turns into an airplane. The airplane is covered with glue. The airplane flies into a cloud of forms and the forms stick to the airplane. ZOOM in on the forms—they are 1040 tax forms for the IRS.

Six items on the day's schedule—you'll remember them all.

EXERCISE

Make a list of 10 items. CURE the items, two at a time. The more ridiculous the connections, the easier it will be for you to recall them.

Repeat the exercise five times.

Mnemonics

Devices that help us to remember—like the CURE method, visualizing, and using stories—are called mnemonics. Here are some more.

Acronyms

An acronym is a device that helps memory by using initial letters to form words. There are *sentence* acronyms and *word* acronyms.

To help you remember the lines on a G Staff—EGBDF—chances are that you learned the sentence acronym: "Every Good Boy Deserves Fun." For the order of the planets, a sentence acronym is, "My Very Easy Method Just Speeds Up Naming Planets" (Mercury, Venus, Earth, Mars, Jupiter, Saturn, Uranus, Neptune, Pluto). And for taxonomic classifications: "King Philip Came Over For Good Soup" (Kingdom, Phylum, Class, Order, Family, Genus, Species).

How about the Great Lakes? HOMES is the word acronym I was taught to connect to the Great Lakes. Each letter is the first letter of one of the five lakes: Huron, Ontario, Michigan, Erie, Superior. Another example would be the acronym in music for the spaces on a G Staff: FACE.

Sentence acronyms are especially helpful when you have a list of items with first letters that do not lend themselves to forming a word, even when shuffled. For example, let's say you are remembering a list of words or terms, and by taking the first letters of each you end up with the following series: a, l, i, h, s, o, h. Make up a sentence using the letters of the series as the first letters of the words, such as: "All Lighthouses In High Seas Offer Help." Now you have a sentence acronym to assist you in remembering the list.

The acronym does not need to make sense. It need only help you to remember. For example, the acronym in Science for remembering the colors of the spectrum in order is ROY G BIV: Red, Orange, Yellow, Green, Blue, Indigo, Violet.

Use acronyms to help you remember. When you are confronted with the challenge of remembering a list or a group, create an acronym, using the first letter of a word, or of a group of words in a sentence, as in the examples above.

EXERCISE

Write down as many acronyms as you can right now. Keep the list handy and let it grow. As you come across more, add them. Make it a habit to create acronyms for yourself regularly, even when it is not necessary—just for practice. The more you use this method, the easier it will become for you to call upon it when you need it. In the meantime, your mind will stay sharp and your memory will improve.

Three Very Important Words: Location, Location, Location

Mnemonics need not come in the form of acronyms formed from letters, words, or sentences. The ancient Greeks had an extremely effective method called *loci,* which used familiarity with locations to help them remember. Learn this method and you will take a giant leap forward in your Intelligence Makeover. You will be able to retain facts more quickly and easily than you ever imagined.

Connect lists or sets of facts to the rooms and areas of your home. For example, if you want to remember the first five presidents of the United States in order, you might want to connect them in order with the first five rooms or areas in your house as you enter and walk through your home. You know your house. The layout is embedded in your memory. The goal now is to connect the presidents to what you already know.

Using the layout of my house, I would visualize Washington in the front hall, Adams in the living room, Jefferson in the dining room, Madison in the family room, and Monroe in the bathroom (with all due respect). Once I have committed the image of each president in his designated space, preferably doing something appropriate to the space (e.g., eating dinner in the dining room; watching TV in the family room), I can always remember the order of their presidencies simply by remembering the order of the rooms in my home.

EXERCISE

Take a group of people you normally have difficulty remembering, and create a mnemonic device to help you remember them from now on.

Perhaps you have difficulty remembering the order of birth of your sister's twelve children (or any 12 members of your family). Determine the correct order and envision each one in his or her particular space in your home, according to its layout. If you do not have 12 rooms, use areas like the front stairs, the patio, the yard, and so on. Designate 12 distinct spaces. (Don't forget the bathrooms.) Once you have assigned each child to a space in the order of your home, according to the birth order, you will not forget the birth order again.

Now try this with the first 12 presidents of the United States. Put the presidents in order through your house, one president assigned to one space. Eventually, use it to remember all the presidents—in order.

Body Zones

Use the areas around your body to help you remember. For example, make a mental note of the six zones within reach—immediately in front of you, immediately behind you, immediately to your right, immediately to your left, on your head, and under your feet.

Place the pieces of information you want to remember in your body zones. Let's say you need to remember six important people—U.S. presidents, or teachers in a school, or executives in a company, or the like. We'll take six great baseball players of the past: Babe Ruth, Willie Mays, Mickey Mantle, Duke Snider, Cal Ripken, and Hank Aaron.

Place the six players in the zones around your body. Let's put Babe Ruth in front of you. Interact with him. Shake his hand or give him a high five. Talk baseball with him. Ask him how he felt when he hit 60 home runs in one season, and so on. Got the picture? Ruth is in front of you.

Right behind you, poking you in the back, is Willie Mays. He keeps saying, "Say, hey." In fact, Willie Mays, was known as the Say Hey Kid. So, he's poking you, and you turn around and talk with him and interact with him. Ask him how he felt when he caught that ball over his head in the World Series. Mays is behind you.

Continue to the point where you are standing on somebody's head, and someone is standing on yours. Remembering these six players—or any other six people—will be easier for you now when you use this method.

The Body Zones method is also good for remembering items. Just place them around you in a memorable way.

Let's take a grocery list. One of the items is ice cream. Put it behind you. It's in a bowl with chocolate syrup on it. Every time you want a spoonful, you have to twist your body so that you can reach behind yourself to get it. Memorable? Yes. Do the same with the other items. Also needed from the store is motor oil. Put it on your head, open it, and let it pour out on you. Yuk. Memorable? Yes. When you think of that body zone, are you likely to forget? No.

Add the Body Zones method to your repertoire of memory techniques.

Written Notes

Writing notes will help you to remember. Write out a list of "things to do." Refer to it regularly to help you remember. Decorate it with stickers or write it in different colored inks. The actual process of writing helps to plant the information into your memory. You have given yourself an additional sense—sight/visualization—to help you to remember.

Notes on the Floor

Put important notes about things to do on the floor where you will be sure to see them. Try placing them in your path—by the bed, in the kitchen, or wherever you are sure to walk during the day. Your natural instinct to notice what is on the floor—a survival instinct that helps you avoid tripping—will permit you to see the note and be reminded of what you wanted to do. This is a highly effective technique (unless you have a paper-eating pet).

Motivate Yourself

Motivate yourself to remember. If you had to remember a list of facts for a test, you probably would have motivation to do so in order to get a good grade. The higher your level of motivation to remember, the better.

Let's see how powerful this can be. Ratchet up the reward. Let's say that if you remembered the list of facts you would receive $100,000, cold cash, right in your hand. I suspect that you would be more motivated and, as a result, more likely to remember the facts.

Always try to find the best motivation for your memory. Consider all the benefits that will be gained from your success in the task.

Remembering State Capitals

Use the CURE technique to remember the 50 state capitals so that you will never forget. Again, creativity and ridiculousness are in order.

An example of CUREing a state to its capital would be New Jersey and Trenton. I simply envision a cow (Jersey) in a tent. Tent is enough for me to remember Trenton, but perhaps you would prefer a different connection (e.g., Ten ton? Train . . . ?).

Another example: I think of a large eye hoeing a field; from nowhere a gang of little boys appears and tramples all that has been hoed. (Idaho: Boise)

Another example: I think of a mountain made of fur peeling like a banana. (Vermont: Montpelier)

You can CURE countries to their capitals as well, of course.

EXERCISE

Write a list of all 50 states and their capitals. CURE them. (You are much more likely to remember them forever if *you* CURE them, rather than if I provide CUREs for you.)

Remembering Names

We forget names of people we meet because we do not make them stand out in our minds when we are introduced. To remember them, we simply have to create a CURE that will trigger them for us.

First, get into the habit of **saying the name aloud** as soon as you hear it. This will insure that you insist on hearing it during an introduction, and that you will ask someone to repeat it if it is mumbled, rather than just letting it go. Similarly, to remember a name when you are reading, say it aloud as you read it.

Saying a name aloud gives you another sense—hearing—to complement the visual image that you will use when you create your CURE. When you try to recall the name, you will be able to draw upon how it sounded when you said it. The more senses you can use when recording a piece of information, the better, because you can use them all in the retrieval process.

Also, connect a name with a face. CURE it to the face.

We remember information and things that we *see*. Our brain takes in the image and stores it for us automatically. Some people say: "I never forget a face." We see faces, and often remember them, but lose the name. You would remember the name if only you had connected it to the face. It follows that if you never forget a face, and if you connected the name and the face, you'd never forget the name either.

While many names are common—that is, used often by many different people—faces usually are distinct from person to person. Again, it is likely that you remember faces, even though you forget names. Right? That is because (1) you SEE faces and, in terms of the senses of seeing and hearing, it is easier for most people to remember what is seen as opposed to what is heard, and (2) while most names are not distinct, almost everyone has some distinct feature in his or her face—a high forehead, long sideburns, big ears, small ears, banana nose, upturned nose, bushy eyebrows, blonde eyebrows, long or curly hair, short or straight hair, and so on.

The next time you are introduced to someone, repeat his name aloud and, as you do so, note a particular prominent feature on his face. If there is a prominent feature presenting itself more readily elsewhere (e.g., a fancy coat), use it, but know that the more permanent the prominent feature, the more permanent the memory trigger. If you rely on a person's clothing or jewelry (e.g., big earrings), you are not likely to see the trigger the next time you see the person in another setting. The face, on the other hand, will remain the same—same big ears, or big nose, or bushy eyebrows, or high forehead, and so on.

Use the prominent feature to CURE the name. For example, you are introduced to Jim. As you stick out your hand to shake, you say the name Jim aloud, and you note (without staring) his balding head. One way to CURE the name Jim to the face in this instance would be to SEE the name Jim nestled into the bald spot on his head. SEE it as you SAY it. See the letters J I M.

Substitution Alternative

For certain names, like Jim, you can see a GYM nestled into the bald spot, a real gym, complete with basketball court, parallel bars, hanging rings, wrestling mats—whatever *your* version of a gym looks like. The next time you see Jim, you will also see the GYM and remember his name.

Jim/Gym is an easy **substitution**, and, though the name itself spelled out in large letters (or small ones, if that works better for you) can work well if you CURE it to a prominent feature of the face, a substitution CURE may make the process just a bit easier.

Other examples of substitutions are: Bill/restaurant bill; Jack/automobile jack; Pat/hand patting; Pete/a patch of peat moss; Mary/marry (picture a bride and groom); John/bathroom (hey, if it works, use it); Peg/wall peg; Carol/caroller (singer); Janet/janitor; and so on.

Let's take one more example, using Jack from above: You are trying to remember his name is Jack and you SEE big, heavy, automobile jacks—the kind they slide under the car when it's at the service station—HANGING FROM HIS EARS, CAUSING HIM TO STOOP FORWARD. Emblazon this image into your mind. The next time you see the face, you will see the jacks hanging from his ears—and you will remember his name.

This method will work for you in trying to remember names of people you meet in person or, perhaps, characters and faces you see in a book. The academic applications are evident.

Of course there are limitations for this method when using it outside of an introduction. Let's say that your goal is to remember a name out of a history book, such as the name of the warrior who invaded England in 1066, William the Conqueror—the initial advice is the same: say the name aloud. But trying to find a picture of William the Conqueror might not be practical. In cases like that, saying the name aloud may have to suffice—but you can still make a mental picture of what he would have looked like.

EXERCISE

Write down 10 more name substitutions. They do not have to be exact—the only criterion is that they work for you. For example, if JUICE will help you to remember JOYCE, then it is perfectly fine. (CURE: She has a glass of juice balanced on her curly-haired head.)

Build a repertoire of names so that when it is time to remember, you will have an established pool from which to draw.

If No Prominent Feature . . .

Not all faces or bodies readily present a prominent feature. Not a problem. Simply remember that your goal is to make **a connection that is unlikely or ridiculous or extraordinary.**

If Jim does not have a prominent feature, give him one. See him with the gym rings in his nose. Or simply imagine that he opens his mouth and a series of gyms, dozens of them, come streaming from his mouth. You are not likely to forget that.

Be creative and ridiculous. You won't get stumped for a good CURE as long as you remember that ANY ridiculous connection can work. If you meet Margaret and you cannot think of a substitute for the name Margaret, and she has no prominent feature, just **say** her name aloud and **see** the name Margaret in large letters coming out of her mouth, or sitting on her nose, or sticking out of her ear.

Take a moment to remember how it feels when someone remembers your name. It makes you feel good, doesn't it? Our names are very personal possessions. We care about them, and we like it when others show care and respect in remembering them. Your Social Intelligence will be enhanced with this device. It will help you in your relations with others. One man used it to remember the names of a dozen search-committee members at a job interview—they were impressed because he used their names when shaking their hands at the end. He got the job.

Review

To Remember Names:

1. SAY NAME ALOUD.

2. CURE IT (with or without a substitution) TO THE FACE (or other prominent feature).

Remembering Numbers and Dates

Have you ever forgotten a telephone number? Your Social Security number? A date? Other numbers? You will never have to worry about forgetting a number again.

The longest number that the average person must remember is either nine or 10 digits—a Social Security number is nine digits long; a telephone number, with area code, is 10 digits long. There are occasions when we may be called on to remember numbers with more digits, but, in fact, seven digits is most likely the longest number we encounter on a regular basis—a telephone number in the same area code as ours.

No matter how long the number, the principles to follow are the same:

Simplify and Reduce

It is easier to remember two or three items than seven or eight or nine items. That is why you should **simplify and reduce** a telephone number, a Social Security number, or any other large number, to just two or three items, rather than try to remember seven or more individual digits.

For example, if the telephone number is 593-2478, you would be creating an unnecessary burden for yourself if you tried to remember each individual digit in sequence: five, nine, three, two, four, seven, eight.

It is easier if you think of the first three digits as a number in the **hundreds**, in this case, five hundred ninety-three, said "five-ninety-three." Not only is one three-digit number easier to remember than three individual digits, but it is also easier to visualize, which is important for another step described below.

In addition, rather than remember the four remaining digits individually, reduce them to one number in the **thousands**, to be pronounced in this case "twenty-four seventy-eight" (as opposed to "two thousand four hundred seventy-eight").

Think and see the four-digit number in the thousands, **but pronounce** it as a series of two-digit numbers.

In sum, what you are doing in the example above is simplifying the seven parts of a telephone number into only two parts—that is, one number in the hundreds and one number in the thousands.

The same principle would apply for larger numbers: Social Security numbers, for example. Take the number 331-28-5796. Simplify and reduce the nine parts into three parts. Remember the number as three-thirty-one, twenty-eight, fifty-seven ninety-six.

EXERCISE

Simplify and reduce the following numbers:

254-8746 (into only two parts)

387-21-9238 (into only three parts)

213-664-2327 (into only three parts)

Repeat Number Aloud

It is very important to repeat the number aloud when you are trying to commit it to memory. Again, as in remembering names, SAYING the number will give you a prominent trigger when you try to recall it: You will be able to draw upon how it sounded when you said it. Saying it only in your mind is not as effective as saying it **aloud**.

Give a Number Meaning If Possible

Though my college days began several decades ago, I will never forget the post office box number I had at Yale Station in New Haven: 5256.

Did I remember it as five, two, five, six? No. I remembered it as fifty-two fifty-six, and by doing so the number took on additional meaning to me.

Though neither history nor political science is my favorite subject, I do remember certain dates very well. One date, for example, is 1066 (ten sixty-six), the year of the Battle of Hastings and the Norman Conquest of England. I also remember that Eisenhower was elected President of the United States in 1952 and in 1956. Sometimes I connect other things in my life to those election dates and to similar pieces of information already engraved in my memory.

When I received Box 5256 as my address at college, I connected the years of Eisenhower's election victories to the box number, and gave it meaning that permitted me to remember it.

Of course, the reverse may be helpful as well. If your post office box were 5256 and you needed or wanted to remember the years that Eisenhower was elected, you would have a ready-made trigger at your fingertips—just remember your P.O. box number. This is merely one example. "Coincidences" like this surround us. Connect numbers that you know to other numbers, give them meaning, make them more memorable. This technique is useful in remembering many kinds of numbers, including dates.

Look for Patterns

In a long series of numbers, determine if there is a pattern that can help you to remember. For example, in the series 22, 17, 12, 7, 2, each number is 5 less than the preceding number. How about 3, 4, 6, 9, 13, 18?

Here a pattern manifests itself by adding 1 to the first number, 2 to the second number, 3 to the third number, 4 to the fourth number, and 5 to the fifth number. If the series continued, we would assume that the next number would be 24, determined by adding 6 to the sixth number (18 plus 6 equals 24). What would the number after that be?

Patterns may turn up in circumstances other than numbers. For example, let's say you receive these driving directions: Make a left on the corner, then two blocks to the stop sign and make a right, three blocks to the light and make a left, and one block to Elm and make a right. The pattern that jumps out is left, right, left, right. At least for that portion of the directions, you should have no problem remembering.

Visualize—Engrave or Chisel

To help you remember a number, **visualize** it as you say it aloud, and, more important, visualize the number being **engraved into a band of gold**, or **chiseled into a slab of cement**. This visual image, coupled with the auditory clues developed when you say the number aloud, will serve as a trigger when you want to recall the number. You want to be able to SEE the engraved or chiseled number and HEAR it pronounced.

Use **VISUALIZATION** in all memory tasks when possible, not just in remembering numbers or when using the CURE technique. Get a picture or an image in your mind. It can help tremendously.

As for numbers, if you have a favorite piece of jewelry, ENLARGE the image of the piece in your mind and SEE the engraving of the number taking place. By using a piece of jewelry that is familiar to you, you will be giving yourself one more trigger to help visualize the number. Likewise, if you prefer to see the number chiseled rather than engraved, perhaps you can visualize the sidewalk in front of your house, or the base of a statue that has meaning for you. SEE the chiseling taking place. Perhaps it would work better for you if you saw yourself taking a stick and engraving the number into wet cement. Or perhaps you can visualize yourself or someone else using a jackhammer to etch it into the ground.

Do not feel limited to engraving or chiseling. If carving wood works better for you, use it. Or perhaps a branding iron. Or a paintbrush on canvas. The principle is still the same: SEE the number, and the process.

Remember also to SAY the number ALOUD as it is being engraved or chiseled (or carved, etc.).

Review

To Remember a Number:

1. Simplify and Reduce it.

2. Say it Aloud.

3. Give it Meaning, if possible.

4. Look for Patterns in it.

5. VISUALIZE IT—Engrave or Chisel it into your mind.

Remembering Speeches

More than once, before I began using this system, I delivered an address and left out one or more important points that I had wanted to make. That does not happen to me anymore, because I use this simple method.

As you review the speech beforehand, list the significant ideas in the sequence in which you will offer them. The list can be as detailed or as distilled as you wish. In the end, however, you will have a list—and you already know that you are capable of committing a list to memory, no matter how long.

The worst possible way to deliver a speech is to read it to the audience, unless, of course, your goal is to put them to sleep. You must commit your speech to memory, but you need not memorize every single word.

Learn the significant ideas. Learn them well enough that you can speak with confidence, in your own words, without having to rely on the written speech itself. You will always be able to refer to the speech or to notes in the event that you need to or want to.

Now that you know the significant ideas, simply list them. If you can reduce them to single words, great. If not, however, phrases or sentences are fine: whatever works best for you, given the speech's content. Now, just as you would remember a grocery list, or a list of random objects, CURE the speech's significant ideas in pairs.

For example, in a speech I gave once at a dinner to honor the success and achievement of a group of salespeople, I broke down the speech into a list of five items to remember: (1) humorous opening about the length of the speech; (2) my definition of success; (3) examples of outstanding success, including a quick story about Abraham Lincoln; (4) a brief account of how the honorees had succeeded; (5) the impact of the honorees' success on the future of the company.

I simply CUREd the elements in pairs.

Humorous opening and definition of success: I envisioned an audience howling in **laughter** (for humorous), and out of their mouths came **dictionaries** (for definitions), actually shooting into the air.

Definition of success and examples: I envisioned the **dictionaries** and ZOOMED in to the covers, and on the covers were old photos of **Lincoln** with just a mustache and no beard, wearing a baseball cap. He looked odd, but that's the point.

Lincoln's success and the honorees' success: Each dictionary, still in the air, with the Lincoln cover, turned into **Lincoln himself**, and now there were dozens of him, and each replica, kicking and flailing, came crashing down with great noise and disruption into the area of tables where the **guests of honor** were seated.

Honorees' success and the future of the company: The **honorees** helped each Lincoln to his feet and removed his baseball cap and replaced it with a **space helmet** and also offered him sophisticated, futuristic, high-tech gadgets, symbols of the **future**, especially for Lincoln.

My CUREs were distilled in my mind:

Laughing audience—dictionaries shooting from their mouths to the air.

Zoom in to a dictionary cover—it's a photo of Lincoln in a baseball cap.

The dictionaries turn into full replicas of Lincoln himself.

Each Lincoln comes crashing into the tables of the honorees.

The honorees replace the baseball caps with space helmets.

I remembered the speech without a problem and it went quite well.

Again, if the significant ideas of the speech can be expressed in one or two words, all the better, as long as it works for you. Your speech may have five significant ideas or twenty significant ideas. No matter. Simply CURE the ideas in pairs, and never fear that you will forget.

Review

To Remember Speeches:

1. List the Significant Ideas.
2. CURE them.

Other Important Techniques

When possible, use **RHYMING** to help you remember. Who can forget the spelling rule: "Use *i* before *e* except after *c* or when sounded like *ay* as in *neighbor* or *weigh*." Or how about, "In fourteen hundred ninety-two, Columbus sailed the ocean blue."

Use **REPETITION**. Practice makes perfect, whether you are trying to play a musical instrument, sharpen athletic skills, or remember facts. Repeating the facts over and over (aloud, if possible) will drill them into your memory.

Be **ACTIVE** when recording information. You are trying to create a trigger for retrieval. If the information goes into your memory passively, it may get lost in the canyons of your mind. On the other hand, if you are active, alert, and aware as you record the information, it will be more readily available when you look for it again.

REVIEW the material you want to remember. How often? As often as possible, but at least twice—as soon as possible after you first memorize it, and as close as possible before you need to retrieve it, such as before a test. Not only will you be assured of passing every time, you will increase your chances of scoring a high grade.

Use **LINKS** whenever possible, linking what is easy to remember to what is difficult to remember. For example, to remember how to spell the word *principal,* the person in charge of a school, think of this link: "The principal is my pal." The word *pal* in the sentence is linked to the spelling of the word. This distinguishes it from *principle,* which means a "truth," "standard," or "rule." Another example is stalagmite and stalactite. If you have a difficult time remembering which of these icicle-shaped cave formations hangs from above or rises from below, use the link "g = ground, c = ceiling." The word *stalagmite* has the *g,* which indicates that it rises from the *ground*. The word *stalactite* has the *c,* which indicates that it hangs from the *ceiling*.

Use **STRUCTURE** to help you remember. Let's say you have a constant problem remembering where you put your keys or where you parked your car. By structuring the event—that is, the placing of the keys or the parking of the car—you will never misplace them again. For example, prepare a specific place near the door as the designated location for your keys, such as a dish on a desk, or a hook on the wall. Dedicate this place for your keys only. Then, when you enter the house, ALWAYS put your keys there—in their special place, the place that was established just for them. The structure that you have provided, with both the specific place and with the consistency of always using it for your keys, will permit you to know where they are at all times.

Likewise, designate a specific location where you will park ALWAYS. In parking lots, for example, tell yourself (and the others around you who can help you to remember, such as family, friends, co-workers, and so on) that from now on you will park to the left of the main entrance of the destination building (as you face it), as close to the building as possible. So, if you are going to Sears at the mall, you will park in the lot to the left of the main entrance to Sears, as you face it, as close to the building as possible. On streets, you may want to designate the specific parking spot as, say, always east of the entrance to the location, or always toward the higher-numbered street or avenue, or always in a straight line away from the location (in other words, no turns involved). What you designate is not as important as committing yourself to the **STRUCTURE** of parking with that guideline ALWAYS. You will never misplace your car again.

Confidence and Knowledge

With the techniques presented in this chapter, your memory will improve significantly. Make these techniques a part of your everyday life and you will be able to meet any memory challenge.

Review and Practice

Review the chapter and practice the techniques. Scan the headings. Reread the sections that seem most important to you, the sections that fit your needs.

Next, we will address writing and speaking, but first another fun quiz. Put the answers in your notebook, and indicate whether you answered each question correctly or incorrectly.

QUIZ #8

1. The first 10 amendments to the U.S. Constitution are known by what term?

2. Two centuries of "Roman Peace" (27 B.C. to A.D. 180) was known by what term?

3. A misanthrope
   a. hates mankind
   b. donates money
   c. preceded Cro-Magnon man
   d. not a, b, or c

4. *Don Quixote* was written by whom?

5. What is the formula to find the area of a rectangle?

6. Who was the German scientist who refined Copernicus' theory by identifying certain orbits as elliptical?

7. This composer wrote *The Marriage of Figaro*.

8. Which baseball pitcher has the all-time career record for wins?

9. A fertilizer made from a mixture of decaying organic matter is:
   a. mulch
   b. compost
   c. defoliant
   d. not a, b, or c

10. Who was not a Renaissance painter
    a. Michelangelo
    b. da Vinci
    c. Durer
    d. all of a, b, and c were Renaissance painters

11. What is the therapy designed to relieve anxiety through gradual exposure to the cause?

12. True or false: The Jewish population in the United States is larger than in Israel.

13. "The medium is the message." Who said it?

YOUR ANSWERS

1. _____

2. _____

3. _____

4. _____

5. _____

6. _____

7. _____

8. _____

9. _____

10. _____

11. _____

12. _____

13. _____

5. Week Three—Simple Steps to Improving Writing and Speaking

It is a sobering thought that each of us gives his hearers and his readers a chance to look into the inner working of his mind when he speaks or writes.

—J. M. BARKER

HAVE YOU EVER HAD A GREAT IDEA that came to you when you least expected it, maybe after waking up one morning? You couldn't wait to tell someone or to write it down. You knew you were really on to something. Then, a funny thing happened when you did try to tell someone or when you did try to write it down: You found that you couldn't articulate it. You couldn't put it together as neatly as it seemed in your head. You ended up thinking that maybe it wasn't such a great idea after all.

Writing and speaking force us to put structure to our thoughts. As thoughts rumble around in our mind, we don't need a high degree of structure. After all, we understand our own thoughts and ideas better than anyone. We may not notice gaps in logic as we think. Putting our thoughts on paper or articulating them orally, however, especially in a public speech, releases them to the world around us and exposes any gaps or flaws.

Writing and speaking, testing and filtering thoughts, make us think more clearly. The more we write and speak, the more practice we get in this clear thinking.

You'll want to devote the next week to this chapter, and to use what you learn in your everyday activities.

Strictly Speaking

When speaking in public, please bear in mind the following fundamentals:

1. MAKE EYE CONTACT TO ESTABLISH A RAPPORT WITH THE AUDIENCE.

Have you ever listened to a speech and had the speaker look you right
in the eye, as if he was talking directly to you? Even if there were 10,000
other people in attendance, for that instant, you felt special as the
object of the speaker's attention.

This is the feeling you want to impart every time you speak. You
want the audience to know that you appreciate them, each and every
one. Look out into the audience. Make eye contact with someone and
hold it for a few seconds. Switch your focus and make contact with
someone else. After a while, switch again to someone else. You are
establishing a bond with these people, one by one, a bond that implies
that you will speak to them if they will listen to you. At the same time,
you are persuading them to be sympathetic to your message, which
they may be inclined to do in return for the special treatment you are
according them.

Speak into a mirror to see exactly what you will look like when
delivering your speech. Remember Robert De Niro in *Taxi Driver*: "You
talking to me?" Yes.

When rehearsing, look at various objects around the room—chairs,
tables, knickknacks, lamps—and imagine that they are people attending your talk. Practice looking directly at them. You can't underestimate
the importance of eye contact in establishing a rapport with the audience.

2. SPEAK LOUDLY ENOUGH TO BE HEARD IN THE FARTHEST CORNER OF THE ROOM.

It would be easy to say "duh" to this. Who doesn't know that it is
important to speak loudly enough to be heard? Well, judging from the
speakers we hear regularly, even if people know they should do this,
they are not doing it.

We hear our own voice when we speak. Our vocal cords are not very far away from our ears. It is easy to assume that if you can hear your own voice, others can hear it too. Of course, this is not so.

When speaking publicly, project your voice to the person sitting farthest away. If that person can hear you, the people close to you will be able to hear you. Determine approximately how far away the farthest audience member will be sitting, and place a tape recorder that far away from you when practicing your speech. When you replay the rehearsal you will get an idea of how effective your projection is.

You have devoted a lot of time to preparing a great speech. Why risk wasting it by failing in a fundamental task? If the audience cannot hear you, you have wasted their time and yours.

3. ABSOLUTELY, POSITIVELY, DO NOT USE "UM" OR "UH" OR OTHER SUCH SOUNDS WHEN PAUSING.

Few other tortures compare to attending a speech or listening to an interview in which the speaker punctuates sentences with "um" or "uh" or other such sounds. Equally maddening is the continuing use— and misuse—of the words *like* and *go* and *sort of*.

"I am really pleased to, like, be here tonight, um, to accept this award. Uhhhh, I do want to thank God for sort of giving me the ability to, like, do all the stuff that, um, I do. I want to thank Bill. He's sort of my right-hand man. It would have been, like, impossible to do what I did without him. I spoke with him earlier tonight and he goes, you're like the best. You deserve this award. And I go like, no, Bill, it's sort of like both of us, um . . ."

This is not the way to give a successful speech.

4. REHEARSE, REHEARSE, REHEARSE.

Even if a speech sounds okay in your head when you read it to yourself, you still need to rehearse it aloud. It may sound good as you think it, but confused when you speak it.

Take advantage of today's technology. Videotape your speech (or use a digital camera, etc.). Play it back to see and hear what you need to improve. Rehearse until it is just right. If any part drags, fix it immediately. If *you* notice a problem, you can be sure that your audience will, too.

Rehearse in front of family or friends. Have them tell you which parts need attention. The object of your speech is to communicate with

listeners; they can tell you how effective it is. If they think certain parts
need fixing, you should consider the feedback.

Writing

Good writing springs from a good grammatical foundation and from
years of practice. Even if you didn't have good teachers or role models,
however, there are some general rules to abide by for good results.

Step 1. Don't Slow the Flow in the Beginning.

This approach pertains to virtually every piece of writing. It is not so
much what you *do,* but what you *think,* as you engage in the writing
process. It is an attitude.

Get the ideas down on paper or onto the computer screen. Do not
worry about ANYTHING in the beginning of the writing project except
to **GET THE PROJECT ITSELF UNDER WAY.** Bogging down the writing process can kill the enthusiasm and creativity necessary for writing
a good piece.

One of the easiest ways to bog down the writing process is to be
overly concerned with details in the beginning stages of the piece, be it
a letter, report, composition, or any other kind of writing. Spelling,
grammar, and punctuation are important to good writing, but you can
review and make changes in the middle and later stages; you need not
worry about them in the beginning, especially while brainstorming,
outlining, or generating first drafts. During the early stages, write down
as much of the big picture as possible. Let the thoughts flow on to the
paper as quickly as they enter your mind. Wait until you are revising to
fine-tune your thoughts.

You don't want a great thought to escape you because you spent too
much time worrying about details or because you attempted to refine a
particular point before moving on to the next. Great thoughts are the
substance of great writing and you cannot afford to let even one escape.

Step 2. See the Big Picture: Brainstorm
and Outline.

Think intensely about the topic, and outline the piece. As you brain-
storm, keep the big picture in view at all times. Write down anything

and everything that comes into your mind. Do not worry about order or structure at this point. Capture as many details as possible in lists or phrases or sentences—whatever feels comfortable. Use NEOTWY to help: Ask Who? What? Where? When? Why? How? Do not worry about excess here. It is better to have too much than not enough. Cover as much ground as you can. In writing the outline, you will keep the appropriate points and discard the points that do not fit.

Many good writers use an outline to sketch out the picture and organize their points before actually beginning to write the text. Outlines can be very helpful in seeing on paper a beginning, a middle, and an end to what you want to express. Outlines can help you test the strength of your ideas, and, if they look weak or odd, you can shift them or change them to suit.

Use an outline structure that works best for you. Keep it simple. Use either sentences, phrases, or single words, and don't get weighed down with details. View it as a **blueprint.** A piece about your vacation in Rio, for example, may follow the example below.

My Vacation in Rio
  I. The trip down (beginning)
  - the odd driver and the hilarious taxi ride to the airport
  - the bumpy airplane ride through patches of clouds
  - the view of Rio from the air as it lay in the sun

 II. The stay in the city (middle)
  - the condition of the city and the beaches
  - the swimwear you noticed
  - the bellhop at the hotel
  - the night you and the other travelers got sick after a meal

III. The trip back (end)
  - the interesting thing that happened on the plane ride back
  - the incredible coincidence of getting the same odd cab driver going home
  - your thoughts in retrospect on the value of the trip

This piece may need a lot of work to pull it together enough to interest a reader more than, say, a home movie of your travels (and you know how boring they can get after a while), but at least the outline above has sketched the big picture in an order that makes sense. It is not the only way to outline this piece; there are dozens of other ways. Here is another outline, with the same essence, but in a slightly different form.

My Vacation in Rio
  I. The trip down (beginning)
    A. to the airport
      1. the hilarious taxi ride
      2. the odd driver
    B. airplane
      1. the bumpy ride through patches of clouds
      2. the view of Rio from the air
        a. as it lay in the sun (weather)
        b. as it lay in the sun (desc. of buildings, beaches, etc.)
  II. The stay in the city (middle)
    A. the condition
      1. of the city
      2. of the beaches
    B. the swimwear you noticed
    C. the bellhop at the hotel
    D. the night you and the other travelers got sick after a meal
  III. The trip back (end)
    A. the interesting thing that happened on the plane ride back
    B. the incredible coincidence of getting the same odd cab driver going home.
    C. your thoughts in retrospect on the value of the trip

Of course, you may approach a story in several different ways, and, as a result, the outlines would be completely different in content, if not in form. For example, you could contrast this vacation to the last one you took—to Australia. Or you could compare it to the last time you were in Rio. Or you could focus exclusively on the people you met during your stay.

Outlines may change as you write the piece. As Viper said to Maverick in *Top Gun*, "A good pilot must constantly reassess." Keep reminding yourself to **keep seeing the big picture**. Regardless of how you approach the piece, or of what you feel you should emphasize, use your outline as a contractor would use a blueprint to build a house or a skyscraper.

Think of writing an outline as pleasant and beneficial. Think of how it helps you establish the structure you will follow and how it will make the overall writing easier for you.

Step 3. State the Point of the Piece Immediately.

When I taught writing at Harvard University, I had my students state the point of each paper in the very first sentence. By the end of the course, I would let them attempt to state it in the second or third sentence, or even in the last sentence of the first paragraph, but rarely, if ever, could they state it later than the first paragraph. In most instances, particularly when you are attempting to improve your skills, the "point sentence" or "thesis sentence" or "topic sentence" should be the very first sentence of the piece.

Many readers—maybe even you fall into this category—often do not read beyond the first paragraph of a piece. Generally, we approach a piece of writing wanting to know immediately what it is about, and as much as possible about how the writer intends to treat the topic. If a reader gets to the end of your first paragraph and still does not know the specific point you are going to make in the piece, you may have missed your only opportunity to state your thoughts.

You may be thinking that it is impossible to state the point of the piece in only one sentence. Nonsense. Simply distill what you are about to say into one clear, concise thought. Whether you are writing a 20-page report or a two-page letter, your writing must have a point, and you must capture that point in one sentence.

Let's say you are writing a report about the state of communism in Eastern Europe today, an assignment for school or an analysis for the international trade department of your business. If you have established the big picture in your mind, preferably in an outline, and the report has a beginning, a middle, and an end, then you must have a point in mind to make to your professor or to your boss and, most important, to yourself. What is it?

Is it that the fall of communism in Eastern Europe has created an enormous, untapped market for Western businesses? Is it that the current state of affairs in Eastern Europe demonstrates conspicuously that communism was the glue that held together the economies of the countries, and that, without it, certain countries are doomed to constant struggle? What do you want to describe, explain, or defend in your 20 pages? Tell us, the readers, clearly, in the very first sentence of the report.

Go back to the outline about the vacation in Rio. The piece as sketched has no significant point. But now you can go back to it and impose that point. Did you, perhaps, see the trip as a metaphor or microcosm of your life? Are the legs of the trip analogous to the legs of the life journey or the spiritual journey or the career journey you are on? Adjust the outline to fit your point.

Let's say you are writing a letter to a corporation. What is the point of your letter? Are you writing a manufacturer to complain about a defective product? Do you want your money back? Do you want to exchange the product for a new one? Do you simply want the satisfaction of knowing that you have brought this matter to the attention of the company? Does the defect cause a safety problem that may jeopardize others?

Distill the message into one clear sentence and state it in the beginning of the letter. You will know then for certain that the reader has been exposed to the essence of your thoughts, whether he or she reads the entire letter or not. Go on to explain, describe, or argue your point further in the letter, but do not fail to state it in the first sentence.

The "point sentence" or "thesis sentence" serves two important functions: First, it forces *you* to think carefully about exactly what you want to say; second, it presents that thought to the readers immediately to help them understand better what is about to be read. You can and should distill your thesis, your opinion, your argument, your description—whatever it is that you want to say—into one sentence and place it in the beginning of the piece. If you cannot put the essence of your thoughts into one sentence, then you may not have a distinct point to make, and if that is so, then you may not have a reader interested enough to engage the piece, at least beyond the first paragraph.

Step 4. Tell Them What You Are Going To Say. Say It. Tell Them What You Said.

This is a tried-and-true method of writing that will give you ample opportunity to be understood. Use it with confidence.

All good writing needs a beginning, a middle, and an end. State the point of the piece in the first paragraph to establish the beginning. In essence, you tell the reader what you are going to discuss in the middle of the piece.

In the middle of the piece, the good writer provides significant support, description, or explanation of the point stated in the opening paragraph. For example, if the point of your piece is that the decline of communism in Europe has devastated the economy of countries X, Y, and Z, then you need to support that contention. Just because you say that something is so does not mean that it is true or that the reader will believe it; you need to support what you say. You may want to provide statistics that clearly demonstrate, for instance, that the economy slipped in countries X, Y, and Z after the decline of communism. If the topic of your piece is the environment and your point concerns the harmful effects that the average person can have on it, you would provide hard evidence from scientific studies.

If your piece is descriptive, the middle is the place for amplifying your description. Say the point of your piece concerns the architectural beauty that generally goes unnoticed in a certain city. In the middle of the piece you would provide examples of architectural highlights in that city—the flying buttresses of a particular church, or the intricate cornice work on particular office complexes, or the bas-relief on certain buildings.

If you are writing an explanative essay—like how a battery works—you would provide details in the middle of the piece. Perhaps you would create an image that nonscientific minds could easily understand: Picture, for example, that there is a pipe that runs through the middle of the battery from end to end. The pipe is just wide enough to accept golf balls. Now picture yourself loading golf balls into the pipe, one after the other, and, as you load one in, it pushes the other balls deeper and deeper into the battery, until, eventually, the first golf ball exits the other end of the pipe. This, you could point out, represents the flow of electricity through a battery, with the golf balls representing electrons.

The more attention you pay to explaining the process in the middle of the piece, the more appreciative the readers will be, and the more likely that they will understand your explanation, which is, of course, the goal of your writing.

What about the end? Good writers know that readers generally remember the end of a piece more readily than any other part. To leave a piece without a proper closing is to leave the reader unsatisfied, perhaps with a sense that your writing is incomplete, which, in effect, clouds your credibility and jeopardizes your success.

The end must relate to the middle and to the beginning. The simplest, most effective method of ending a piece successfully is to summarize briefly what you said and to draw a conclusion that repeats the point you stated in the opening paragraph. Summarizing is not the same as simply repeating. An effective summary is brief, containing only key words and phrases from the body of the piece, and covering all points made in the body. Draw a conclusion from it. A good summary **distills** the information presented into prominent pieces that fit together into a one- or two- or three-sentence foundation that supports your main point.

For example, in your communism piece, you may wish to close by summarizing the facts demonstrated by the statistics you provided: "As the statistics clearly demonstrate in countries X, Y, and Z, after the demise of communism, unemployment rose, the gross national product declined, and inflation more than quadrupled." This easily flows into the final sentence, which reaffirms the point stated in the opening paragraph: "There can be no doubt that the fall of communism in these countries contributed significantly to the devastation of their economies."

By sandwiching your argument, explanation, or description between a "point/thesis" sentence and a summary, you offer yourself three opportunities to communicate with the reader.

Step 5. Revise, Revise, Revise.

There are two kinds of writers in the world: "Mozartians" and "Beethovenites." Mozartians, like Mozart, can write the first draft of a piece from beginning to end with minimal hesitation in the process, revising in their minds as they go. The Beethovenites, like Beethoven, need to revise the first draft of a piece over and over before considering it respectable and comprehendible.

Whether you see yourself as a Mozartian or a Beethovenite, when you write your first draft, know full well that you will need to review it and revise it several times before others can appreciate it. Think of the revision stages as **opportunities** to fine-tune a piece and to make any corrections and improvements it needs. Even if you revise in your mind as you write, you should write a first draft and then keep revising until you are comfortable that you no longer can improve the piece significantly. Every English teacher to have stepped into a classroom has had a fair share of students who hand in compositions without ever bothering to revise. You can be sure that those are not the "A" students.

Some writers may need to revise less than others, but every piece requires a review and revision. Even if you articulate the thoughts well, you may have a misspelling, omission, typographical error, or logic gap. Humans make mistakes.

The Secret to Successful Revision

Put your consumer cap on for a moment. Virtually every product we buy has been tested extensively before it reaches the store. From food products to sunglasses to automobiles, manufacturers test the quality and form of the product, and their marketing analysts test the expected public response to it. After all, manufacturers are in business to make money, and if the product does not sell, it will no longer be produced.

The inherent goal that the writer has in mind when he or she launches a piece is to communicate thoughts successfully to the reader. If the reader cannot understand your piece, you cannot consider it successful.

The best method of testing for success before you launch your writing into the world is to: **Let readers read it, and pay attention carefully to what they say about it.**

When I taught writing, I used peer review to help students revise their papers. Students were divided into groups of three and shared their assigned essays in draft stages. Each student reviewed the papers of the two other members of the group and also received feedback on his or her own writing from those same group members. Even though the students liked this exercise, some who felt that their ability to write was superior to the others in their group initially questioned whether they could gain anything from the feedback of less accomplished writers. At first they also questioned whether any student could have enough expertise to offer credible feedback.

I explained that no student was expected to have significant expertise as a writer, but each was to *read* the paper and offer comments on how well the paper communicated. The peer reviewers served as an **audience**. They didn't need expertise in writing to serve successfully in that role. If they discovered parts of the paper that were difficult to read or understand—for whatever reason—they were to point out those parts. The peer reviewers were not to judge whether any particular part of the paper was good or bad writing, but only to make comments that reflected their **reactions as readers**. The writers had to respect the comments of the peer reviewers, their audience, though they were not forced to accept suggested changes.

To be successful in everything you write, build into your writing process a revision stage that includes getting feedback from readers, family, friends, or co-workers. Ask them to tell you if they notice any parts that are not clear or that seem tangled, confusing, or incomplete. While they are at it, they may also notice spelling errors or typos. Explain that you would appreciate it if they did not make judgments about the writing: you are interested in their opinions as readers. Ask them to confine their comments to how they were able to read the piece from beginning to end. Be patient with those who agree to help you. It may take a while for them to give you what you seek. But having a regular group of readers will help you to write and revise better.

You can write well. Practice the above steps this week. Write every day. After this week, continue to hone your skills. Writing fosters clear thought. Get a notebook devoted exclusively to writing, and write in it every day. Write whatever you wish—descriptions of the day's events, your thoughts and opinions on world issues, your blockbuster novel. Anything. Not only will you be practicing to become a better writer, you will be moving one step closer to completing your Intelligence Makeover.

It's time for another fun quiz. Score each question in the quiz section of your notebook when you're finished.

QUIZ #9

1. What significant world event occurred on 12/7/41?

2. What is today's name for the city that was once called Byzantium and Constantinople?

3. If anything is incorrect in the following sentence, correct it: Irregardless of the injury to his hand, he used the calculator to count the amount of marbles on the table.

4. Shakespeare's title character Macbeth was:
    a. a Danish prince
    b. an Italian merchant
    c. a Scottish widow
    d. not a, b, or c

5. Pi equals:
    a. 3.04
    b. 3.14
    c. 3.24
    d. 3.34

6. What is the geocentric theory?

7. Who created *The Pirates of Penzance* and *The Mikado*?

8. In men's tennis, who has the most career wins in Grand Slam Singles?

9. Which is a conifer?
    a. pine
    b. spruce
    c. fir
    d. a, b, and c are all conifers

10. What country is associated with the following: Goya, Dali, Picasso?

11. Identify: "Stimulation following a response, which increases the likelihood that the same response will be made in the future under similar circumstances."

12. Has there been a Catholic president of the United States? If so, who?

13. "When you come to a fork in the road, take it." Who said it?

YOUR ANSWERS

1. _____

2. _____

3. _____

4. _____

5. _____

6. _____

7. _____

8. _____

9. _____

10. _____

11. _____

12. _____

13. _____

6. Your New Path: The Individualized Makeover Plan

CONSIDER THIS STORY ABOUT Albert Einstein on a train: As the conductor moved through each car, asking passengers for tickets, Einstein reached into the inside pocket of his jacket for his ticket, which was not there. He dug into his other pockets without success. By the time the conductor reached him, the renowned man of science was standing by his seat, his pants pockets turned inside out and their contents strewn across two cushions.

Sympathetic, the conductor told him to take his time, and moved into the next car, promising to return.

Einstein lifted the cushions and checked the overhead racks, still to no avail. The conductor returned to find him bent to the floor, searching beneath the seats.

"Please don't worry, Mr. Einstein," the conductor said. "I trust you. I'm sure you purchased a ticket."

Einstein looked up and said, "It's not a matter of trust. It's a matter of direction. Without my ticket, how am I going to know where I'm going?"

Direction is an important element at this point in your Intelligence Makeover. You need a plan to know where you are going. Now it is time to confirm the subjects you want to explore.

The subjects covered in the final section include U.S. History, World History, English, Literature, Math, Science, Music, Sports, Gardening/Nature, Art History, Psychology, Religion, and Quotations. You may choose to explore any or all of them. You can skim them or delve deeply. To help you decide, this chapter will digest your testing results and collate the other information you have provided.

But first, please take this last fun quiz. Score it in the quiz section of your notebook as soon as you're finished.

QUIZ #10

1. Which decision by the U.S. Supreme Court established the right of judicial review?

2. Who fought in the Peloponnesian War?

3. What, if anything, is wrong with this sentence: He likes to listen to music alot.

4. Who wrote the short story "The Cask of Amontillado"?

5. What ancient mathematician and physicist discovered the value of pi?

6. James Watson, Francis Crick, and Maurice Wilkins shared the Nobel Prize in 1962 for what discovery (made in 1953)?

7. In 2002, for the first time since 1980, a musical artist won Grammies in the same year for Single of the Year, Album of the Year, and Best New Artist. Who was it?

8. Who won the Tour de France bicycle race for the sixth consecutive year in 2004?

9. The largest phylum in the animal world is
    a. insects
    b. arthropods
    c. crustaceans
    d. spiders
    e. none of these

10. Mary Cassatt belonged to which artistic movement in 19th-century France?

11. Which "Humanist" psychologist developed a theory that humans have a "Hierarchy of Needs"?

12. In the Church of England, which high-ranking position serves as "Primate of All England"? (Hint: George Carey served from 1991 to 2002 and was followed by Rowan Williams.)

13. "A little learning is a dangerous thing." Who said it?

YOUR ANSWERS

1. _____

2. _____

3. _____

4. _____

5. _____

6. _____

7. _____

8. _____

9. _____

10. _____

11. _____

12. _____

13. _____

Quiz Results

Let's take a look at your quiz results to see how you fared, with the understanding that the ultimate decision on direction always rests with you. If you haven't corrected all of your quizzes, please do that now. The answers are provided at the back of the book. For each question in each of the 10 quizzes, put a mark next to your responses to indicate whether you answered the question correctly or incorrectly. You will be tallying your score for each individual answer (more on this below). Now tally the number of correct and incorrect responses for each quiz— it should always total 13. So, for Quiz #1, for example, you may have answered 9 questions correctly and 4 questions incorrectly. In Quiz #2, perhaps the tally is 6 correct, 7 incorrect. In your notebook, record this information for each quiz.

Do not continue until you have scored all the quizzes.

The quizzes followed a distinct pattern. Each quiz contained 13 questions—one question in each of 13 subject areas. For example, every Question #1 focused on U.S. History. Every Question #2 focused on World History. See the distribution below.

For your cumulative tally, you will need to keep track of how you fared with each question on each quiz. For example, over the 10 quizzes, how did you do on all the Questions #1? All together, there were a total of 10 Questions #1. How many of the 10 did you get correct? In your notebook, copy the list below. Indicate how many correct responses you made over the 10 quizzes and how many incorrect. When you have scored all 10 quizzes, you should have a total of 10 responses for each question, some in the "correct" column, some in the "incorrect" column.

Keep Track of the 10 Quizzes

QUESTION #/SUBJECT	CORRECT + INCORRECT	=	TOTAL
1. U.S. History	+		= 10
2. World History	+		= 10
3. English	+		= 10
4. Literature	+		= 10
5. Math	+		= 10
6. Science	+		= 10
7. Music	+		= 10
8. Sports	+		= 10
9. Nature	+		= 10
10. Art History	+		= 10
11. Psychology	+		= 10
12. Religion	+		= 10
13. Quotations	+		= 10
TOTAL	+		= 130

Again, with 10 quizzes in all, your final tally for each question number should always equal 10, as indicated above. For example, in the end you may discover that the tally for all the Question #6 responses (Science) equals 7 correct and 3 incorrect, and for all the Question #9 responses (Nature), the tally was 2 correct and 8 incorrect.

When you have determined your grand totals for each of the 13 questions on all 10 quizzes, tally on the bottom line the total number of correct and the total number of incorrect—it should add up to 130 (10 quizzes x 13 questions = 130).

ABOUT THE RESULTS

You now have an indication of the level of your strength in 13 different subject areas. With a total of 10 questions in each area, it is relatively simple to score. For example, a score of 8 correct in an area is equivalent to getting 80 percent of the questions correct. A score of 5 correct is equivalent to 50 percent. Simply add a zero to the number correct in order to determine the percentage.

Look at your results for Question #1. How many were correct, and how many were incorrect? All of these questions focused on U.S. History. Now look at how you did overall on Question #2. All of these questions focused on World History. By tallying your scores on the individual questions, you can see how you fared in each of the 13 different subject areas.

Keep the quiz results in perspective. These results are not meant to be the end-all in determining your prowess. The tallies indicate your overall score on 10 quizzes covering 13 subject areas, and your individual score in each subject area. While this is useful information, and can guide you in forming your Makeover Plan, your scores might be different on another set of 10 quizzes in the same subject areas. Perhaps you would score higher in some areas and lower in others. Again, these results are simply meant to be a guide, not a definitive measure of your fundamental knowledge.

A score of 2 correct and 8 incorrect in U.S. History could confirm your sense that this is an area that needs to be shored up. Or, say, scoring 10 of 10 correct in Music may indicate that you need no further exploration in that subject, unless of course you wish to venture into it for pure pleasure or enrichment.

In the end, you may wish to explore all 13 areas, regardless of how you fared on the quizzes. That would be fine. The final chapters offer you the opportunity to explore as many or as few subjects as you choose.

Record your scores in percentages in the list below and in your notebook. Simply add a zero to the number of correct responses you had in a question, and therefore in a subject area, over the course of the 10 quizzes.

SUBJECT	SCORE (PERCENTAGE CORRECT IN 10 QUIZZES)
1. U.S. History	%
2. World History	%
3. English	%
4. Literature	%
5. Math	%
6. Science	%
7. Music	%
8. Sports	%
9. Nature	%
10. Art History	%
11. Psychology	%
12. Religion	%
13. Quotations	%

This list should provide insight into your comparative strengths.

Intellectual Dreams

A review of your intellectual dreams can help you decide where to spend your time and energy in your makeover. In Chapter 2, you recorded in your notebook thoughts of where you felt you stood intellectually at the moment, and where you felt you would like to be in the future. Here's where you start to make concrete plans to make those dreams a reality. Even if the dream is a long-term goal, you can begin the journey here. For example, if your intellectual dream includes reading 20 books over the next five years, or getting a law degree, or completing a course of study in preparation for a career change, you may be expecting to spend the next three to five years fully engaged in the effort. But make your first step right now.

Review the notes you recorded about your dreams. Pay particular attention to anything that you marked with a star or other symbol to indicate importance. Consider where you want to be intellectually in five years, 10 years, and at retirement. You may want to refer to Chapter 2, Intellectual Dreams, from time to time to refresh your memory.

Learning Style, Likes, Dislikes, Strengths, Weaknesses

Because you have characteristics that make you special, different from everyone else, as you develop your Makeover Plan, consider the following: your personality, schooling, body of knowledge, creativity, idiosyncrasies, problem-solving ability, social intelligence, and personal history.

You are the best judge of which characteristics should weigh most heavily in formulating the optimum plan for a makeover. As you map out your strategy, take into account all of the pertinent information about yourself, your interests, your dreams, your unique nature, your abilities, and how you learn best.

Of particular importance are the answers to these questions: What is your learning style? Do you learn best by touching, smelling, tasting, seeing, hearing, saying, or doing? What are your needs and desires, likes and dislikes, strengths and weaknesses?

ROUTINE

In order to draw up the most efficient, most feasible plan, you need to determine the routine that will work best for you, and you need to commit yourself to sticking with it. In other words, what is the NEOTWY that will permit you to work regularly on the makeover, without distractions and without missing sessions?

WHEN

What time of day or night is optimum for reading or for visiting the Internet? What day(s) of the week can you devote routinely to visiting physical locations, like museums and libraries? Which specific calendar dates will permit optimum effort?

WHERE

What location will afford you quiet, undisturbed hours?

WHO

Whose cooperation will you need to pull this off?

WHAT

What arrangements might you have to make—like reserving space—in order to have the ideal set-up for reading, studying, Web surfing, and so on? What else will you need? What are you striving for?

HOW

How will you accommodate this routine? For example, will you need babysitters? Will you need money to buy books or materials? What potential obstacles may arise, and just how do you intend to manage them? It is better to anticipate than to react.

WHY

Are you firm on why you are moving forward? Do you have motivation? If not, do you have a plan for establishing and maintaining motivation? Can you insert the motivational sources into the routine, returning regularly to spur you on? The more you keep the carrot in view, the easier will be the walk. And the easier the walk, the easier the overall journey.

The Plan

Every journey begins with the first step. You have taken that step, and now can map out your plan for continuing your makeover. Fill in the blanks and keep this plan handy. It is a physical representation of your commitment to change, to reinvent yourself. It is a path, a route designed just for you, a route that will take you from where you are now to where you want to be. Review it often.

On the top of each page you will write: "I learn best by———." More than one response is acceptable. This will be a constant reminder for you to accommodate your learning style. If, for example, you learn best by seeing, then you may consider spending much of your time reading, or watching instructional videos or DVDs, or visiting museums where you can actually *see* the object(s) you read about. If you learn best by hearing, you may want to consider devoting more of your energy to listening to tapes, CDs, or lectures. If you learn best by doing, you may plan to get out a lot and make appointments for engaging in activities related to the subject. You get the idea. Tailor this plan in a way that gives you the best chance to reach your goals most efficiently and effectively. With that in mind, it is time to map out your intellectual future.

The complete document will be made up of a series of pages. They are, by design, simple and nonintimidating. In your notebook, dedicate a section specifically to the plan. The first page looks at the big picture—what is your ultimate goal? Is it to teach Shakespeare in college, or to read a dozen books this year, or to change careers? What is it that will change for you? Taking a step back, what do you need to do to reach that ultimate goal? Focus on the big picture. Use the format below for convenience, or create your own form—whatever will work best for you.

Working backward, devote the next page to related goals. For example, if your ultimate goal is to teach, your penultimate goal may be to earn a degree that will get you hired. Perhaps you need a master's. What are the details? How will you work toward this?

Regardless of how long your ultimate goal will take, devote a page to cover your plans for the next months. Use the following template pages to cover your plans for each month (make 12 copies, one for each month). And devote the other template pages to cover weekly and daily activities, making copies as appropriate.

The Individualized Makeover Plan   **BIG PICTURE**

NAME: _____   DATE BEGUN: _____

I LEARN BEST BY: _____

The Ultimate Goal: _____

People I need to see/contact to accomplish this ultimate goal:

Locations free of distractions for my routine reading, writing, study, Internet time, etc.:

Where I will travel, visit, etc.:

Estimated Time/Date of Achieving Ultimate Goal:

Specifics: List materials and locations to engage, such as books, tapes, CDs, DVDs, libraries, museums, cities, etc.:

What arrangements need to be made to achieve this ultimate goal (e.g., costs, babysitting, travel, time off work, vacation, etc.):

The Individualized Makeover Plan | INTELLECTUAL DREAMS |

NAME: _____ TODAY'S DATE: _____

I LEARN BEST BY: _____

Briefly, what my life will be like 5 years from now:

Briefly, what my life will be like 10 years from now:

Briefly, what my life will be like 20 years from now:

Briefly, what my life will be like next year:

Briefly, what my life will be like next month:

Briefly, what my life will be like next week:

In regard to achieving my goal, what specifically I am going to do tomorrow:

The Individualized Makeover Plan | THIS COMING YEAR |

NAME: _____ TODAY'S DATE: _____

I LEARN BEST BY: _____

The Goal for the Year: _____

People I need to see/contact this year to accomplish the goal:

Locations free of distractions for my routine reading, writing, study, Internet time, etc.:

Where I will travel, visit, etc.:

Estimated Time/Date of Achieving Goal:

Specifics: List materials and locations to engage, such as books, tapes, CDs, DVDs, libraries, museums, cities, etc.:

What arrangements need to be made to achieve this goal (e.g., costs, babysitting, travel, time off work, vacation, etc.):

The Individualized Makeover Plan

> **MONTH**

NAME: _____ TODAY'S DATE: _____

I LEARN BEST BY: _____

The Goal for the Month: _____

People I need to see/contact this month to accomplish the goal:

Locations free of distractions for my routine reading, writing, study, Internet time, etc.:

Where I will travel, visit, etc.:

Estimated Time/Date of Achieving Goal:

Specifics: List materials and locations to engage, such as books, tapes, CDs, DVDs, libraries, museums, cities, etc.:

What arrangements need to be made to achieve this goal (e.g., costs, babysitting, travel, time off work, vacation, etc.):

The Individualized Makeover Plan

WEEK

NAME: _____ TODAY'S DATE: _____

I LEARN BEST BY: _____

The Goal for the Week: _____

People I need to see/contact this week to accomplish the goal:

Locations free of distractions for my routine reading, writing, study, Internet time, etc.:

Where I will travel, visit, etc.:

Estimated Time/Date of Achieving Goal:

Specifics: List materials and locations to engage, such as books, tapes, CDs, DVDs, libraries, museums, cities, etc.:

What arrangements need to be made to achieve this goal (e.g., costs, babysitting, travel, time off work, vacation, etc.):

The Individualized Makeover Plan

DAY

NAME: _____   TODAY'S DATE: _____

I LEARN BEST BY: _____

The Goal for the Day: _____

People I need to see/contact today to accomplish the goal:

Locations free of distractions for my routine reading, writing, study, Internet time, etc.:

Where I will travel, visit, etc.:

I will begin today at what time?

Estimated Time of Achieving Today's Goal:

Specifics: List materials and locations to engage, such as books, tapes, CDs, DVDs, libraries, museums, cities, etc.:

What arrangements need to be made to achieve this goal (e.g., costs, babysitting, travel, time off work, vacation, etc.):

. . . All You Need to Know

PART III

FOUNDATIONAL KNOWLEDGE

These final chapters provide a wealth of resources to help you plant your feet and get your bearings in your quest for knowledge. Foundational Knowledge covers thirteen different subject areas, with essays and facts that will serve as starting points and conversation pieces. Reading lists, Web sites, and numerous other resources point you to where to go for deeper explorations.

This section's information will help you determine what you want to explore further, and grounds you so that you can venture out on your own. The aim here is to give you a launching pad in that subject. You can learn more by using the complete set of resources provided.

The particular facts listed in each subject are significant and worth knowing, even if they are not necessarily the most important facts, since *most important* is a relative term. If 100 "experts" in a given field were asked to choose 25 "most important facts in that subject, the lists would likely not agree. There would be accord on some, but there also would be stark differences. I chose these nuggets as valuable pieces of information integral to the subject, not too elementary, not too sophisticated. Since every subject contains hundreds of thousands, if not millions, of facts, all cannot be listed in a volume like this, but a relative handful can give you a reasonable starting point.

The titles offered in the "Reading" sections come from a wide variety of sources. Some are best-sellers. Some are used in syllabi at Harvard, Yale, and other universities. Many are well-known standards, while others are best-kept secrets. Quite a few are included in almost any version of *The Western Canon,* and a sprinkling are obscure treasures from my personal library.

In baseball, a common chant to the hitter from his teammates tells him to look over the pitches carefully—"It only takes one." Don't worry about the score. Don't let the fact that your team is losing distract you. Don't worry about anything but the one pitch that is next. Because it only takes one. One good swing can put the ball in play. One timely hit can begin a rally, regardless of the inning. It is no different here. It only takes one. One good book can light a fire in your heart. One enlightening moment, one timely thrill of intellectual success, can turn a day around, indeed a career, or a life. These books may lead to others. These Web sites may click you through to another world. These resources may ignite a passion that has been hiding within you for years. With a little perseverance, the right book, or idea, or "aha!" is sure to cross your path. It only takes one.

You can approach the following chapters from any direction. Please do not feel compelled to start at the beginning. If you are interested in a subject positioned in the middle, jump right in. The hope is that you will have fun as you get smarter.

Cheers.

7. U.S. History

A GOOD STARTING POINT FOR REVISITING U.S. History is a basic, broad-based book to brush up on individual topics. You'll refresh your memory of many names, dates, and events, and you'll discover details that escaped you in the past. Once you've looked through a wide lens, you'll want to focus on particular people, places, and events that strike you as worthy of closer inspection.

Begin with *A History of the American People,* by Paul Johnson (New York: HarperCollins, 1999), 1,100 pages from a British historian who writes about social issues rather than about generals and battles. The *Los Angeles Times* calls it "A fresh, readable and provocative survey." You'll also want to take a look at *The Timetables of American History,* by Laurence Urdang (New York: Touchstone, 2001), which, in timetable format, chronicles the nation's history through events in politics, arts, science, and technology, simultaneously viewing world events in the same areas.

Web sites can help you, too. You'll find lists of sites on U.S. History at History Matters (**http://historymatters.gmu.edu/browse/wwwhistory**) and at the Yahoo Directory (**http://dir.yahoo.com/Arts/Humanities/ History/U_S__History/**). Visit the Library of Congress at **http://www. memory.loc.gov/** for a gateway to primary source materials. And try the History Channel's site at **http://www.historychannel.com/**, which offers articles, discussions, videos, and quizzes.

Other books, Web sites, and resources are listed later in the chapter.

Starting Points and Conversation Pieces

U.S. Supreme Court Cases

❖ *Marbury v. Madison* (1803): Established the right of "judicial review"—that is, that the Supreme Court had the constitutional right to interpret the constitutionality of a law.

❖ *McCulloch v. Maryland* (1819): Established the doctrine of "implied powers"—that is, that Congress had the authority, albeit implied and not specifically stated in the Constitution, to carry out the powers expressly declared in the Constitution.

❖ *Plessy v. Ferguson* (1896): The court held that "separate but equal" laws were constitutional—that is, that it was reasonable to allow state laws that said that blacks could be separated from whites as long as they were accorded equal accommodations.

❖ *Brown v. Board of Education* (1954): Rejected the decision of *Plessy v. Ferguson*. In this decision, the court said that segregating blacks in public schools was a violation of the equal protection rights of the Fourteenth Amendment.

❖ *Mapp v. Ohio* (1961): Search-and-seizure limitations of the Fourth Amendment applied to both state and federal governments.

❖ *Miranda v. Arizona* (1966): Minimum standards established to protect the rights of those in police custody, who were to be informed of their rights prior to questioning, including that they have the right to remain silent, that anything they say may be used against them, and that they have the right to an attorney.

❖ *The New York Times Co. v. the United States* (1971): The court permitted publication of the "Pentagon Papers," a classified report on the Vietnam War.

❖ *Roe v. Wade* (1973): The court ruled that states could not unduly restrict abortion.

❖ *Bush v. Gore* (2000): The court halted a recounting of votes in Florida in the presidential election of 2000. Bush won the state and the presidency.

Terms to Remember

❖ *Federalism*: The philosophy espousing that the national and state governments should share powers.

❖ *Carpetbagger*: Term (usually uncomplimentary) used by Southerners for Northerners who relocated to the South after the Civil War, and who often carried their belongings in a carpetbag.

❖ *Manifest Destiny*: As the boundaries of the country expanded from the eastern colonies in the 19th century, many Americans believed that it was their right to claim and settle the western part of the continent.

❖ *The Great Depression*: A time of severe economic trouble, beginning with the stock market crash of 1929 and carrying through in succeeding years with high rates of unemployment, bank failures, bankruptcy, and poverty.

❖ *New Deal*: In his first term (1934–38), President Franklin D. Roosevelt promised to bring America out of the Great Depression with a "New Deal"—via a series of government-sponsored programs—which would restore confidence and provide relief as the country battled its economic woes.

Notables

❖ *Horace Mann* (1796–1859) is often referred to as the Father of American Public School Education. He was the first Secretary of the Massachusetts State Board of Education and helped to establish a system of free public schools. In 1839 he established the first teacher-training college, called a "Normal" school.

❖ *W. E. B. DuBois* (1868–1963), the first African-American to receive a Ph.D. from Harvard University, was the founder of the NAACP (the National Association for the Advancement of Colored People).

Politics

❖ The *Democratic Party* has its roots in the Democratic Republican faction of Jefferson and Madison. The *Republican Party* has its roots in the Federalist faction of Alexander Hamilton and John Adams.

Documents

❖ From the *Declaration of Independence*: "We hold these Truths to be self-evident, that all Men are created equal, that they are endowed by their Creator with certain unalienable Rights, that among these are Life, Liberty and the Pursuit of Happiness."

❖ Preamble to the *Constitution of the United States*: "We the people of the United States, in order to form a more perfect union, establish justice, insure domestic tranquility, provide for the common defense, promote the general welfare, and secure the blessings of liberty to ourselves and our posterity, do ordain and establish this Constitution for the United States of America."

Key Amendments to the Constitution

❖ *Bill of Rights* (first 10 amendments, which guarantee personal liberties and restrict government power). 1. Freedom of religion, speech, press, and assembly. 2. The right to keep and bear arms. 3. No quartered soldiers without homeowner's consent. 4. No unreasonable searches or seizures. 5. No person subject to double jeopardy, or to be a witness against himself. The right to due process of law. 6. The right to a speedy and public trial. 7. The right to a trial by jury. 8. No cruel or unusual punishment. 9. Constitutional rights shall not deny or disparage other rights. 10. The powers not delegated to the United States by the Constitution are reserved to the states.

❖ *Fourteenth* (affirms and protects citizens' rights to "due process of law" and "equal protection under the law").

❖ *Nineteenth* (women granted the right to vote).

World Wars

❖ *World War I* began in 1914 and ended in 1918. The United States, disturbed in 1915 by the sinking of the ship *Lusitania*, entered in 1917 in response to Germany's escalating submarine warfare.

❖ The United States entered *World War II* (1939–45) following the Japanese bombing of Pearl Harbor on December 7, 1941.

Presidents

❖ Presidential succession in the event of the death of the president: vice president, speaker of the house, president pro tempore of the Senate, secretary of state, cabinet officers in the order that the departments were first established.

❖ Two U.S. presidents have been impeached (officially accused of wrongdoing): Andrew Johnson (1868) and Bill Clinton (1998). Both were acquitted.

❖ Here is a list of all U.S. Presidents and their dates in office: 1. George Washington (1789–97) 2. John Adams (1797–1801) 3. Thomas Jefferson (1801–1809) 4. James Madison (1809–1817) 5. James Monroe (1817–25) 6. John Quincy Adams (1825–29) 7. Andrew Jackson (1829–37) 8. Martin Van Buren (1837–41) 9. William Henry Harrison (1841—served one month and died) 10. John Tyler (1841–45) 11. James K. Polk (1845–49) 12. Zachary Taylor (1849–50—died in office) 13. Millard Fillmore (1850–53) 14. Franklin Pierce (1853–57) 15. James Buchanan (1857–61) 16. Abraham Lincoln (1861–65—assassinated) 17. Andrew Johnson (1865–69) 18. Ulysses S. Grant (1869–77) 19. Rutherford B. Hayes (1877–81) 20. James A. Garfield (1881—assassinated) 21. Chester A. Arthur (1881–85) 22. Grover Cleveland (1885–89) 23. Benjamin Harrison (1889–93) 24. Grover Cleveland (1893–97) 25. William McKinley (1897–1901—assassinated) 26. Theodore Roosevelt (1901–1909) 27. William Howard Taft (1909–1913) 28. Woodrow Wilson (1913–21) 29. Warren G. Harding (1921–23—died in office) 30. Calvin Coolidge (1923–29) 31. Herbert Hoover (1929–33) 32. Franklin D. Roosevelt (1933–45—died in office) 33. Harry S. Truman (1945–53) 34. Dwight D. Eisenhower (1953–61) 35. John F. Kennedy (1961–63—assassinated) 36. Lyndon B. Johnson (1963–69) 37. Richard M. Nixon (1969–74—resigned) 38. Gerald R. Ford (1974–77) 39. Jimmy Carter (1977–81) 40. Ronald Reagan (1981–89) 41. George H. W. Bush (1989–93) 42. William J. Clinton (1993–2001) 43. George W. Bush (2001–)

Resources for Further Exploration

READING

The Colonial Era
Marrin, Albert. *George Washington and the Founding of a Nation*. New York: Dutton, 2003.
McCullough, John. *John Adams*. New York: Simon and Schuster, 2001.

Classics
Franklin, Benjamin. *Autobiography*. New York: Penguin, 1986.
Hamilton, Alexander, John Jay and James Madison. *The Federalist Papers*. New York: Signet, 2003.
Paine, Thomas. *Rights of Man, Common Sense and Other Political Writings*. Oxford: Oxford University Press, 1998.
Tocqueville, Alexis de. *Democracy in America*. New York: Signet, 2001.

The Civil War Era

Douglass, Frederick. *Life and Times of Frederick Douglass*. New York: Library of America, 1996.
Foote, Shelby. *The Civil War: A Narrative: Fort Sumter to Perryville, Fredericksburg to Meridian, Red River to Appomattox*. New York: Vintage, 1986.
McPherson, James M. *Battle Cry of Freedom: The Civil War Era*. New York: Ballantine Books, 1989.
Sandburg, Carl. *Abraham Lincoln: The Prairie Years and the War Years*. San Diego: Harvest Books, 2002.
Washington, Booker T. *Up from Slavery*. Oxford: Oxford University Press, 2000.

Presidents

Ambrose, Stephen. *Undaunted Courage: Meriwether Lewis, Thomas Jefferson, and the Opening of the American West*. New York: Touchstone, 1996.
Anderson, David. *Trapped By Success: The Eisenhower Administration and Vietnam, 1953–1961*. New York: Columbia University Press, 1991.
Kennedy, Robert F. *Thirteen Days: A Memoir of the Cuban Missile Crisis*. New York: W. W. Norton & Company, 1999.
Woodward, Bob, and Carl Bernstein. *All the President's Men*. New York: Touchstone, 1994.

20th Century America

Cohen, Warren I. *America in the Age of Soviet Power, 1945–1991* (vol. 4 of the Cambridge History of American Foreign Relations). New York: Cambridge University Press, 1995.
Galbraith, John Kenneth. *The Great Crash, 1929*. Boston: Houghton Mifflin, 1997.
Iriye, Akira. *The Globalizing of America, 1913–1945* (vol. 3 of the Cambridge History of American Foreign Relations). New York: Cambridge University Press, 1995.
McMahon, Robert J. *Major Problems in the History of the Vietnam War*. Boston: Houghton Mifflin, 2003.

World War II—D-Day

Ryan, Cornelius. *The Longest Day*. New York: Touchstone, 1994.

Documents

Mayflower Compact (1620)—the foundation of government at Plymouth, MA.
The Declaration of Independence (1776).
The Constitution of the United States (ratified, 1788).
The Bill of Rights (1791)—first 10 amendments to the Constitution.
Emancipation Proclamation (1863)—issued by Lincoln, freeing slaves.
Gettysburg Address (1863)—Lincoln's memorial to heroes and country.

PULITZER PRIZE FOR HISTORY, 1990–2004

2004 *A Nation under Our Feet : Black Political Struggles in the Rural South from Slavery to the Great Migration,* by Hahn, Steven (Cambridge, MA: Belknap Press, 2003).

2003 *An Army at Dawn: The War in North Africa, 1942–1943,* by Atkinson, Rick (Henry Holt & Co., 2002).

2002 *The Metaphysical Club,* by Menand, Louis (Farrar Straus & Giroux, 2002).

2001 *Founding Brothers: The Revolutionary Generation,* by Ellis, Joseph J. (Alfred A. Knopf, 2000)

2000 *Freedom from Fear: The American People in Depression and War, 1929–1945,* by Kennedy, David M., and C. Vann Woodward (Oxford University Press, 1999).

1999 *Gotham: A History of New York City to 1898,* by Burrows, Edwin G., and Mike Wallace (Oxford University Press, 1998).

1998 *Summer for the Gods: The Scopes Trial and America's Continuing Debate Over Science,* by Larson, Edward J. (Harvard University Press, 1998).

1997 *Original Meanings: Politics and Ideas in the Making of the Constitution,* by Rakove, Jack N. (Vintage Books USA, 1997).

1996 *William Cooper's Town: Power and Persuasion on the Frontier of the Early American Republic,* by Taylor, Alan (Vintage Books USA, 1996).

1995 *No Ordinary Time: Franklin and Eleanor Roosevelt: The Home Front in World War II,* by Goodwin, Doris Kearns (Simon & Schuster, 1995).

1994 No award.

1993 *Radicalism of the American Revolution,* by Wood, Gordon S. (Vintage Books USA, 1993).

1992 *The Fate of Liberty: Abraham Lincoln and Civil Liberties,* by Neely, Mark E., Jr. (Oxford University Press, 1992).

1991 *A Midwife's Tale: The Life of Martha Ballard, Based on Her Diary, 1785–1812,* by Ulrich, Laurel, and J. Laslocky (Vintage Books USA, 1991).

1990 *In Our Image: America's Empire in the Philippines,* by Karnow, Stanley (Ballantine Books, 1990).

WEB SITES

General Resources and Relevant Sites

http://www.loc.gov/—The Library of Congress home page.

http://americanhistory.si.edu/—Smithsonian National Museum of American History.

http://www.americanrhetoric.com/—Audio and video of well-known speeches.

http://www.ukans.edu/carrie/docs/amdocs_index.html—Documents for the study of American History.

http://www.americaslibrary.gov/cgi-bin/page.cgi—Fun site from the Library of Congress, with young people in mind.

http://www.ushistory.org/—Mostly early Philadelphia focus: Ben Franklin, Liberty Bell, Independence Hall, etc.

http://www.historyplace.com/—General resource, beginning with the American Revolution and heavy with war information.

http://www.thehistorynet.com/—History magazines, with a wide variety of article topics, such as the Wild West, the Civil War, Vietnam, Aviation History and British History.

http://historymatters.gmu.edu/—American Social History Project, City University of New York, Graduate Center. "Gateway to Web resources" for teaching U.S. History.

http://www.yale.edu/ynhti/curriculum/units/1998/4/98.04.04.x.html—Focus on the Great Depression and FDR's New Deal of the 1930s.

http://docsouth.unc.edu/—University of North Carolina site focuses on the American South of the 18th, 19th, and 20th centuries.

http://www.hti.umich.edu/m/moagrp/—Digital library of primary sources related to American society from antebellum to reconstruction. Collaboration of University of Michigan and Cornell University.

http://www.digitalhistory.uh.edu/—Resource Guides, Biographies, Primary Sources (digital), hosted by the University of Houston.

http://www.pbs.org/history/—Complement/supplement to PBS programming.

http://www.cnn.com/SPECIALS/—Historical background on current events.

Historic Locations

http://www.nps.gov/bost/Bunker_Hill.htm—*Freedom Trail, Bunker Hill monument.*

http://www.history.org/—*Official Web site of Colonial Williamsburg.*

Presidential Libraries

http://www.nara.gov—*National Archives, Office of Presidential Libraries.*

http://www.reagan.utexas.edu—*Ronald Reagan library.*

http://www.clintonlibrary.gov—*Bill Clinton library.*

Maps

http://memory.loc.gov/ammem/gmdhtml/gmdhome.html—*Map collections, 1500–2004, from the Library of Congress.*

http://www.lib.utexas.edu/maps/histus.html—*Map collection.*

Law and Courts

http://www.oyez.org/oyez/frontpage—*Reviews U.S. Supreme Court cases.*
http://jurist.law.pitt.edu/issues/issue_scotus.htm—*Law research site, including U.S. Supreme Court opinions. Hosted by University of Pittsburgh School of Law.*
http://www.law.umkc.edu/faculty/projects/ftrials/ftrials.htm—*Focus on famous trials, from Socrates to Scopes "Monkey" to O. J. Simpson.*

OTHER RESOURCES

Library of Congress
On Capitol Hill in southeast Washington
Washington, D.C. 20540
202-707-5000
http://www.loc.gov/

Smithsonian Institution
National Museum of American History
On the National Mall, 14th Street and Constitution Avenue NW
Washington, D.C. 20560
Open daily, 10 A.M. to 5:30 P.M. Free admission.
202-633-1000
http://americanhistory.si.edu/

Colonial Williamsburg, Williamsburg, VA—Colonial days preserved.
Midway between Richmond and Norfolk on I-64 (exit 238).
1-800-HISTORY
http://www.history.org/

Fort Sumter National Monument, Charleston, SC—First shots fired in
Civil War.
Visitor information: 843-883-3123
http://www.nps.gov/fosu/

Ronald Reagan Library
40 Presidential Drive
Simi Valley, CA 93065
http://www.reagan.utexas.edu

William J. Clinton Presidential Materials Project
1000 LaHarpe Boulevard
Little Rock, AR 72201
http://www.clinton.archives.gov

The National Museum of the American Indian
At Independence and 4th on the National Mall
Washington, D.C. 20024
(800) 400-6624
http://www.americanindian.si.edu

8. World History

A REFRESHER COURSE IN WORLD HISTORY begins with a broad overview. Get *The New Penguin History of the World,* by John M. Roberts (New York: Penguin, 2004), a hefty tome of more than 1,200 pages and 90 maps, which the *Sunday Telegraph* hails as "a work of outstanding breadth and scholarship . . . nothing better of its kind." Also take a look at *Millennium Year by Year: A Chronicle of World History from A.D. 1000 to the Present* (New York: Dorling Kindersley, 1999), which uses a clever newspaper style to tell the world's story, with articles on wars, politics, scientific discoveries, and cultural development, and which the editors at Amazon.com say is "difficult to put down." A must-read is *The Timetables of History: A Horizontal Linkage of People and Events,* by Bernard Grun (New York: Touchstone, 1991), which, in a standard timetable format, allows you to see the world evolve through a variety of lenses, such as history, politics, literature, and religion.

In a subject with such an enormous span of years and vast array of people, places, wars, and cultures, you eventually will want to select more narrow, more manageable topics to explore. If, for example, you have a particular interest in modern Europe, read John Merriman's *A History of Modern Europe* (New York: W. W. Norton, 1996), which comprehensively chronicles the European experience from the Renaissance to the present. For other suggestions, see the lists below, including General Resources, Classics, Middle Ages, and Histories of Countries.

To explore topics and eras on the Web, use directories such as Yahoo's Directory of Directories (**http://dir.yahoo.com/Arts/Humanities/History/Web_Directories/**), which links to directories for Ancient, European, Middle Ages, and Military, or HyperHistory (**http://www.hyperhistory.com/**), which covers 3,000 years of world history and includes maps, timelines, and lifelines, or the History Place

(http://www.historyplace.com/), which offers enough history to satisfy even the hungriest buff.

For a nutshell look at the early empires, read the piece that follows.

Empire-State Building: A Crash Course in the Most Notable Early Empires
From the Rise of the Persian Empire to the Fall of the Roman Empire

THE PERSIAN EMPIRE—SIXTH CENTURY B.C. TO FOURTH CENTURY B.C.

Today's greater Middle East, and particularly Iran, stood at the heart of
the lands comprising the ancient Persian Empire. At its peak, the whole
of the empire stretched across the breadth of Mesopotamia from Macedon (north of Greece) to Egypt to the borders of India.

The Persian Empire came into existence when the Persian tribe,
under **Cyrus the Great** (c. 580 B.C.—c. 530 B.C.), conquered the lands of
Media, Lydia, Chaldea, and Babylonia. While conquering territories
had not been an uncommon pursuit for a variety of powerful tribes and
countries before this, Cyrus established himself as the first leader in history to aspire to conquering the world. However, before he could
accomplish that ambitious goal, he died in battle and his son, **Cambyses** (ruled 530 B.C.–522 B.C.), assumed leadership. Cambyses continued
the expansion and conquered Egypt.

The rulers of the empire were tolerant, permitting the conquered
lands to retain most of their laws and cultural practices. Though Zoroastrianism thrived among the Persians, their territories were free to follow
their own religions.

Darius I (c. 521 B.C.—486 B.C.), who followed Cambyses to the
throne, divided the empire into 20 provinces, called satrapies, and Persian culture flourished with advancements in writing, irrigation, and
transportation. Sensing a threat from the Greeks, Darius launched an
attack on Athenian forces in **490** B.C., and, though the Persians far outnumbered their foe, the Greeks won a decisive victory in the **Battle of
Marathon**.

This may have been the most important military victory in Greek
history, if not world history. Had the Greeks lost this battle, the classic
Greek culture that went on to give birth to Western Civilization and to

influence the world as we know it today would have been inexorably changed, no doubt seasoned heavily with a Persian flavor.

Xerxes (ruled c. 486 B.C.–465 B.C.) followed Darius and continued the wars with Greece. Time and time again Greek forces, though heavily outnumbered, defeated the Persians, most notably at Plataea (479 B.C.) and at Mycale (478 B.C.). The Persians withdrew from Europe but remained a threat to the Greeks for more than a century, until the rise of Alexander the Great.

ALEXANDER THE GREAT—FOURTH CENTURY B.C.

In the ancient kingdom of Macedon, which included portions of today's Macedonia, Greece, and Bulgaria, **Philip II** (c. 382 B.C.–336 B.C.) rose to power through military victories, aided by his son, **Alexander** (c. 356 B.C.–323 B.C.). When Philip was assassinated in 336 B.C., Alexander assumed the throne at 20 years of age and surpassed even the high level of military success achieved by his father.

Schooled by the best available teachers of the time, including the renowned Aristotle, Alexander developed a love of learning and a deep appreciation of the arts and sciences, politics and athletics. But no area of his life shone more conspicuously than that which permitted exercise of his skills as a warrior and commander of armies.

In continuing campaigns that pitted him against a variety of foes over more than a dozen years, Alexander defeated enemy after enemy, ever widening his empire. From the squelching of uprisings in "poleis," city states in Greece such as Thebes and Ionia, to victories over the Persians and Egyptians, Alexander at one point ruled the kingdoms of Macedon, Persia, Babylon, Egypt, and many of the city-states in the Greek League. Along the way, he established numerous cities, not the least of which was the port of Alexandria (332 B.C.) at the mouth of the Nile in Egypt.

It is important to note that the empire built by Alexander, a champion of Greek culture, shifted the world's focus for the first time from the East to the West. Had he lived a little longer, many scholars conjecture that he may have made Greece the seat of his domain. Indeed, Western Civilization as we know it today may trace its roots back to this significant period in history. The rise of the Roman Empire that followed served further to strengthen the connection.

Ironically, the valiant warrior Alexander the Great did not die of battle wounds but of a fever—probably malaria—in 323 B.C. His legend, however, still lives to this day.

THE ROMAN EMPIRE—FOURTH CENTURY B.C. TO FIFTH CENTURY A.D.

Though scholars do not agree about the exact dates of the era called "The Roman Empire," there is no shortage of details about the history of Rome itself. The city was founded in 753 B.C. by Romulus, and by 509 B.C. had formed a republic. Through colonization and outright military aggression, Rome gained control of the whole of Italy, and then expanded its borders in virtually all directions.

Rome acquired its first provinces during the **Punic Wars** with Carthage, a Mediterranean power in coastal North Africa. The First Punic War lasted 23 years (264–241 B.C.) and resulted in Rome's building a dominant fleet to complement its potent armies. With its victory in this war, Rome now had its first provinces, Sicily, Corsica, and Sardinia. The Second Punic War (218–201 B.C.) saw Carthage's commander **Hannibal**, with elephants and army, cross the Alps into Italy, winning battles and skirmishes well into the southern regions, but never actually penetrating Rome. Again Rome rose to victory in the end, and in doing so gained control of Spain. By the end of the Third Punic War (149–146 B.C.), Rome had soundly defeated its rival and had gained control of Carthage itself and all of its territories.

From this point, Roman control expanded to Greece, Macedon, Egypt, and Asia Minor. Through the rise of generals such as Marius, Sulla, Pompey, and **Julius Caesar** (102–44 B.C.), Rome's conquests grew steadily until at its peak the empire controlled virtually the whole of the civilized territories of the Mediterranean and beyond. In 60 B.C., Caesar, Pompey, and Crassus formed the **First Triumvirate** to lead Rome.

Between 58 and 50 B.C., Caesar successfully led assaults against Gaul (France) and Britain. The Triumvirate began to fall apart with the death of Crassus in battle in 53 B.C., and by 48 B.C. Caesar had wrested complete control from Pompey and the senate. After a foray to the East, where he had his infamous affair in Egypt with Cleopatra, sister of King Ptolemy XII, Caesar returned to Rome in 45 B.C. On the Ides of March (i.e., March 15) in 44 B.C., Caesar was stabbed to death by a group of senators who feared he was growing too strong politically.

Political unrest ensued, with the temporary rise to power of Caesar's supporter, Marc Antony, and then the formation of the **Second Triumvirate**, Octavian, Antony, and Lepidus. Antony found his way to Egypt, where he fell in love with star-crossed Cleopatra, and both eventually committed suicide in Alexandria.

With Lepidus having been forced out of leadership, and with Antony dead, Octavian now ruled alone. In **27 B.C.**, Rome crowned its first emperor—Octavian, whose title became **Augustus**, the name attached to him throughout history. Many scholars would argue that this is the date that makes the most sense as marking the actual beginning of the Roman Empire.

Despite significant challenges during his reign (27 B.C. to A.D. 14), Augustus succeeded in developing an overall sense of calm and stability in the often tense, battle-ravaged empire. This *Pax Romana* (Roman Peace) lasted for more than two centuries (c. A.D. 180) through the reign of 15 more emperors.

After Augustus, the leadership passed in succession to four emperors with direct family ties to Julius Caesar and Augustus: **Tiberius** (A.D. 14), **Caligula** (A.D. 37), **Claudius** (A.D. 41), and **Nero** (A.D. 54).

Under **Diocletian** (A.D. 284–305) the rule was shared among four leaders and the empire was divided, with a seat in the East and a seat in the West. In A.D. 306, **Constantine** (ruled A.D. 306–337) ascended into one of the shared positions and in A.D. **313** issued the **Edict of Milan**, which sanctioned Christianity as a lawful religion. Constantine converted to Christianity and in A.D. **325** assembled the **First Council of Nicaea**, where the Nicene Creed was issued, unifying and openly declaring Christian beliefs. In A.D. 324, Constantine took complete control of the throne and in A.D. 330 designated the eastern city of Byzantium as the capital of the empire, renaming it **Constantinople** (today's Istanbul).

In addition to achievement in military affairs over the course of the empire's existence, the Romans set high standards and demonstrated high levels of success in other matters as well, such as law, language, and civil engineering. A good portion of their roads and architecture, for example, endured for many centuries. In fact, the heart of the Roman culture would live on for centuries after the fall of the empire, and carve its signature into the grain of the developing Western Civilization.

In A.D. 476, under the pressing weight of civil unrest, barbarian invasions, declining economy, shrinking population, disease, migration, division, corruption, and other significant societal ills, the last Western emperor, Romulus Augustulus, was ousted, and the empire collapsed.

Starting Points and Conversation Pieces

- *Mesopotamia*: Archaeologists' digs indicate that the world's earliest civilizations (c. 5000 B.C.) lived in this area between the Tigris and Euphrates Rivers, in what is today's Iraq.

- *Sumerians* (circa 4,000 B.C.): Inhabitants of Babylon, credited with the earliest forms of writing, done on clay tablets.

- Having been most influential in key victories over Persia, *Athens* became the dominant city in Greece circa 478 B.C. This was followed by the lengthy Peloponnesian War between Athens and Sparta, ultimately won by Sparta.

- In 325 *Constantine* called for the Council of Nicea, at which Christian bishops created a fundamental statement of beliefs—the Nicene Creed—which is still in use today.

- *Charlemagne* was crowned the first Holy Roman Emperor on Christmas Day in 800.

- In Europe in the Middle Ages (c. 1000), *feudalism* arose, in which landowners granted temporary use of parcels of land in exchange for services and loyalty.

- The *first university* in Europe was established in Bologna, Italy in 1088.

- The *Magna Carta,* sanctioned under duress by England's King John in 1215, guaranteed personal liberties and civil rights for the common people, becoming a model for subsequent democracies.

- The *Black Death*—a devastating outbreak of bubonic plague in Europe from 1347 to 1351—killed between one-third and one-half of the population.

- When *Martin Luther* formally questioned Catholic practices in 1517 with the publication of his "Ninety-five Theses," the Protestant Reformation was born.

❖ *Henry VIII* of England was born in 1491 and died in 1547. His six wives were: Catherine of Aragon; Anne Boleyn; Jane Seymour; Anne of Cleves; Catherine Howard; and Catherine Parr.

❖ In 1789, during the French Revolution, the Bastille (prison) was stormed by the common people on *July 14,* which is commemorated as a national holiday in France today.

❖ In the late 1790s in France, *Napoleon* rose to power, and in 1804 was declared Emperor.

❖ *Gross National Product*: The total market value of a nation's total production of goods and services in a specified period, usually a year. (In the United States, expressed in dollars.)

❖ *John Maynard Keynes* (1883–1946): English economist. Among other theories, advocated government programs to stimulate the economy and increase employment in down times. Authored the classic, *The General Theory of Employment, Interest, and Money.*

Resources for Further Exploration

READING

General Resources and Relevant Books

Crampton, R. J. *Eastern Europe in the Twentieth Century*. New York: Routledge, 1997.

Diamond, Jared. *Guns, Germs, and Steel: The Fates of Human Societies*. New York: W. W. Norton & Co., 1997.

Linz, Juan, and Alfred Stepan. *The Breakdown of Democratic Regimes: Europe*. Baltimore: Johns Hopkins University Press, 1978.

Moore, Barrington, Jr. *The Social Origins of Dictatorship and Democracy*. Boston: Beacon Press, 1964.

Polanyi, Karl. *The Great Transformation: Political and Economic Origins of Our Time*. Boston: Beacon Press, 2001.

Ponting, Clive. *World History: A New Perspective*. London: Chatto and Windus, 2000.

Spielvogel, Jackson J. *Western Civilization, vols. 1 and 2*. Belmont, CA: Wadsworth Publishing, 2002.

Classics

Descartes, René. *Meditations*. Translated by Desmond Clark. New York: Penguin, 1999.

Herodotus. *The Histories* (This edition titled *The History*). Translated by David Grene. Chicago: University of Chicago Press, 1987.

Locke, John. "The True End of Civil Governement." In *Locke: Two Treatises of Government*. Cambridge: Cambridge University Press, 1988.

Machiavelli, Niccolo. *The Prince*. New York: Signet, 1999.

Montaigne, Michel de. *Michel de Montaigne: The Complete Essays*. Translated and edited by M. A. Screech. New York: Penguin, 1993.

Plato. *The Republic*. Translated by Desmond Lee. New York: Viking, 1976.

Plutarch. *Lives of the Noble Grecians and Romans, vol. 1*. New York: Modern Library, 2001.

Rousseau, Jean-Jacques. *The Social Contract*. Translated by Maurice Cranston. New York: Penguin, 1968.

Thucydides. *The Peloponnesian War*. Translated by Steven Lattimore. Indianapolis: Hackett, 1998.

Near-Classic

Gibbon, Edward. *The History of the Decline and Fall of the Roman Empire*. New York: Penguin, 2001.

USSR (Atrocities)

Solzhenitsyn, Alexander I. *The Gulag Archipelago*. Abridged by Edward E. Erickson, Jr. New York: HarperCollins, 2002.

Leading Personalities

Cracraft, James. *The Revolution of Peter the Great*. Cambridge, MA: Harvard University Press, 2003.

Rossabi, Morris. *Khubilai Khan, His Life and Times*. Berkeley, CA: University of California Press, 1990.

Strachey, Lytton. *Queen Victoria*. San Diego, CA: Harcourt, 1983.

Histories of Countries

DeBary, William Theodore, et al., eds. *Sources of Chinese Tradition, vol. 1*. New York: Columbia University Press, 2001.

Duggan, Christopher. *A Concise History of Italy*. Cambridge: Cambridge University Press, 1994.

Evtuhov, Catherine, et al., eds. *A History Of Russia: Peoples, Legends, Events, Forces*. Boston: Houghton Mifflin, 2003.

Freeze, Gregory. *Russia, A History*. Oxford: Oxford University Press, 2002.

Hansen, Valerie. *The Open Empire: A History of China to 1600*. New York: W. W. Norton & Company, 2000.

Hoffmann, Stanley, et al. *In Search of France*. New York: Harper, 1963.

Hume, David. *The History of England, vols. 1 to 6.* Indianapolis: Liberty
Fund, 1985.
Karnow, Stanley. *Vietnam: A History.* New York: Penguin, 1997.
Morgan, Kenneth O., ed. *The Oxford Illustrated History of Britain.* Oxford:
Oxford University Press, 2001.
Orlow, Dietrich. *A History of Modern Germany: 1871 to Present.* Upper Saddle
River, New Jersey: Prentice Hall, 1987.
Perkin, Harold. *The Origins of Modern English Society, 1780–1880.* London:
Routledge and Kegan Paul, 1969.
Riasanovsky, Nicholas V. *A History of Russia.* Oxford: Oxford University
Press, 1999.
Ropp, Paul S., ed. *Heritage of China: Contemporary Perspectives on Chinese
Civilization.* Berkeley, CA: University of California Press, 1990.
Stone, Lawrence. *The Causes of the English Revolution, 1529–1642.* New
York: Harper, 1972.

The Middle Ages
Geary, Patrick J. *Readings in Medieval History.* Peterborough, Ont.: Broad-
view, 1989.
Howarth, David. *1066: The Year of Conquest.* New York: Viking, 1981.
Rosenwein, Barbara. *A Short History of the Middle Ages.* Orchard Park, NY:
Broadview Press, 2001.
Tierney, Brian. *The Middle Ages, Volume I: Sources of Medieval History.* New
York: McGraw-Hill, 1992.
Tuchman, Barbara. *A Distant Mirror: The Calamitous Fourteenth Century.*
New York: Ballantine, 1987.

World War II
Allen, William Sheridan. *The Nazi Seizure of Power: The Experience of a Single
German Town, 1922–1945.* New York: Watts, 1984.
Ambrose, Stephen E. *D Day: June 6, 1944: The Climactic Battle of World War
II.* New York: Simon & Schuster, 1995.

Stark Contrasts
Hitler, Adolf. *Mein Kampf.* Boston: Houghton Mifflin, 1998.
Marx, Karl, and Friedrich Engels. *The Communist Manifesto.* New York: Pen-
guin, 1998.
Weisel, Elie. *All Rivers Run to the Sea: Memoirs.* New York: Random House,
1995.

Document
The Magna Carta (1215)

WEB SITES

General Resources and Relevant Sites

http://www.thehistorynet.com/—Offers articles on history of world, United States, military, etc.

http://www.cr.nps.gov/—National Parks Service "Links to the Past."

http://www.hpol.org/—Limited audio archive of speeches includes Lyndon Johnson, Nixon, M. L. King, JFK, FDR, Churchill, and Khrushchev.

http://www.fordham.edu/halsall/mod/modsbook.html—Modern History Sourcebook. From the Reformation to modern day.

http://oi.uchicago.edu/OI/MUS/QTVR96/QTVR96_Tours.html—Oriental Institute Museum. University of Chicago. Virtual tour.

http://www.bbc.co.uk/worldservice/africa/features/storyofafrica/index.shtml—BBC's "The Story of Africa." In-depth look.

http://www.pbs.org/wgbh/pages/frontline/shows/muslims/—PBS's Frontline looks at Muslims.

http://www.pbs.org/wonders/—PBS's "Wonders of the African World."

http://www.bbc.co.uk/religion/interactive/civilisations/—BBC's extensive focus on human history using "flash" technology.

http://www.wsu.edu:8080/~dee/WORLD.HTM—Review of World Civilizations. Washington State University.

http://www.historylearningsite.co.uk/—Broad world-history site.

http://www.kn.pacbell.com/wired/fil/pages/listdocumentpa.html—Primary source materials.

Ancient History

http://www.fordham.edu/halsall/ancient/asbook.html—Internet Ancient History Sourcebook.

http://www.pbs.org/wgbh/nova/lostempires/—PBS's "Secrets of Lost Empires" attempts to answer questions about Stonehenge and other ancient mysteries.

http://eawc.evansville.edu/index.htm—Introduction to ancient world cultures.

http://www.perseus.tufts.edu/—Perseus Digital Library from Tufts University covers ancient times to the sixteenth century.

http://dir.yahoo.com/Regional/Regions/Middle_East/Arts_and_Humanities/Humanities/History/By_Time_Period/Ancient_History/Persian_Empire/—Yahoo Directory for Persian Empire.

http://www.wsu.edu:8080/~dee/MESO/PERSIANS.HTM—Washington State University—Persian Empire.

http://www.roman-empire.net/diverse/faq.html—Roman Empire.

http://www.bartleby.com/65/ro/RomeIt.html—Bartleby on the Roman Empire.

http://www.exovedate.com/ancient_timeline_one.html—Timeline.

Medieval History

http://www.fordham.edu/halsall/sbook.html—Internet Medieval Sourcebook.
http://www.georgetown.edu/labyrinth/labyrinth-home.html—Medieval studies, hosted by Georgetown University.

Reformation and Renaissance Era

http://www.crrs.ca/—Center for Reformation and Renaissance Studies.
http://www.medici.org/—Medici Archive Project.
http://www.loc.gov/exhibits/bnf/bnf0001.html—Traces French culture and politics through Bibliothèque Nationale de France via the Library of Congress.
http://www.educ.msu.edu/homepages/laurence/reformation/index.htm—The Reformation Guide.

Exploration

http://www.win.tue.nl/cs/fm/engels/discovery/—Focus on 15th- and 16th-century explorers.
http://muweb.millersville.edu/~columbus/—"Columbus and the Age of Discovery." Over 1,100 articles.
http://www.collectionscanada.ca/2/8/index-e.html—North American exploration—Library and Archives, Canada.
http://www.pbs.org/opb/conquistadors/home.htm—PBS on The Conquistadors.

French and English History

http://www.tudorhistory.org/—All about the Tudors.
http://www.luminarium.org/renlit/eliza.htm—Life and works of Elizabeth I.
http://www.olivercromwell.org/—Life and times of Oliver Cromwell.
http://www.pipeline.com/~cwa/TYWHome.htm—The Thirty Years War.
http://chnm.gmu.edu/revolution/—Welcome to the French Revolution.
http://www.wsu.edu:8080/~dee/ENLIGHT/ENLIGHT.HTM—European Enlightenment.
http://www.britannia.com/history/euro/1/2_2.html—Britannia's take on the French Revolution.
http://www.pbs.org/empires/napoleon/—PBS on Napoleon.
http://www.napoleon.org/en/home.asp—Bilingual site (French and English) on Napoleon.
http://www.napoleonseries.org/—Napoleon encore.
http://www.spartacus.schoolnet.co.uk/—British History.
http://www.bbc.co.uk/history/—BBC's history site.
http://www.victorianweb.org/—Victorian era.
http://victorianresearch.org/—Victorian research.
http://www.learningcurve.gov.uk/politics/default.htm—British political history, 19th century.

http://www.bbc.co.uk/history/society_culture/industrialisation/index.shtml—BBC
   on the Industrial Revolution.
http://www.history1700s.com/—Focus on the 18th century.
http://www.british-civil-wars.co.uk/—British Civil Wars, 1638–60.
http://library.byu.edu/~rdh/eurodocs/uk.html—Primary documents from the
   history of the United Kingdom.
http://www.people.virginia.edu/~eas5e/Irish/Famine.html—Interpreting the
   Irish Famine, 1849–50.
http://www.bbc.co.uk/history/games/through_time/index.shtml—BBC's exploration of kings and queens through time.

Early Modern History
http://www.lib.umd.edu/ETC/LOCAL/emw/emw.php3—Early modern women.
http://www.earlymodernweb.org.uk/—Early modern resources, 1500–1800.

OTHER RESOURCES

The Resistance Museum
Bygning 21
Akershus Festning
0015 Oslo Norway
telephone 23 09 32 80
http://www.mil.no/felles/nhm/start/eng

The British Museum
Great Russell Street
London WC1B 3DG
(The British Museum was founded in 1753.)
telephone (+44) 020 7323 8000 (switchboard) or (+44) 020 7323 8299
   (information desk)
http://www.thebritishmuseum.ac.uk/index.html

Bygones Victorian Museum
Fore Street, St. Marychurch
Torquay, England. TQ1 4PR
telephone +44(0)1803 326108
http://www.bygones.co.uk/

Smithsonian Institution
On the National Mall
14th Street and Constitution Avenue NW
Washington, D.C. 20013
202-633-1000
http://www.si.edu/

9. English

EVERY HOME LIBRARY SHOULD INCLUDE the following two books: *English Composition and Grammar,* by John Warriner (New York: Holt, Rinehart and Winston, 1988), and *The Elements of Style,* by William Strunk and E. B. White (Upper Saddle River, NJ: Pearson, 2000). These will give you the essentials of English grammar and writing style.

Warriner's book breaks down all the components of grammar and composition, such as parts of speech, punctuation, and spelling, and provides details for traditional methods of learning in this subject, like diagramming sentences. If you don't know a gerund from a dangling participle, this is definitely the book for you.

Strunk and White's book is a classic. Brief by design, its aim is to guide the writer with fundamentals like "rules of usage," "principles of composition," "matters of form," and "words and expressions commonly misused." Own it; enjoy it.

In addition to these staples, many journalists rely on *The Chicago Manual of Style,* by the University of Chicago Press staff (Chicago: University of Chicago Press, 2003), which explains how to format letters, papers, and all manner of documents. If your aim is to write a term paper or dissertation, you'll want *A Manual for Writers of Term Papers, Theses, and Dissertations,* by Kate L. Turabian (Chicago: University of Chicago Press, 1993), which will guide you and answer all your questions about form and process.

Online, go to **http://dir.yahoo.com/Reference/Dictionaries/**—the Yahoo Directory of dictionaries, and **http://dir.yahoo.com/Reference/Thesauri/**—the Yahoo Directory of thesauri.

For precise definitions, I prefer the *American Heritage Dictionary* (Boston: Houghton Mifflin, 2000), which has more than 200,000 entries, 3,000 photos and illustrations, and good tips on usage. *The New York Times Book Review* says that it is "more suited to our national character than any other previous dictionary." I keep a hard copy on my desk, and I refer to the online version regularly, **http://www.bartleby.com/64/**.

Another highly regarded text is the *Concise Oxford English Dictionary* (New York: Oxford University Press, 2004). With more than 1,700 pages and 200,000 words and phrases, it offers clear definitions, historical insight on word origins, and useful advice on grammar.

For a general reference site, one of the best is **http://www.refdesk. com**, which describes itself as "free and family friendly," and which offers a treasure chest of countless links to dictionaries, encyclopedias, search engines, news organizations, libraries, and reference resources. Bookmark it.

Scan the resources below for a variety of other helpful tools.

Starting Points and Conversation Pieces

WORDS AND SPELLINGS OFTEN CONFUSED

❖ *It's v. its*: "It's" means "it is." "Its" is the possessive pronoun.

❖ *Irregardless*: There is no such word. The correct word is "regardless."

❖ *Semiannual*: Half-year. *Note*—a *biannual* event occurs every two years (bi = 2), while a semiannual event occurs every half-year, or twice a year.

❖ *Stationary v. stationery*: "Stationary" means standing still. "Stationery" is writing paper.

❖ *Desert v. dessert*: Think of strawberry shortcake—"ss"—to remember how to spell "dessert." A "desert" (noun) is a dry, desolate place, and "to desert" (verb) means "to leave."

❖ *Capitol v. Capital*: "Capitol" is the building. "Capital" is the city. Also, "capital" as a noun means "money" or "property" and as an adjective means "quite significant" or "most important."

❖ *Led v. lead*: "Led" is the past tense of the verb "to lead." "Lead" (noun) is a metal. Because they sound alike, "lead" is often used mistakenly for "led."

❖ *Amount v. number*: Use "number" when you can count the discreet parts or when referring to a plural word. (E.g., I'm counting the number of dimes in my pocket.) Use "amount" when not counting discreet parts or when the word you are referring to is singular. (E.g., That's an enormous amount of information.)

VOCABULARY AND GRAMMAR

❖ Studying prefixes, roots, and suffixes can improve your vocabulary enormously. If, for example, you knew that "mis" meant "hate" and "anthropo" meant "mankind," then you would be able to figure out that a "misanthrope" is a person who hates mankind.

❖ Helpful prefixes, roots, and suffixes:
  ❖ ante: before   post: after   sub: under   ex: out of
  ❖ biblio: book   phile: love   ology: study of   psych: mind
  ❖ bio: life   geo: earth   sci: know   omni: all

❖ *Symbiotic*: Mutually beneficial.

❖ *Tantamount*: The same as or equal to.

❖ *Egregious*: Flagrant, glaring.

❖ *Dichotomy*: Division into two parts.

❖ *Obsequious*: Submissive, to follow fawningly.

❖ *The Eight Parts of Speech*: Noun, pronoun, adjective, verb, adverb, conjunction, preposition, interjection.

❖ Palindromes are words or numbers that read the same backward and forward. (E.g., "A man, a plan, a canal—Panama." "Borrow or rob." "Madam, I'm Adam." "3773.")

❖ It is "between him and me," not "between him and I," and not "between he and I." The word "between" here is a preposition. Prepositions take objects, and objects of a preposition must use the objective case—in this instance, "him and me."

❖ It is "whet your appetite," not "wet your appetite."

❖ The plural of "alumnus" is "alumni." You alone may be an alumnus, but you alone cannot be alumni.

❖ It is "dire straits," not "dire straights."

❖ If there is one, it is a "criterion." If more than one, they are "criteria."

❖ The heavenly creature is spelled "angel," not "angle," which is the math term, as in "the triangle has a right angle."

❖ It is "insofar as," not "insofaras."

❖ "Oral" relates to what is said, while "aural" relates to what is heard.

❖ The female is the "masseuse." The male is the "masseur."

❖ An "auger" is a tool for boring. "To augur" is to predict.

❖ It is "I should have said . . ." Not "I should of said . . ."

❖ It is "a lot," not "alot." To remind yourself, think of how you do not use "alittle."

❖ It is "basically," not "basicly."

❖ It is "beyond the pale," not "beyond the pail." "Pale" in this context means "fence" or "boundary."

❖ It is "asterisk," from the Greek *asteriskos*. It is not "asterick."

❖ The possessive pronoun is "whose," not "who's." Example: "Whose turn is it?"

Resources for Further Exploration

READING

English Usage
Fowler, Henry, et al. *A Dictionary of Modern English Usage*. New York: Oxford University Press, 2003.
Irmscher, William F. *The Holt Guide to English*. New York: Holt, Rinehart and Winston, 1981.
O'Conner, Patricia T. *Woe is I*. New York: Riverhead, 1998.
Walraff, Barbara. *Your Own Words*. New York: Counterpoint-Perseus, 2004.

Vocabulary and Spelling
Beck, Isabel L., et al. *Bringing Words to Life: Robust Vocabulary Instruction*. New York: Guilford Press, 2002.
Lewis, Norman. *Word Power Made Easy*. New York: Pocket Books, 1991.
Proctor, William. *The Terrible Speller*. New York: Quill, 1995.

Robinson, Adam. *Word Smart: Building an Educated Vocabulary*. New York: Princeton Review, 2001.

WRITING

Bernstein, Theodore M. *The Careful Writer: A Modern Guide to English Usage*. New York: Free Press, 1995.

Brande, Dorothea. *Becoming a Writer*. Los Angeles: J. P. Tarcher, 1981.

Daigh, Ralph. *Maybe You Should Write a Book*. Upper Saddle River, NJ: Prentice Hall, 1979.

Elbow, Peter. *Writing With Power*. New York: Oxford University Press, 1981.

———. *Writing Without Teachers*. New York: Oxford University Press, 1973.

Hiers, James, et al. *The Research Paper: Sources and Resources*. Lexington, MA: D.C. Heath, 1986.

Kane, Thomas S. *The New Oxford Guide to Writing*. New York: Oxford University Press, 1994.

Marius, Richard. *A Writer's Companion*. New York: Knopf, 1985.

Murray, Donald. *A Writer Teaches Writing*. Boston: Houghton Mifflin, 1985.

———. *Write to Learn*. New York: Holt, Rinehart and Winston, 1987.

Nordquist, Richard F. *Writing Exercises*. New York: Macmillan, 1985.

Zinser, William. *Writing to Learn*. New York: HarperResource, 1993.

———. *On Writing Well, 25th Anniversary*. New York: HarperResource, 2001.

Dictionary and Thesaurus

American Heritage Dictionary. *The American Heritage Dictionary of the English Language*. Boston: Houghton Mifflin, 2000.

Kipfer, Barbara Ann. *Roget's 21st Century Thesaurus: Updated & Expanded 2nd Edition*. New York: Dell, 1999.

Partridge, Eric. *Origins: A Short Etymological Dictionary of Modern English*. New York: Macmillan, 1983.

General Resources and Relevant Books

Adler, Mortimer J. *How to Speak, How to Listen*. New York: Touchstone, 1983.

Hirsch, E. D. *Cultural Literacy: What Every American Needs to Know*. Boston: Houghton Mifflin, 1987.

WEB SITES

Writing

http://www.oualline.com/style/—An abbreviated version of the classic book *Elements of Style*.

http://webster.commnet.edu/mla/index.shtml—A Guide to Writing Research Papers Based on MLA Documentation.

http://webster.commnet.edu/apa/index.htm—A Guide for Writing Research Papers—American Psychological Association Style.

English Usage

http://www.wsu.edu/~brians/errors/—Common Errors in English.
http://community-2.webtv.net/solis-boo/Grammar1/—Armchair Grammarian. Links to libraries, etc.
http://www.papyr.com/hypertextbooks/engl_126/book126.htm—The HyperText-book Modern English Grammar book online.
http://www.geocities.com/gene_moutoux/diagrams.htm—How to diagram sentences.
http://www.bartleby.com/185/—The American Language.
http://www.westegg.com/cliche/—Cliché finder.
http://www.columbia.edu/cu/cup/cgos/idx_basic.html—Columbia University Press Style Guide.
http://www.ccc.commnet.edu/grammar/—Guide to Grammar and Writing.
http://andromeda.rutgers.edu/~jlynch/Writing/—Guide to Grammar and Style.
http://www.english.uiuc.edu/cws/wworkshop/grammar_handbook.htm—University of Illinois Grammar Handbook.

Dictionaries and Thesauri

http://www.m-w.com/—Merriam-Webster Online.
http://www.oed.com—Oxford English Dictionary.
http://www.rhymezone.com/—Rhyming dictionary and thesaurus.
http://www.bartleby.com/62/—Roget's II, The New Thesaurus.
http://thesaurus.reference.com/—Online thesaurus.
http://dictionary.reference.com/—Online dictionary.

Vocabulary and Spelling

http://www.perseus.tufts.edu/cgi-bin/resolveform?lang=Latin—Latin dictionary. Help with Greek, too.
http://www.zdaily.com/vocabulary.htm—Daily vocabulary quiz.
http://www.esldesk.com/esl-quizzes/misspelled-words/misspelled-words.htm—Commonly misspelled words.
http://www.mywordaday.com/—Word-a-day vocabulary builder.
http://spotlightongames.com/quote/chinesewords.html—English words from Chinese origin.
http://spotlightongames.com/quote/japanesewords.html—English words from Japanese origin.
http://www.oed.com/cgi/display/wotd—Oxford English Dictionary Word of the Day.

Libraries
http://www.ipl.org/—Internet Public Library.
http://www.nypl.org/—New York Public Library.
http://lib.harvard.edu/—Harvard University Libraries.
http://www.library.yale.edu/—Yale University Library.

NCTE and SAT
http://www.ncte.org/—National Council of Teachers of English.
http://www.kaptest.com/repository/templates/ArticleInitDroplet.jhtml?_relPath=/
repository/content/College/SAT-PSAT/Class_of_2006/Special_Features
/CO_sat_practiceSAT.html&ProductId=—practice SAT.

10. Literature

IF C. S. LEWIS WAS CORRECT when he said "We read to know we're not alone," then be prepared for plenty of company as you explore the vast canyons of literature. In this chapter you will touch on prose and poetry from hundreds of writers, even if only to read the titles of their work. I suspect that you will not limit yourself to that.

Any worthwhile foray into literature includes a taste of the classics, and for that reason I have listed 101 titles of important works. These are familiar titles—classics, by definition, command world attention and acclaim—some of which you may have read, some of which you wish you had. There is no time like the present. After the chapters on Super Tools, you read faster and better now than you ever have. Take advantage of your skills.

Whether you want to read a recent prize-winning book, like Nobel winner *Disgrace*, by J. M. Coetzee, or National Book Award winner *The Singing Poems*, by C. K. Williams, or prefer to immerse yourself in a treasure of the past, such as Robert Penn Warren's *All the King's Men*, or Mark Twain's *Huckleberry Finn*, or Shakespeare's *Hamlet*, you will find a wide variety of selections below.

Should you wish only to browse in this chapter, you will also find helpful Web sites and numerous other resources.

Starting Points and Conversation Pieces

FAMOUS LINES FROM LITERATURE

- ❖ "Call me Ishmael." Opening of Herman Melville's *Moby Dick*.

- ❖ "All animals are equal, but some animals are more equal than others." *Animal Farm*, by George Orwell.

- ❖ "God bless us, every one." *A Christmas Carol*, by Charles Dickens.

❖ "There is no joy in Mudville—mighty Casey has struck out."
"Casey at the Bat," by Ernest Lawrence Thayer.

❖ "All for one and one for all." *The Three Musketeers*, by Alexandre
Dumas.

PHENOMENON

J. K. Rowling—*Harry Potter*. Series. (Underdog boy goes to wizard school
and fights the evil creature responsible for his parents' death.)

Resources for Further Exploration

READING

General Resources and Relevant Books
Adler, Mortimer J., and Charles Van Doren. *How to Read a Book: The Classic
Guide to Intelligent Reading*. New York: Touchstone, 1972.
Baldick, Chris. *The Concise Oxford Dictionary of Literary Terms*. New York:
Oxford University Press, 2001.
Bloom, Harold. *The Western Canon: The Books and School of the Ages*. New
York: Harcourt Brace, 1994.
Crystal, David. *The Cambridge Encyclopedia of Language*. New York: Cam-
bridge University Press, 1997.
Cuddon, J. A., and Claire Preston. *The Penguin Dictionary of Literary Terms
and Literary Theory*. New York: Penguin, 2000.
Hoad, T. F. *The Concise Oxford Dictionary of English Etymology*. New York:
Oxford University Press, 1993.
McArthur, Tom, and Roshan McArthur. *The Concise Oxford Companion to
the English Language*. New York: Oxford University Press, 1996.

101 IMPORTANT WORKS

> *A good book is the precious lifeblood of a master spirit.*
>
> —JOHN MILTON

The following texts likely would find their way into most collections of
important works of literature. The list runs from ancient times to modern times, and includes a variety of forms: fiction, nonfiction, short stories, essays, poetry, and drama. Many great books and great writers are
not included simply because there is no room. And, of course, with

thousands of worthy texts from which to choose, another valid list of important works could shape up completely differently.

In any event, for any number of reasons, all of these works and authors are prominent in the body of world literature. All should be readily available at most libraries.

Should you choose to take on the entire list, and read actively every week, you may find yourself busily engaged for a couple of years. And when this list runs dry, you can devour the other lists provided in these pages: National Book Awards, Pulitzer Prizes, and so on. Should you wish to take on an even more demanding schedule over a longer period, pick up a copy of *The Western Canon,* by Harold Bloom, long-time Yale professor, and tackle the enormous list that he offers. That should keep you busily engaged for a dozen years or more.

Anonymous (c. 2000 B.C.). *Epic of Gilgamesh.* (Touch antiquity with this epic poem, dating back to the days of Babylon, found on ancient tablets. King Gilgamesh wrestles with the notion of death.)

Homer (c. 800 B.C.). *The Iliad.* (Epic poem. Hero, Achilles, endures gods, prophesies, and revenge in the midst of the Trojan War.) *The Odyssey.* (Epic poem. Hero, Odysseus, encounters gods and monsters at sea for 10 years in efforts to get home to his wife, Penelope, and son, Telemachus.)

Aeschylus (525–455 B.C.). *Oresteia.* (Ancient Greek tragedies of guilt, murder, and revenge. Trilogy.)

Sophocles (496–406 B.C.). *Oedipus the King; Oedipus at Colonus; Antigone.* (Ancient Greek tragedies. Freud found his name for the "Oedipus Complex" from a primary theme here: man kills his father, marries his mother.)

Plato (428–348 B.C.). *Dialogues.* (On the life and death of Socrates. Read *Apology* and *Republic.*)

Virgil (70–19 B.C.). *Aeneid.* (Epic poem. Trojan hero, Aeneas, follows fate and founds Rome.)

Augustine, Saint (354–430). *Confessions.* (An autobiography of life and soul. A calling described.)

Anonymous (c. 1000). *Beowulf.* (Epic poem. Hero kills monsters and saves Danes.)

Dante (1265–1321). *The Divine Comedy.* (Epic poem. Dante travels through hell to save his soul.)

Chaucer, Geoffrey (1342–1400). *The Canterbury Tales.* (Epic poem. During their journey to Canterbury in the 1300s, pilgrims compete for a prize by telling stories, at times ribald. Read the Prologue and tales of the Knight, Miller, Pardoner, and Wife of Bath.)

Cervantes, Miguel de (1547–1616). *Don Quixote.* (Accompanied by his dim-witted squire, a romantic Spaniard finds adventure by reading novels, tilting at windmills, and searching for love.)

Spenser, Edmund (1552–99). *The Faerie Queene.* (Allegorical epic poem. A search for Truth in the face of Evil. In the Preface, the poet says that the aim of the book is to show how a virtuous man should live.)

Shakespeare, William (1564–1616). *Hamlet.* (A Danish prince seeks revenge for his father's murder.) *Macbeth.* (An ambitious Scottish general becomes a ruthless villain as he seeks to be king.), *Romeo and Juliet.* (Star-crossed lovers, whose family ties prevent union in life, find union in death.) *Julius Caesar.* (Brutus conspires to kill Caesar, fearing he will become king.) *Richard III.* (Opens with "Now is the winter of our discontent." Deceitful, deformed Richard becomes king, but his ambition ultimately kills him.) *A Midsummer Night's Dream.* (Love matures in the midst of chaos, with a little help from fairies and magic.)

Donne, John (1573–1631). Poems: *Holy Sonnets* ("Death be not proud . . .") and *Devotions* ("No man is an island . . . never send to know for whom the bell tolls; it tolls for thee.")

Milton, John (1608–74). *Paradise Lost.* (Epic poem. Tempted by a complex, charismatic Satan, Adam and Eve sin, losing paradise as a result.)

Molière (1622–73). *The Misanthrope.* (A biting, 17th-century comedy that shakes a finger at hypocrisy and extremism.)

Swift, Jonathan (1667–1745). *Gulliver's Travels.* (Satire. Through his travels, the title character turns from a gullible idealist to a misanthrope.)

Voltaire (1694–1778). *Candide.* (Both a satire and a philosophical romance, this novel follows the title character's development from naïve optimist to hardworking pragmatist.)

Fielding, Henry (1707–1754). *The History of Tom Jones, a Foundling.* (If for no other reason, read this comic story of a wild young man because of its importance as an early novel.)

Goethe, Johann Wolfgang von (1749–1832). *Faust.* (In this two-part dramatic tragedy, the title character, meant to symbolize Mankind, sells his soul to the devil, but redeems himself.)

Austen, Jane (1775–1817). *Pride and Prejudice.* (In the early 1800s in rural England, a witty young woman and a dashing young man overcome their pride and prejudice to find love. Virginia Woolf described Jane Austen as "the most perfect artist among women.")

Irving, Washington (1783–1859). *The Legend of Sleepy Hollow.* (Teacher, Ichabod Crane, meets a headless horseman in upstate New York.)

Hugo, Victor (1802–1885). *Les Misérables.* (Epic novel. In post-Revolution France, Jean Valjean runs from the police as he raises his daughter, Cosette. See the play, too.)

Hawthorne, Nathaniel (1804–1864). *The Scarlet Letter.* (In Puritan Boston, Hester Prynne, who has mothered an illegitimate child, is forced to wear the letter *A* on her dress.)

Poe, Edgar Allen (1809–1849). Poems and stories. (Best known for his gothic themes in poems such as "The Raven," and short stories like "The Murders in the Rue Morgue," "The Pit and the Pendulum," and "The Cask of Amontillado.")

Tennyson, Alfred, Lord (1809–1892). *Poems.* (You'll remember the great lines, like those from "The Charge of the Light Brigade": "Half a league, half a league, Half a league onward. All in the valley of death Rode the six hundred." "Theirs not to reason why, Theirs is but to do and die." Also read "The Lotos-Eaters" for its connection to Homer's *Odyssey* and for its rhyme scheme, similar to Spenser's *Faerie Queene.*)

Dickens, Charles (1812–70). *Great Expectations.* (As he grows up near London in the 19th century, a poor boy named Pip reconciles his great expectations of wealth with the realities of life.) *David Copperfield.* (As a successful writer, the title character looks back at the challenges of his youth and development. The story parallels Dickens' own life.) *A Tale of Two Cities* ("It was the best of times, it was the worst of times." London and Paris at the time of the French Revolution.) *Bleak House.* (A story of illegitimate children, lovers, and hidden identities. Worth reading to note that the legal costs and entanglements of Dickens' day rival those of today.)

Brontë, Charlotte (1816–55). *Jane Eyre.* (In the early 19th century, Jane matures as she falls in love with her employer and faces the inevitable challenges that result.)

Melville, Herman (1819–91). *Moby Dick.* (Ahab and the whale. One represents good, one, evil. You make the match.) *Billy Budd.* (Evil Claggart falsely accuses handsome, innocent Billy of mutiny.)

Whitman, Walt (1819–92). *Leaves of Grass.* Poems. (Poet responsible for, "I hear America singing." "When lilacs last in dooryard bloomed." "O Captain, My Captain.")

Flaubert, Gustave (1821–80). *Madame Bovary.* (Emma's marriage to a doctor does not fulfill her romantic fantasies, which leads her to an unfaithful life and a sad death.)

Dostoyevsky, Fyodor (1821–81). *Crime and Punishment.* (In the middle of the 19th century a young Russian with a dual personality commits murder and wrestles with his guilt.)

Tolstoy, Leo (1828–1910). *Anna Karenina.* (Anna abandons her family for an affair that ultimately destroys her.)

Ibsen, Henrik (1828–1906). *A Doll's House.* (Social play. At first a devoted wife and mother, by play's end Nora yearns for self-identity enough to abandon her family.)

Dickinson, Emily (1830–86). Poems. (Known as the Belle of Amherst, she wrote hundreds of untitled poems. A recluse, one of her lines reads: "A Prison gets to be a friend.")

Twain, Mark (1835–1910) (real name, Samuel Langhorne Clemens). *Huckleberry Finn* (This book gets more profound with each reading. Naïve youth finds raucous fun on the Mississippi prior to the Civil War as he and a slave seek freedom and adventure.) *Tom Sawyer.* (Fun-loving young boy finds adventure in a small town on the Mississippi in the 1840s.)

Hardy, Thomas (1840–1928). *The Return of the Native* (With ideals and aspirations, successful man returns to his native moors in England, only to find heartache and tragedy. Hardy is a master at describing landscapes.)

James, Henry (1843–1916). *The Portrait of a Lady*. (Isabel, an intellect from Albany, New York, travels through 19th-century Europe and struggles with love, independence, and marriage.)

Chopin, Kate (1851–1904). *The Awakening*. (In Louisiana's Creole country, tragic figure Edna Pontellier tries to awaken her inner passion and find her true self.)

Wilde, Oscar (1854–1900). *The Picture of Dorian Gray*. (Dorian sells his soul for youth and beauty, but sinks into depravity and can't live with his withering picture.) *The Importance of Being Earnest*. (Play with a play on words. The women want to marry men named Ernest because it sounds so aristocratic, which causes problems for suitors Jack and Algernon.)

Shaw, George Bernard (1856–1950). *Pygmalion*. (Play. Professor Higgins wagers that he can turn the cockneyfied Eliza Doolittle into a polished, well-spoken lady. "By George, she's got it.")

Conrad, Joseph (1857–1924). *Heart of Darkness*. (Short novel set in Africa. Undoubtedly the inspiration for Francis Ford Coppola's film *Apocalypse Now*. The evil Kurtz inhabits both.)

Wharton, Edith (1862–1937). *Ethan Frome*. (In attempting to escape his wife, henpecked Ethan becomes disabled and, ironically, finds himself under her care.)

Wells, H. G. (1866–1946). *The War of the Worlds*. (Unfriendly Martians land in the English countryside. Wells was the master of early sci-fi.)

Masters, Edgar Lee (1868–1950). *Spoon River Anthology*. (Poems. About the "ordinary" people buried on a hill overlooking Spoon River.)

Crane, Stephen (1871–1900). *The Red Badge of Courage*. (How Henry Fleming comes to be wounded and find his courage during the Civil War.)

Cather, Willa (1873–1947). *My Antonia*. (Life on the unforgiving American prairie for immigrants at the turn of the 20th century.)

Frost, Robert (1874–1963). (Poems. Poet included in virtually every anthology. New England flavor. If you read nothing else, read "The Road Not Taken," "Mending Wall," and "Stopping by Woods on a Snowy Evening.")

Sinclair, Upton (1878–1968). *The Jungle* (A socialist novel aimed at exposing the ills of the meatpacking industry in Chicago in the early 1900s.)

Stevens, Wallace (1879–1955). (Poems. Read the award-winning collections: *Auroras of Autumn* and *The Necessary Angel*.)

Forster, E. M. (1879–1970). *A Passage to India*. (Exploration of racial tensions in English-Indian relations through an assault accusation in India in the early 20th century.)

Joyce, James (1882–1941). *Portrait of the Artist as a Young Man*. (At the turn of the 20th century in Ireland, Stephen is torn between a career in religion or art.)

Woolf, Virginia (1882–1941). *To the Lighthouse*. (This is a story of a family trying to bring order to its life, but read it for its manageable "stream-of consciousness" style.)

Kafka, Franz (1883–1924). (Stories. You can't know Kafka without reading "The Metamorphosis," a story of a man transformed into an insect.)

Lewis, Sinclair (1885–1951). *Arrowsmith*. (Doctor/researcher Martin Arrowsmith fights temptations to bow to pressures in the world of American health care in the early 20th century.)

Fitzgerald, F. Scott (1886–1940). *The Great Gatsby*. (The rise and fall of the American dream. In the bootlegging days of the 1920s, Gatsby gains wealth and lives quite well, but cannot find true love.)

O'Neill, Eugene (1888–1953). *Long Day's Journey into Night*. (Play. Family's struggles revolve around tuberculosis, morphine addiction, and excessive drinking.)

Pasternak, Boris (1890–1960). *Doctor Zhivago*. (In Revolution-era Russia, Yury Zhivago, though married to Tonya, falls in love with Lara.)

Huxley, Aldous (1894–1963). *Brave New World*. (Picture of industrialized humanity, controlled by leaders of a world state, six hundred years into the future. Title taken from a line in Shakespeare's *The Tempest*.)

Faulkner, William (1897–1962). *Light in August*. (Pregnant girl finds racial tension in a Mississippi town as she searches for the baby's father.) *The Sound and the Fury*. (Using a "stream-of-consciousness" style,

Faulkner tells of the deterioration of the Compsons, an aristocratic family of Mississippi.)

Wilder, Thornton (1897–1975). *Our Town.* (Play. Daily activity in a small town transcends time and keys the importance of appreciating each moment of life.)

Remarque, Erich Maria (1898–1970). *All Quiet on the Western Front.* (Antiwar novel about a "lost generation" of German soldiers in World War I.)

Hemingway, Ernest (1899–1961). *A Farewell to Arms.* (The circumstances and consequences of an officer's decision to leave the army and his lover in the middle of World War I.) *The Old Man and the Sea.* (Fisherman Santiago thinks his luck is bad when he catches nothing for 84 days, but it gets even worse when he finally does catch a marlin and has to fight sharks to keep it.)

Steinbeck, John (1902–1968). *Of Mice and Men.* (Tragic story of how Lennie didn't mean to do "a bad thing," and how his friend George does what he must to give Lennie peace.) *The Grapes of Wrath.* (When the Dust Bowl forces a family out of Oklahoma during the Great Depression, they move to California as migrant workers.)

Orwell, George (1903–1950). *Animal Farm.* (Farm animals seek freedom through rebellion, only to find themselves living in a dictatorship after all.) *1984.* (This is the book that made "Big Brother" a part of the vernacular. Still timely, despite title.)

West, Nathanael (1903–1940). *Miss Lonelyhearts.* (Miss Lonelyhearts, a man who writes an advice column for a New York newspaper, searches unsuccessfully for love, religion, and happiness.)

Warren, Robert Penn (1905–1989). *All the King's Men.* (The rise and fall of Southern politico Willie Stark; explores the dirty side of American politics. No writer can beat Robert Penn Warren's ability to structure a sentence.)

Beckett, Samuel (1906–1989). *Waiting for Godot.* (Play. Before *Seinfeld,* there was this story about "nothing.")

Wright, Richard (1908–1960). *Native Son.* (Racism makes Bigger Thomas angry and violent, and he must face the consequences.)

Williams, Tennessee (1911–83). Plays. *A Glass Menagerie*. (After her mother arranges a disastrous visit from a "gentleman caller," shy, crippled Laura becomes as fragile as her glass collection.) *A Streetcar Named Desire*. (It's hard to think of this play and not conjure the familiar image of Marlon Brando calling "Stella." When Blanche Dubois visits her sister Stella in New Orleans, Stella's husband, Stanley, helps to show just how dysfunctional a family can be.)

Camus, Albert (1913–60). *The Plague*. (Threatened by a plague, which represents the Nazis, the inhabitants of a French town discover the importance of unity.)

Miller, Arthur (1915–). Plays. *The Crucible*. (Ostensibly about a 17th-century Massachusetts witch hunt, but parallels a 20th-century Washington witch hunt.) *Death of a Salesman*. (Willy Loman remembers the good old days, but can't re-create them.)

Solzhenitsyn, Alexander (1918–). *One Day in the Life of Ivan Denisovich*. (How a prisoner sees the "good fortune" that befalls him one day in a Siberian prison camp.)

Dickey, James (1923–97). Poems and novels. (Read the poetry that won a National Book Award, *Buckdancer's Choice*, and the intense Southern novel, *Deliverance*, which will make you think twice about your next rafting trip.)

Lee, Harper (1926–). *To Kill a Mockingbird*. (In an Alabama town, a little girl named Scout learns about racial tension, justice, and the wisdom of her father's advice.)

A book that does not appear on any of the lists in this section but that deserves mention as a personal favorite is Laura Hillenbrand's *Seabiscuit* (New York: Ballantine, 2001). It's too soon after publication to be dubbed a classic, but it's masterfully written. More than a story about a thoroughbred race horse, this is a book about the spirit of America in the 1930s. It is at once entertaining and enlightening.

BOOKS ABOUT BOOKS

Among the Gently Mad. Nicholas A. Basbanes. (Henry Holt, 2002)
Books of the Century. Charles McGrath, ed. (Three Rivers Press, 2000)
Great Books. David Denby. (Touchstone, 1997)

The New Lifetime Reading Plan. C. Fadiman and J. S. Major. (HarperResource, 1999)

A Passion for Books. H. Rabinowitz and R. Kaplan, eds. (Three Rivers Press, 2001)

The Well Educated Mind. Susan Wise Bauer. (W. W. Norton, 2003)

WEB SITES

American Literature

http://www.americanliterature.com/—American Literature. American Literary Classics.

http://www.jstor.org/journals/00029831.html—American Literature. (JSTOR-subscription).

WINNERS OF THE NOBEL PRIZE FOR LITERATURE, 1990–2004

2004 Novels and plays (no specific work cited), by Jelinek, Elfriede.

2003 *Disgrace,* by Coetzee, J. M. (Penguin, 2003).

2002 *Fateless,* by Kertesz, Imre, Katharina Wilson, and Christopher Wilson (Hydra Books, 1996).

2001 *Half a Life,* by Naipaul, V. S. (Alfred A. Knopf, 2001).

2000 *The Other Shore,* by Xingjian, Gao, and C. F. Fong (Chinese University Press, 1999).

1999 *My Century,* by Grass, Gunter, and Michael Henry Heim (Harvest Books, 2000).

1998 *Blindness,* by Saramago, Jose, and Giovanni Pontiero (Harvest Books, 1999).

1997 *Tricks of the Trade,* by Fo, Dario (Theatre Arts Books, 1991).

1996 *View with a Grain of Sand: Selected Poems,* by Szymborska, Wisawa, Szymborska, Wislawa, and Clare Cavanagh (Harcourt, 1995).

1995 *Door Into the Dark,* by Heaney, Seamus (Faber & Faber, 1995).

1994 *The Silent Cry,* by Oe, Kenzaburo,and S. Shaw (Kodansha International—Japan, 1994).

1993 *The Bluest Eye,* by Morrison, Toni (Plume, 2000).

1992 *Omeros,* by Walcott, Derek (Noonday Press, 1992).

1991 *Jump and Other Stories,* by Gordimer, Nadine (Penguin, 1992).

1990 *The Collected Poems of Octavio Paz, 1957–1987,* by Paz, Octavio, Elizabeth Bishop, and Eliot Weinberger (New Directions Publishing Corporation, 1991).

http://www.nagasaki-gaigo.ac.jp/ishikawa/amlit/—American Literature on the
  Web.
http://www.yale.edu/lawweb/avalon/chrono.htm—American History—A Documentary Record. Yale University.
http://www.nagasaki-gaigo.ac.jp/ishikawa/amlit/21/f_authors21.htm—
  American Authors Since 1945.
http://www.bartleby.com/cambridge/—Cambridge History of English and American Literature.
http://www.lang.nagoya-u.ac.jp/~matsuoka/AmeLit.html—American Authors on
  the Web.
http://guweb2.gonzaga.edu/faculty/campbell/enl311/litfram.html—American
  Authors. Literary Movements.
http://www.calstatela.edu/academic/english/ala2/—American Literature Association.
http://www.wwnorton.com/naal/—Norton Anthology of American Literature.
http://etext.lib.virginia.edu/railton/—Mark Twain in his Times.
http://www.nypl.org/links/index.cfm?Trg=1&d1=592&d3=Authors%2C%20Poet
  s%2C%20and%20Playwrights—New York Public Library's Authors,
  Poets, and Playwrights (American and British).
http://www.top20americanliterature.com/—"Top 20" American Literature Sites.
http://guweb2.gonzaga.edu/faculty/campbell/enl311/timefram.html—Brief
  Timeline of American Literature and Events, 1620–1920.
http://www.nagasaki-gaigo.ac.jp/ishikawa/amlit/20/timeline.htm—American
  Literature Timeline, 1914–1945.

British Literature
http://www.luminarium.org/lumina.htm—Texts from Medieval, Renaissance,
  and 17th-Century British Literature.
http://www.victorianweb.org/—Victorian literature and more.
http://chemicool.com/Shakespeare/—Complete Shakespeare online.
http://www.bartleby.com/70/— The Oxford Shakespeare.
http://www.shakespeares-globe.org/—Shakespeare's Globe Theater.
http://www.wfu.edu/~tedforrl/shakespeare/—Electronic Shakespeare. Resource
  for Researchers.
http://www.shakespeare-online.com/—Shakespeare Online.
http://www.bardweb.net/—Shakespeare Resource Center.
http://sites.micro-link.net/zekscrab/—Shakespeare Study Guide.
http://www.shakespearemag.com/—Shakespeare Magazine Online.
http://www.shu.ac.uk/emls/emlshome.html—Early Modern Literary Studies.
  Journal.
http://www.nypl.org/branch/books/—New York Public Library's Recommended Reading, Booklists, and Book Reviews.

http://vos.ucsb.edu/browse.asp?id=3—Voice of the Shuttle Directory—Literature (British and American).

http://www.studyguide.org/brit_lit_timeline.htm—British Literature Timeline.

World Literature

http://www.csdl.tamu.edu/cervantes/V2/CPI/index.html—Cervantes Project. Bilingual site (Spanish and English).

http://www.virginia.edu/cla/split.htm—Spanish Literature. Listings, links, book reviews.

http://www.bartleby.com/65/ge/Germanli.html—Columbia Encyclopedia—German Literature.

http://www.berlinerzimmer.de/eliteratur/—Handbook of German Literary Magazines and Ezines (in German).

http://histrom.literature.at/—The German Historical Novel Project.

http://www.columbia.edu/cu/lweb/indiv/africa/cuvl/aflit.html—African Literature on the Internet.

http://web.uflib.ufl.edu/cm/africana/writers.htm—African Writers: Voices of Change.

http://hapax.be.sbc.edu/—HAPAX: French Resources on the Web.

http://gallica.bnf.fr/Classique/—Gallica Classique. French texts in French.

http://www.crs4.it/HTML/Literature.html—Italian Literature.

http://www.lib.uchicago.edu/efts/IWW/—Italian Women Writers.

http://www.lib.virginia.edu/wess/etexts.html—Electronic Text Collections in Western European Literature.

http://info.wlu.ca/~wwweng/faculty/jwright/irish/—Bibliography of 19th-century Irish Literature.

http://www.lysator.liu.se/runeberg/—Project Runeberg. Classic Swedish Literature (in Swedish).

http://www.canlit.ca/index.html—Canadian Literature: A Quarterly of Criticism and Review (in French or English).

http://www.umanitoba.ca/canlit/—Canadian Literature Archive.

http://setis.library.usyd.edu.au/oztexts/ozlit.html—Australian Studies—Australian Literary and Historical Texts.

http://mclc.osu.edu/—Modern Chinese Literature and Culture.

http://mockingbird.creighton.edu/english/worldlit/wldocs/japan.htm—Japanese Literature Resources Page.

http://www.classics.ox.ac.uk/—Faculty of Classics, University of Oxford.

http://www.ipl.org/div/litcrit/—Internet Library's Literary Criticism.

Classics

http://www.artsci.wustl.edu/~cwconrad/classics.html—Classics Resources. Includes links for Greek and Latin.

http://gilgamesh.psnc.pl/—Gilgamesh. Epic poem. Digital Library book.
http://classics.mit.edu/index.html—Internet Classics Archive.
http://www.perseus.tufts.edu/—Perseus Digital Library. Tufts University.
http://www.nypl.org/links/index.cfm?Trg=1&d1=594&d3=Classical%20Litera
 ture—New York Public Library Directory for Classical Literature.

OTHER RESOURCES

Folger Shakespeare Library
201 East Capitol Street SE
Washington, D.C. 20003
(202) 544–4600
http://www.folger.edu/Home_02B.html

NATIONAL BOOK AWARDS FOR POETRY, 1991–2004

2004 *Door in the Mountain,* by Valentine, Jean (Wesleyan University Press, 2004).

2003 *The Singing Poems,* by Williams, C. K. (Farrar, Straus and Giroux, 2003).

2002 *In the Next Galaxy,* by Stone, Ruth (Copper Canyon Press, 2002).

2001 *Poems Seven,* by Dugan, Alan (Seven Stories Press, 2001).

2000 *Blessing the Boats: New and Selected Poems, 1988–2000,* by Clifton, Lucille (BOA Editions, 2000).

1999 *Vice: New and Selected Poems,* by Ai (W. W. Norton & Co., 1999).

1998 *This Time: New and Selected Poems,* by Stern, Gerald (W. W. Norton & Co., 1998).

1997 *Effort at Speech: New and Selected Poems,* by Meredith, William (Northwestern University Press, 1997).

1996 *Scrambled Eggs and Whiskey: Poems, 1991–1995,* by Carruth, Hayden (Copper Canyon Press, 1996).

1995 *Passing Through: The Later Poems New and Selected,* by Kunitz, Stanley (W. W. Norton & Co., 1997).

1994 *Worshipful Company of Fletchers,* by Tate, James (Ecco, 1995).

1993 *Garbage: A Poem,* by Ammons, A. R. (W. W. Norton & Co., 1994).

1992 *New and Selected Poems,* by Oliver, Mary (Beacon Press, 1993).

1991 *What Work Is: Poems,* by Levine, Philip (Alfred A. Knopf, 1992).

Shakespeare's Globe Theater
21 New Globe Walk
Bankside
London SE1 9DT
Telephone: +44 (0)20 7902 1400
http://www.shakespeares-globe.org/

The Library of Congress
101 Independence Avenue SE
Washington, D.C. 20540
(202) 707-5000
http://www.loc.gov/

READING LIST

Suggested Anthologies
The American Tradition in Literature. George Perkins, ed. (McGraw-Hill,
    2002).
The Norton Anthology of World Masterpieces. Maynard Mack, ed. (W. W.
    Norton & Co., 1997).
Perrine's Literature. Thomas R. Arp, ed. (Heinle, 2001).
Stories and Poems for Extremely Intelligent Children of All Ages. Harold Bloom.
    (Scribner, 2001).

11. Math

There are three kinds of people in the world:
those who can count and those who can't.

LOOK UP AT THE SKY AT NIGHT. COUNT a hundred million stars. That might seem impossible, even if you devoted your entire life to it, but, in fact, counting at a reasonable rate of two stars a second, it would take you only about a year and a half. The point is not that you should devote every second of your next year and a half to counting stars, but only that math can make possible what at first seems impossible. We send spacecraft hundreds of millions of miles through the universe with remarkable precision. They send back revealing information and close-up images of distant worlds. We have landed rovers on Mars and put one of our vehicles—*Cassini,* a craft as big as a bus—into orbit around Saturn, a journey of 900 million miles that took seven years.

Math is more than a lot of numbers and formulas. Math is a concept meant to help us with our problems and challenges. It's practical, useful, beneficial. It's a valuable tool that you can use regularly to save precious time, money, and energy.

If you want to remind yourself of what you need to know in math, or perhaps tackle a new area, the best route is to review basic guides or textbooks in the specific subjects. In algebra, see *Introductory and Intermediate Algebra for College Students,* by Robert Blizter (Upper Saddle River, NJ: Prentice Hall, 2004), or *Algebra: Structure and Method,* by Richard G. Brown, et al. (Evanston, IL: McDougal Littell/Houghton Mifflin, 2000), both of which provide a strong foundation in the subject through clear explanations and exercises. In geometry, try *Introduction to Geometry,* by H. S. M. Coxeter (Indianapolis: Wiley, 1989), which has self-contained chapters full of illustrations, or *Glencoe Geometry,* by Joe Cummings, et al. (Westerville, Ohio: Glencoe/McGraw-Hill, 1998), which offers numerous practical applications. For trigonometry, take a look at *Trigonometry Demystified,* by Stan Gibilisco (New York: McGraw-Hill, 2003), which caters to the beginner as it lays out the fundamentals and general concepts. And for calculus get *The Complete Idiot's Guide to Calculus,* by Michael W. Kelley (New York: Alpha Books, 2002), which offers an accessible overview of key concepts.

There's support online at Math2.org (**http://www.math2.org/ index.html**), which begins at multiplication tables and reaches to advanced calculus, and at World of Math Online (**http://www.math. com/**), which covers everything from fractions and decimals to transforms and recursive formulas. Get extra help at any of the dozens of sites listed in the resources area below. There's even a math museum you can visit in New York (**http://www.mathmuseum.org/**) that features a variety of programs and attractions, such as puzzles, video spheres, and origami instruction.

Doing Certain Kinds of Math in Your Head Faster than a Calculator

Knowledge crushes fear and boosts confidence. And you can master select pieces of knowledge about math rather simply. If you're afraid of math, know this: By the time you finish this section, you will have tools that will permit you to tame that fear.

TAMING YOUR FEAR

Let's say you are buying a carpet today. The space to be covered measures 11 feet by 16 feet. By using the basic techniques outlined below, you would know IMMEDIATELY that the area to be covered is 176 square feet. IMMEDIATELY! This type of everyday problem does not require paper and pencil, or calculator, or computer. This is the kind of challenge that can be figured out INSTANTLY in your head, as long as you know the simple techniques to use. In a few minutes, as you read this chapter, you will know not only how to find the area of a rectangle but also how to multiply by 11 in your head faster than a calculator. While you're at it, you'll also learn how to multiply by 5 faster than a calculator.

AIMS AND MEANS

There are hundreds of tools that can help you breeze through math problems. In the following pages, for example, there are "starting points" for you to review and master. Some of them don't even contain numbers. They refer to people. Rule #1 in math: It's not a problem until it's a problem.

You're not aiming at becoming a math scholar at this point, but at attaining fundamentals that will permit you to solve everyday problems and hold your own in a conversation in which math pops up.

The following are just two techniques of many that exist. Learn how to multiply by 5 and by 11 FAST, FAST, FAST. Master these techniques. Build your repertoire. Conquer the world.

MULTIPLYING BY 5

Here is a technique that has the potential to help you virtually every day of your life—multiplying by 5 in your head faster than a calculator.

Memorize this: **When you want to multiply a number by 5, simply add a zero to the number and then divide by 2.**

For example: How much is 4862 times 5?

Conventional method:

$$
\begin{array}{r}
4862 \\
\times\ \ 5 \\
\hline
24310
\end{array}
$$

Easier method—you can do this in your head

Add a zero to 4862, making it 48620. Half of 48620, or 48620 divided by 2, equals 24310.

(Here is how your mind may approach it: half of 48 is **24**; half of 6 is **3**; half of 20 is **10**.)

It makes no difference if the number to be multiplied is odd or even.

For example: How much is 243 times 5?

Conventional method:

$$
\begin{array}{r}
243 \\
\times\ 5 \\
\hline
1215
\end{array}
$$

Easier method—do it in your head

Add a zero to 243, making it 2430. Half of 2430, or 2430 divided by 2, equals 1215.

(Here is how you may approach it: Half of 24 is **12**; half of 30 is **15**. This is the kind of calculation you can do in your head, no?)

So, here is the principle to follow:

WHEN YOU WANT TO MULTIPLY A NUMBER BY 5, SIMPLY ADD A ZERO TO THE NUMBER AND THEN DIVIDE BY 2.

Perhaps you want to multiply a number by 50 or 500. No problem. Same fundamental principle with slight, logical variations.

WHEN YOU WANT TO MULTIPLY A NUMBER BY 50, SIMPLY ADD TWO ZEROES TO THE NUMBER AND THEN DIVIDE BY 2.

WHEN YOU WANT TO MULTIPLY A NUMBER BY 500, SIMPLY ADD THREE ZEROES TO THE NUMBER AND THEN DIVIDE BY 2.

For example:

$$\begin{array}{r} 648 \\ \times\ 50 \\ \hline 32400 \end{array}$$

OR

Add two zeroes to 648, making it 64800, and then divide by 2. Half of 64800, or 64800 divided by 2, equals 32400.

Let's try 500:

$$\begin{array}{r} 865 \\ \times\ 500 \\ \hline 432500 \end{array}$$

OR

Add three zeroes to 865, making it 865000, and then divide by 2. Half of 865000, or 865000 divided by 2, equals 432500.

Let's take a quick step back. How about multiplying by .5? Easy. Simply take half of the number, or divide it by 2. Do not add any zeroes. For example, .5 times 20 equals 10. (And half of 20 is 10.) And .5 times 100,000 equals 50,000. (And half of 100,000 is 50,000.)

So, **.5 multiplied by any number is the same as dividing by 2.**

Think of how handy and practical this information can be. For most people, most of the time, dividing by 2, or taking half of a number, is an easy process, certainly easier than actually multiplying by .5, or 5, or 50, or 500. It is so easy, in fact, that most people—including you—probably already do it in their heads regularly.

Shoppers, for example, regularly encounter sales of "buy one and get

one for half price." So, if the item is $4, then the one for half is $2 . . .
right? Or how about if the sale is simply "half off"? Then the item that
originally costs $6 now costs $3.

And how about routine chores around the house. Let's say your goal is
to put a border around the middle of the wall in a bedroom. The wall is 8
feet high. You know immediately that the middle of the wall is at 4 feet.

This is basic stuff that gives you control. Reminding yourself that
you already know it and use it regularly helps you feel a little more
CONFIDENT about math.

With just a little practice you will master it. You may never use the
conventional method again when you need to multiply by .5 or 5 or 50
or 500. Why do so, when it is so much easier to add some zeroes, if necessary, and then divide by 2?

MULTIPLYING BY 11

Here's the deal: When multiplying a two-digit number by 11, simply
add the two digits together and insert the sum in between the two
digits.

For example:

> 11 × 63
> take the 6 and add it to the 3 to get 9
> insert the 9 between the 6 and the 3 (that is, 6–9–3)
> thus, 11 × 63 = 693

Try another:

> 11 × 52
> add the 5 and 2 to get 7
> insert the 7 between the 5 and the 2 (that is, 5–7–2)
> 11 × 52 = 572

Try these:

> a. 11 × 44
> b. 11 × 26
> c. 11 × 70
> d. 11 × 18

(Answers: a. 484; b. 286; c. 770; d. 198)

Practice a while and it will become second nature to you. Practice
often and you will become a whiz. It is so easy that you can do it in
your head, right? In fact, it is easier to do in your head than with a cal-

culator. Believe it—by the time you push the buttons of a calculator, you already will have come up with the answer in your head.

NOTE: What if the two digits add up to 10 or more, such as 11 × 57? No problem.

> 11 × 57
> add the 5 and the 7 to get 12
> insert the 2 between the 5 and 7 and carry the 1
> add the 1 to the 5 to get 6
> thus, 11 × 57 = 627 (that is, 6-2-7)

Try another:

> 11 × 78
> add the 7 and 8 to get 15
> insert the 5 between the 7 and 8, carry the 1
> add the 1 to the 7 to get 8
> thus, 11 × 78 = 858 (that is, 8-5-8)

Another way to look at it would be:

> 11 × 78
> add the 7 and 8 to get 15
> insert the 15 between the 7 and 8, noting that the 1
>   gets added to the 7
> (7+1)-5-8 = 8-5-8
> 11 × 78 = 858

How about 11 × 93?

> add the 9 and 3 to get 12
> insert the 2, carry the 1
> add the 1 to the 9 to get 10
> thus, 11 × 93 = 1023 (that is, 10-2-3)

Try these:

> a. 11 × 84
> b. 11 × 99
> c. 11 × 68
> d. 11 × 19

(Answers: a. 924; b. 1089; c. 748; d. 209)

Surrounded by the Number 11

Learning to multiply by 11 quickly will help you. You'd be surprised how many times that number appears in your day-to-day life. In a world of counting carbs and calories, for example, it will come up—and in sales, school, the office, room measurements, wall measurements, carpet measurements. The number 11 is quite common. Take an ordinary piece of paper, for example, or a letter in the mail—the dimensions are 8½ inches by 11 inches. Even if you haven't noticed how often the number pops up, rest assured that once you master this technique, you will be amazed at how often it will come in handy.

MORE ADVANCED

Let's look at three-digit numbers. The thinking is consistent: The rule for three or more digits is to add and insert from the right.

For example:

11×436

STARTING FROM THE RIGHT, add the 3 and the 6 to get 9

insert the 9

add the 4 and the 3 to get 7

insert the 7

the middle digit is **replaced** by the insertions

thus, $11 \times 436 = 4796$ (that is, 4-7-9-6)

Note that the digits on the end, that is, the 4 and the 6, have remained the same, while the digit in the middle, that is, the 3, has been **replaced** by the insertions (7 and 9).

Try another:

11×218

STARTING FROM THE RIGHT, add the 1 and the 8 to get 9

insert the 9

add the 2 and the 1 to get 3

insert the 3

thus, $11 \times 218 = 2398$ (that is, 2-3-9-8)

Again, the digits on the end, that is, the 2 and the 8, have remained the same, while the digit in the middle, that is, the 1, has been replaced by the insertions (3 and 9).

Of course, the more digits you are working with, the more practice you will need to master the technique. Once mastered, however, it will be like learning how to ride a bicycle—you'll never forget how to do it and you can always use the skill when needed.

Try these for practice, remembering to insert and carry if the addition comes to 10 or more:

a. 11 × 327
b. 11 × 516
c. 11 × 933
d. 11 × 111

(Answers: a. 3597; b. 5676; c. 10263; d. 1221)

Starting Points and Conversation Pieces

FORMULAS AND TERMS

- ❖ The perimeter of a rectangle: 2 × lengths + 2 × widths (P=2l+2w).

- ❖ The area of a rectangle: length × width (A=lw).

- ❖ The perimeter of a square: 4 × side (P=4a).

- ❖ The area of a square: side × side (A=a²) (side squared).

- ❖ The perimeter of a triangle: add the length of the three sides (P=a+b+c).

- ❖ The area of a triangle: ½ of the base × the height (A=½bh).

- ❖ Pi = 3.14 (π=3.14) (transcendental number; approximate).

- ❖ The distance around a circle is called the circumference. The distance across the middle of a circle is called the diameter. The distance from the center to a point on the circle is called the radius.

- ❖ The diameter of a circle: 2 × radius (d=2r).

- ❖ The circumference of a circle: pi × diameter or 2 × pi × radius (C=πd or C=2πr).

- ❖ The area of a circle: pi × radius squared (A=πr²).

- ❖ Once around a circle measures 360 degrees (360°).

- ❖ The shortest distance between two points is a straight line.

- ❖ Angles that have the same number of degrees are called *congruent* angles.

- ❖ A line that crosses two parallel lines is called a *transversal*.

- ❖ The sum of the angles of a triangle always equals 180 degrees.

- ❖ A right triangle is a triangle with an angle of 90 degrees.

- ❖ The longest side of a right triangle (i.e., the side opposite the right angle) is called the *hypotenuse*.

- ❖ An *isosceles triangle* is a triangle with at least two equal sides.

- ❖ A triangle with all sides equal is called an *equilateral triangle*.

- ❖ A triangle with no sides equal is called a *scalene triangle*.

HISTORY OF MATH

- ❖ The abacus was invented in 500 B.C.

- ❖ Euclid's *Elements* were published in 300 B.C., melding thought in mathematics and philosophy.

- ❖ The number "zero" was used for the first time in Europe in A.D. 976.

- ❖ Tim Berners-Lee is credited with inventing the World Wide Web in 1989.

Resources for Further Exploration

READING

Math History
Beckmann, Petr. *A History of Pi*. New York: St. Martin's Griffin, 1976.
Boyer, Carl B., and Isaac Asimov. *A History of Mathematics*. Indianapolis: Wiley, 1991.
Bryson, Bill. *A Short History of Nearly Everything*. New York: Broadway, 2003.

General Resources and Relevant Books
Courant, Richard, et al. *What Is Mathematics?: An Elementary Approach to Ideas and Methods*. New York: Oxford University Press, 1996.
Dehaene, Stanislas. *The Number Sense: How the Mind Creates Mathematics*. New York: Oxford University Press, 1999.
Devlin, Keith J. *The Language of Mathematics: Making the Invisible Visible*. New York: Owl Books, 2000.
Devlin, Keith J. *The Math Gene: How Mathematical Thinking Evolved & Why Numbers Are Like Gossip*. New York: Basic Books, 2001.

Dunham, William. Journey *Through Genius: The Great Theorems of Mathematics*. New York: Penguin, 1991.

Eves, Howard. *Foundations and Fundamental Concepts of Mathematics*. Mineola, New York: Dover, 1997.

Glazer, Evan M., and John W. McConnell. *Real-Life Math*. Westport, Connecticut: Greenwood Press, 2002.

Kline, Morris. *Mathematics and the Physical World*. Mineola, New York: Dover, 1981.

———. *Mathematics for the Nonmathematician*. Mineola, New York: Dover, 1985.

Livio, Mario. *The Golden Ratio: The Story of PHI, the World's Most Astonishing Number*. New York: Broadway, 2003.

Paulos, John Allen. *A Mathematician Reads the Newspaper*. New York: Anchor, 1996.

Seife, Charles, and Matt Zimet. *Zero: The Biography of a Dangerous Idea*. New York: Penguin, 2000.

Selby, Peter H., and Steve Slavin. *Practical Algebra: A Self-Teaching Guide*. Indianapolis: Wiley, 1991.

Slavin, Steve. *All the Math You'll Ever Need*. Indianapolis: Wiley, 1999.

Sobel, Dava. *Longitude: The True Story of a Lone Genius Who Solved the Greatest Scientific Problem of His Time*. New York: Penguin, 1996.

Spiegel, Murray R. *Schaum's Mathematical Handbook of Formulas and Tables*. New York: McGraw-Hill, 1998.

Stewart, Ian. *Concepts of Modern Mathematics*. Mineola, New York: Dover, 1995.

Astronomy
Seeds, M. A. *Foundations of Astronomy*. Pacific Grove, CA: Thomson Brooks/Cole, 2003.

Statistics
Huff, Darrell, and Irving Geis. *How to Lie with Statistics*. New York: W. W. Norton, 1993.

Patterns
Devlin, Keith J. *Mathematics: The Science of Patterns*. New York: Owl Books, 1996.

Computers
Gralla, Preston. *How the Internet Works*. Upper Saddle River, NJ: Pearson, 2003.

Miller, Michael. *Absolute Beginner's Guide to Computer Basics*. Upper Saddle River, NJ: Pearson, 2002.

WEB SITES

General Resources and Relevant Sites
http://mathworld.wolfram.com/—Mathworld—Theorems and formulas and
    more.
http://www.mathforum.org/dr.math/—Ask Dr. Math. Service to solve com-
    mon math problems.
http://www.mathaddicts.org/tiki-index.php—Math Addicts Anonymous.
http://www.math.com/—Math.com. General resources.
http://www.forbesfield.com/bdf.html—Blue Dog—solves math problems.
http://www.mathforum.org/—The Math Forum. Drexel University.
http://www.mathnotes.com/aw_basicmath.html—Basic College Math.
http://www.ics.uci.edu/~eppstein/junkyard/topic.html—The Geometry Junkyard.
http://www.cs.uidaho.edu/~casey931/new_knot/index.html—New Ideas About
    Knots.
http://www.clarku.edu/~djoyce/wallpaper/—Plane Symmetry Groups.
http://dept.physics.upenn.edu/courses/gladney/mathphys/Contents.html—Inter-
    active Textbook.
http://www.math-net.org/links/show?collection=math.museum—Math museum
    online.

Directories
http://www.tc.cornell.edu/Edu/MathSciGateway/—Math and Science Gateway.
http://www.geocities.com/jayjay99_us/TheMathematicalEquation.html—Links.

History
http://www-history.mcs.st-and.ac.uk/history/Indexes/HistoryTopics.html—The
    history of math.

Fun and Games
http://www.coolmath.com/.—Designed for fun math. Geared to youth.
http://www.cs.uidaho.edu/~casey931/conway/games.html—Clever Games for
    Clever People.
http://www.cs.uidaho.edu/~casey931/—Math puzzles.

Algebra, Geometry, Trigonometry, Calculus
http://www.math2.org/index.html—Help with algebra, geometry, trig, calc,
    etc.
http://www.sosmath.com/—Math help—from algebra to differential equations.
http://www.calc101.com/—Automatic Calculus and Algebra.
http://colbycc.edu/www/math/math.htm—General math resources—algebra,
    geometry, trig.
http://www.math.niu.edu/~beachy/aaol/frames_index.html—Abstract Algebra
    Online.

http://www2.hawaii.edu/suremath/intro_algebra.html—Algebra Story and
   Word Problems.
http://www.calculus.net/ci2/?tag=—Calculus@Internet.
http://www.ima.umn.edu/~arnold/graphics.html—Calculus graphics.

Technology
http://www.cnn.com/TECH/—CNN tech news.
http://msnbc.msn.com/id/3033055/—MSNBC Technology and Science.
http://abcnews.go.com/sections/scitech/index.html—ABC SciTech News.
http://www.newscientist.com/—New Scientist— science and technology news
   service.
http://scientificamerican.com/news_directory.cfm—Scientific American. Science and technology news.
http://story.news.yahoo.com/news?tmpl=index&cid=528—Technology AP. News
   on technology.
http://story.news.yahoo.com/news?tmpl=index&cid=581—Reuters. Technology news.
http://news.com.com/—CNET tech news.
http://zdnet.com.com/2001–11–0.html?legacy=zdnn—ZDNet. Tech news and
   white papers for IT professionals.
http://www.pcworld.com/—PC World.
http://story.news.yahoo.com/news?tmpl=index&cid=74—TechWeb. Tech news.
http://www.pcmag.com/—PC Magazine.
http://story.news.yahoo.com/news?tmpl=index&cid=77—MacCentral.
http://story.news.yahoo.com/news?tmpl=index&cid=711—USA Today tech news.
http://news.yahoo.com/news?tmpl=index2&cid=1804—Washington Post Technology.
http://scitechdaily.com/—SciTech Daily Review.

Astronomy
http://www.museumspot.com/categories/planetariums.htm—Planetariums.
http://www.griffithobservatory.org/—Griffith Observatory.
http://www.amnh.org/rose/haydenplanetarium.html—Hayden Planetarium.
http://www.astronomycafe.com/—Discussion Forum for the Amateur Astronomer.
http://www.astronomy.com—Star charts, space pictures, astronomy news.

OTHER RESOURCES

Griffith Observatory
2800 East Observatory Road
Los Angeles, CA 90027
(323) 664–1181
http://www.griffithobservatory.org/

VIDEO AND DVD

Want a fun and fascinating look at math and science? From your library, pick up the video or DVD *Powers of Ten*, by Charles and Ray Eames (Pyramid Media). Embark on a fantastic trip that takes a camera's point of view beginning with a couple on a picnic blanket in Chicago and moving away—up toward the sky, farther and farther—ten times farther every ten seconds until we are looking at Earth from outer space and then the galaxy and then other galaxies. As the camera reverses direction and moves back toward Earth, we eventually zoom in on the hand of the man lying on the picnic blanket. As if looking through a supermicroscope, we zoom in with ten times magnification every ten seconds, deeper and deeper, until we are inside a protein of an atom within a DNA molecule. The entire video runs only nine minutes but offers entertaining and intriguing perspective on the world around us.

There's a complementary book with the same journey, *Powers of Ten*, by Philip and Phylis Morrison (New York: Scientific American Library, 1982).

Hayden Planetarium
American Museum of Natural History
79th Street and Central Park West
New York, NY 10023
(212) 313-7278
http://www.amnh.org/rose/haydenplanetarium.html

Goudreau Math Museum
Herricks Community Center
999 Herricks Road, Room 202
New Hyde Park, NY 11040-1353
 (516) 747-0777
info@mathmuseum.org
http://www.mathmuseum.org/

12. Science

BEGIN A REFRESHER IN SCIENCE with the essay below, which gives an overview of the foundations of early scientific thought. The "starting points" that follow provide fundamental information on terms like *inertia* and *osmosis* and people like Copernicus, Kepler, Galileo, and Newton.

It's good to have a reference book handy, and *The New York Public Library Science Desk Reference,* by Patricia Barnes-Svarney (New York: Macmillan, 1995), will serve you well. It covers all major topics. The *Library Journal* says that "you could not find a more comprehensive and readable, desk-sized, one-volume science encyclopedia."

Go online to find information on virtually every area imaginable, from oceans and atmosphere (**http://www.noaa.gov/**—National Oceanic and Atmospheric Administration), to microbiology (**http://www.microbes.info/**—The Microbiology Information Portal), to frog dissection (**http://www-itg.lbl.gov/ITG.hm.pg.docs/dissect/info.html**—Virtual Frog Dissection Kit).

A Very Brief and Basic History of Science (The Early Years)
Theories about the Universe from the Heaviest Hitters of Early Scientific Thought

No doubt you know people who think the world revolves around them. (Don't we all?) That attitude may be described as "egocentric" (ego = I, centric = the center of). Whole cultures and nations have had similar attitudes; ancient Chinese cultures, for example, believed (with some justification) that the world revolved around them.

It seems understandable, then, that in the early development of science, the primary issue of explaining how the universe works generated many theories that viewed the Earth as the center of the cosmos.

A history of how the world viewed the structure of the universe is, in many ways, a history of science itself. Perhaps no other topic earned as much attention in the early centuries of science as celestial movements and their bearing on the various cultures that studied them.

Let's first look at ancient Greece. Though the prevalent theories of the day in the seventh century B.C. and earlier adhered to the belief that Zeus and the other Olympian gods controlled every detail of life and every celestial movement of the universe, a few learned philosophers— none more notable than **Thales** (c. 620–550 B.C.)—dared to stray, thinking that there might be natural forces at work. (Note: philosophers and scientists were often one and the same in the early centuries.) Eclipses, thunder, and lightning, for example, may have been attributed to the work of the gods in the seventh century B.C., but gave cause for alternate theories and explanations in succeeding centuries. This was no small moment in the history of science, that is, seeing the workings of the universe as a result of an ordered Nature, rather than as a result of the impulses of the gods, for worldly events then might be predicted and explained with reason and logic.

Perhaps no early civilization rightfully deserves credit for the critical development of scientific thought more than the world of ancient Greece. The Babylonians and Egyptians made contributions, but a vibrant curiosity and genuine passion for learning were the marks of the early Greek culture. **Democritus** (c. 460–370 B.C.), for example, as early as the fifth century B.C. theorized that all matter must have its smallest, most fundamental form, which he referred to as "atomon," the root of the word *atom*.

Ancient Greek philosopher-scientists like **Aristotle** (384–322 B.C) studied the heavens and reasoned that all that could be seen revolved around the Earth—that is, the stars, the sun, the planets. Mother Earth, therefore, was the center of the universe. Aristotle, a most influential scholar of ancient Greece, firmly believed this "geocentric" theory to be true, and through the centuries this view dominated all others. Refined by second-century Egyptian scientist **Ptolemy** (c. A.D. 90–168), the theory reigned supreme until the 1500s.

Few challenged the theory during the rule of the Roman Empire, whose scholars focused more on literature and law, art and architecture.

In the latter stages of the Roman Empire, a dominant Christianity shifted the focus from the current world to the world to come. Arabs of the Byzantine Empire, however, valued the scientific accomplishments of the Greeks, preserving the language and the documents. For centuries, into the Middle Ages, Arabs thrived as caretakers of the scientific world. Math, in particular, flourished in the Byzantine Empire, with the development of algebra, trigonometry, and "Arabic numerals." Astronomy developed also, as Arabs charted the skies and studied the stars.

At the turn of the 16th century, however, **Nicholas Copernicus** (1473–1543) studied the heavens, analyzed the Aristotle/Ptolemy model, and departed from the prevailing "geocentric" theory. He saw that, in fact, the center of the universe was not the Earth but the sun. (Ironically, this was not a new theory, but one that had surfaced and faded in ancient Greece.) Though this "heliocentric" idea (helio = sun) caught on in some circles, many of the top scientists of the day were not convinced, preferring to hold on to the Aristotelian outlook. Change does not come easily in the scientific world.

Copernicus' theory held that the orbiting bodies traveled in circles, which caused irritating irregularities in mathematical calculations and left some aspects of the theory open to interpretation and vulnerable to criticism. In the 1600s, however, **Johannes Kepler** (1571–1630), a German scientist who had originally studied to be a Lutheran minister, refined Copernicus' theory by determining that the orbits were not circular but elliptical. This adjustment immediately closed the nagging gaps, making the theory simpler, more airtight, more elegant, and, as a result, more credible.

Not long after the telescope was invented, **Galileo Galilei** (1564–1642), an Italian astronomer and mathematician, fashioned his own telescope, perhaps the most powerful instrument of his day, and used it to observe and measure the skies. What he saw and recorded confirmed Copernicus' theory. Indeed, it was a heliocentric universe.

Isaac Newton (1642–1727), a British mathematician and scientist, developed cogent and indisputable mathematical laws about motion and gravity that further simplified and validated what Galileo had observed and what Copernicus had theorized.

Slowly and steadily, amidst healthy resistance from the world's scientific community, the theory of the heliocentric universe forged by Copernicus, refined by Kepler, and supported by the work of Galileo and Newton, replaced the geocentric theory established by Aristotle and Ptolemy. In the centuries since then, with constant advancements of technology, further refinements and clarifications have been made. And the beat goes on—even today, with all the powerful computers and precision instruments that may be used to study the structure of the universe, we do not know as much as we will know tomorrow.

Starting Points and Conversation Pieces

TERMS

* *Osmosis:* The process by which fluid passes through a membrane, establishing an equal concentration of fluid on both sides.

* *Inertia:* Law articulated by Newton—unless acted upon by an outside force, an object at rest tends to stay at rest, and an object in motion tends to stay in motion.

* *Natural Selection:* Darwin's theory—survival of the fittest—that is, fit organisms survive, while unfit organisms die away.

* *Nano-technology:* Technology with an emphasis on small, tiny, minuscule (e.g. very, very small, practically invisible, computer chips)—"nano," from the Greek, means "one-billionth."

SCIENTISTS OF NOTE

* *Hippocrates of Cos* (460–370 B.C.): Greek known as the Father of Medicine.

* *Archimedes* (d. 212 B.C.): Ancient mathematician and physicist who discovered the lever, the value of pi, and the principle of liquid displacement.

* *Galileo Galilei* (1564–1642): First astronomer to use a telescope for scientific observations and often referred to as the Father of Mathematical Physics.

* *Isaac Newton* (1642–1727): Best known for discovering gravity, inventing calculus, and articulating the Laws of Motion, including the Law of Inertia.

❖ *Charles Darwin* (1809–1882): In his *The Origin of Species,* he posited the theory of evolution and the process of natural selection.

❖ *Jonas Salk* (1914–95): American biologist responsible for a polio vaccine.

❖ The structure of DNA was discovered in 1953 by *James Watson, Francis Crick,* and *Maurice Wilkins.* All shared the Nobel Prize in 1962.

OTHER ITEMS OF INTEREST

❖ The first recycling law (bottles) was enacted in 1972 in Oregon.

❖ Why does an hour contain 60 minutes? The ancient Sumerians, responsible for the earliest forms of writing and counting, used 60 as a base in their counting. Thus, an hour was divided into 60 minutes and a minute was divided into 60 seconds.

❖ The Sumerians are also credited with having invented the wheel.

❖ The invention of the magnifying glass is credited to Roger Bacon in 1250.

❖ It is estimated that the Great Pyramid in Egypt was completed circa 2600 B.C.

❖ Circa 2296 B.C., the first observation of a comet was made by astronomers in China.

❖ The nucleus of a comet is composed of ice, gas, and dust.

❖ The tail of a comet always points away from the sun.

❖ The first recording of a solar eclipse was circa 2136 B.C. in China.

❖ The first recording of a lunar eclipse was circa 2000 B.C. in Ur, Mesopotamia.

❖ Circa 1500 B.C., the sundial was developed to measure time in Egypt.

❖ The earliest recording of an earthquake dates back to the eighth century B.C. in China.

❖ In 500 B.C., Pythagoras challenged common belief by declaring that the Earth was not flat, but a sphere.

❖ Sirius, called the "dog star" by the ancient Greeks, is the brightest fixed star in the sky.

❖ The word *gas* is taken from the Flemish word for "chaos."

❖ *Columbia,* the first space shuttle, was launched in the United States in 1981.

Resources for Further Exploration

READING

General Resources and Relevant Books

Einstein, Albert. *Ideas and Opinions.* New York: Bonanza, 1954.

Evans, Colin. *The Casebook of Forensic Detection: How Science Solved 100 of the World's Most Baffling Crimes.* Indianapolis: Wiley, 1998.

Gleick, James. *Chaos: Making a New Science.* New York: Penguin, 1987.

Gould, Stephen Jay. *Bully for Brontosaurus: Reflections in Natural History.* New York: New Millennium Press, 2000.

Greene, Brian. *The Elegant Universe: Superstrings, Hidden Dimensions, and the Quest for the Ultimate Theory.* New York: Vintage, 2000.

Hall, Marie Boas. *The Scientific Renaissance.* London: Fontana Press, 1970.

Sagan, Carl. *Cosmos.* New York: Ballantine, 1993.

Watson, James D. *The Double Helix: A Personal Account of the Discovery of the Structure of DNA.* New York: Touchstone, 2001.

Biology and Physics

Asimov, Isaac. *Understanding Physics.* New York: Dorset Press, 1966.

Feynman, Richard P., et al. *Six Easy Pieces: Essentials of Physics Explained by Its Most Brilliant Teacher.* New York: Perseus, 1996.

Feynman, Richard P., et al. *"Surely You're Joking, Mr. Feynman!": Adventures of a Curious Character.* New York: W. W. Norton, 1997.

Gleick, James. *Genius: The Life and Science of Richard Feynman.* New York: Vintage, 1993.

McCormmach, Russell. *Night Thoughts of a Classical Physicist.* Cambridge, MA: Harvard University Press, 1982.

Thomas, Lewis. *The Lives of a Cell: Notes of a Biology Watcher.* New York: Penguin, 1995.

———. *The Medusa and the Snail.* New York: Penguin, 1995.

Ecology and Environmental Science

Cronon, William. *Changes in the Land: Indians, Colonists, and the Ecology of New England*. New York: Hill and Wang, 1983.

Krech, Shepard, III. *The Ecological Indian: Myth and History*. New York: W. W. Norton, 1999.

Merchant, Carolyn. *Major Problems in American Environmental History*. Boston: Houghton Mifflin, 2004.

Strasser, Susan. *Waste and Want: A Social History of Trash*. New York: Metropolitan Books, 1999.

Science History

Delsemme, A. *Our Cosmic Origins*. New York: Cambridge University Press, 1998.

Falk, Dan. *Universe on a T-Shirt*. New York: Arcade Publishing, 2002.

Hawking, Stephen W. *A Brief History of Time*. New York: Bantam, 1998.

Holton, Gerald. *Thematic Origins of Scientific Thought: Kepler to Einstein*. Cambridge, MA: Harvard University Press, 1988.

Lindberg, David C. *The Beginnings of Western Science*. Chicago: University of Chicago Press, 1992.

Atomic Science

Jungk, Robert. *Brighter Than a Thousand Suns: A Personal History of the Atomic Scientists*. New York: Harvest, 1970.

Rhodes, Richard. *The Making of the Atom Bomb*. New York: Simon & Schuster, 1988.

WEB SITES

Space

http://science.nasa.gov/—NASA.

http://story.news.yahoo.com/news?tmpl=index&cid=96—Space.com. Yahoo news on space.

General Resources and Relevant Sites

http://www.fordham.edu/halsall/science/sciencesbook.html—Internet History of Science Sourcebook.

http://es.rice.edu/ES/humsoc/Galileo/—Galileo Project. All about the life and work of Galileo.

http://web.clas.ufl.edu/users/rhatch/pages/03–Sci-Rev/SCI-REV-Home/—Scientific Revolution, Professor Robert A. Hatch, University of Florida. Focus on scientific development in Europe from 1550 to 1700.

THE LOS ANGELES TIMES BOOK PRIZE
SCIENCE AND TECHNOLOGY, 2004–1993

2004 *Protecting America's Health: The FDA, Business, and One Hundred Years of Regulation,* by Hilts, Philip J.

2003 *Rosalind Franklin: The Dark Lady of DNA,* by Maddox, Brenda.

2002 *The Invention of Clouds: How an Amateur Meteorologist Forged the Language of the Skies,* by Hamblyn, Richard.

2001 *The Rise and Fall of Modern Medicine,* by Le Fanu, James D.

2000 *Galileo's Daughter: A Historical Memoir of Science, Faith, and Love,* by Sobel, Dava.

1999 *Blood: An Epic History of Medicine and Commerce,* by Starr, Douglas.

1998 *How the Mind Works,* by Pinker, Steven.

1997 *The Demon-Haunted World: Science as a Candle in the Dark,* by Sagan, Carl.

1996 *Naturalist,* by Wilson, Edward Osborne, Brian Taylor, and Alastair Graham.

1995 *The Beak of the Finch: A Story of Evolution in Our Time,* by Weiner, Jonathan.

1994 *Fuzzy Logic: The Revolutionary Computer Technology That Is Changing Our World,* by McNeill, Daniel, and Paul Freiberger.

1993 *The Third Chimpanzee: The Evolution and Future of the Human Animal,* by Diamond, Jared.

http://es.rice.edu/ES/humsoc/Galileo/Catalog/catalog.html—Catalog of the Scientific Community, 16th and 17th centuries.

http://www.chemicool.com/—Periodic table.

http://www.tc.cornell.edu/Edu/MathSciGateway/—Math and Science Gateway.

http://www.kolmogorov.com/Frontiers_in_Physics.html—Frontiers in Physics Series.

http://www.museumspot.com/—Museums, zoos, national parks, etc.

http://naturalscience.com/dsqhome.html/—Dictionary of Scientific Quotations.

http://aa.usno.navy.mil/data/docs/MoonPhase.html—Moon Phases.

http://www.sciencedaily.com/—Science Daily Magazine.

http://www.digitaldutch.com/unitconverter/—Unit Converter.

http://www.chemie.fu-berlin.de/cgi-bin/abbscomp—Abbreviations of Chemical Compounds.

http://my.unidata.ucar.edu/content/staff/blynds/rnbw.html—About Rainbows.

http://www.timeline.aps.org/APS/home_HighRes.html—A look at the last century in Physics.

http://www.drscience.com/—Ask Dr. Science.

http://www.liv.ac.uk/Chemistry/Links/links.html—Links for Chemists.
http://tolweb.org/tree/phylogeny.html—Diversity and history of Earth's
　　organisms.
http://www.exploratorium.edu/sunspots/—Guide to Sunspots.
http://www.pbs.org/wnet/brain/—The Secret Life of the Brain.

Medicine
http://www.sciencekomm.at/advice/dict.html—Science-medical dictionary.
http://www.bartleby.com/107/—Gray's Anatomy.
http://mtdesk.com/wordlist.shtml—Science/medical word lists.
http://www.nlm.nih.gov/—National Library of Medicine.

Weather
http://www.intellicast.com/LocalWeather/World/—Weather around the world.
http://www.weather.com/—The Weather Channel.

Science News
http://scientificamerican.com/news_directory.cfm—Scientific American.
　　Science news.
http://story.news.yahoo.com/news?tmpl=index&cid=624—Science AP.
http://story.news.yahoo.com/news?tmpl=index&cid=585—Reuters. Science news.
http://news.bbc.co.uk/1/hi/sci/tech/default.stm—BBC. Science news.
http://www.newscientist.com/—New Scientist—science and technology news
　　service.

Technology
http://msnbc.msn.com/id/3033055/—MSNBC Technology and Science.
http://abcnews.go.com/sections/scitech/index.html—ABC SciTech News.
http://scitechdaily.com/—SciTech Daily Review.

OTHER RESOURCES

Jet Propulsion Laboratory
4800 Oak Grove Drive
Pasadena, CA 91109–8099
(818) 354–9314
http://www.jpl.nasa.gov/

Johnson Space Center
Houston, TX 77058
(281) 244-2105
http://www.jsc.nasa.gov/

Kennedy Space Center
Cape Canaveral, Florida, east of Orlando
Spaceport U.S.A.
Kennedy Space Center
FL 32899–0001
(321) 452-2121
http://www.nasa.gov/centers/kennedy/index.html

NASA Headquarters
300 E Street SW
Washington, D.C. 20546
(202) 358-0000
http://www.hq.nasa.gov/

Museum of Science
Science Park
Boston, MA 02114
(617) 723-2500
information@mos.org
http://www.mos.org/—Museum of Science, Boston.

Museum of the History of Science
Old Ashmolean Building, Broad Street
University of Oxford
Oxford, England OX1 3AZ
telephone (+44) [0]1865 277280
http://www.mhs.ox.ac.uk/

13. Music

WHAT'S YOUR GOAL IN MUSIC? If your interest lies in learning how to play an instrument—like piano or guitar—begin with a basic text or video like *Mel Bay's Fun with the Guitar* (Pacific, MO: Mel Bay Publications, 1970) or *Play Piano Overnight* (video—La Quinta, CA: Xebex Productions/Thane Marketing, 1987).

In his nonintimidating booklet, Mel Bay starts with the fundamentals—such as holding the guitar and fingering the frets—and guides you to playing easy chords and songs, like "Home on the Range," and "Oh, Susanna." Note that this is an elementary, introductory text for beginners of all ages. Alternatives include the package by American Legacy Guitar, which includes an acoustic/electric guitar, an amplifier, and lessons on DVD by guitarist Esteban (**http://www.americanlegacygui tar.com**), or online video instruction at Guitar School (**http://www. guitarschool.net**), which features interactive sessions.

The 45–minute piano video, which emphasizes that "you don't need to know how to read music," is in *The Overnight Music Series,* and the goal is to teach you how to play simple tunes by the time you finish the tape. An alternative would be Scott Houston's *Play Piano in a Flash: Play Your Favorite Songs Like a Pro—Whether You've Had Lessons or Not,* which comes in book, video, or DVD. Houston's instructional specials have been aired numerous times on PBS.

If you are more interested in learning or relearning about history or theory than playing an instrument, start with a general reference like *Music Theory Made Easy,* by David Harp (New York: Music Sales Corporation, 1999), which covers scales and chords for jazz, rock, and other types of music, or *HarperCollins College Outline History of Western Music,* by Hugh M. Miller (New York: HarperResource, 1991), which presents historical timelines and easy-to-follow study aids that span the major offerings in college curriculums.

On the Web, begin at the music directories at Google (**http://direc tory.google.com/Top/Arts/Music/**), Lycos (**http://music.lycos.com/**), or Yahoo (**http://dir.yahoo.com/entertainment/music/index.html**), all of which offer links to dozens of sites on a wide variety of topics.

Also, see the additional resources listed below.

Starting Points and Conversation Pieces

IMPORTANT CLASSIC COMPOSERS AND THEIR WORKS

❖ Johann Sebastian Bach (1685–1750); German

Works include:

- ❖ *Brandenburg Concertos*
- ❖ *Christmas Oratorio*
- ❖ Numerous cantatas
- ❖ Cello suites
- ❖ Mass in B Minor

❖ Ludwig van Beethoven (1778–1827); German/Austrian

Works include:

- ❖ Symphonies No. 3 (*Eroica*); No. 5; No. 6 (*Pastoral*); No. 9 (*Choral*)
- ❖ Sonata No. 14 (*Moonlight*)
- ❖ Piano Concerto No. 5 (*Emperor*)
- ❖ *Für Elise*

❖ Wolfgang Amadeus Mozart (1756–1791); Austrian

Works include:

- ❖ *The Marriage of Figaro* (opera)
- ❖ *Requiem* (choral music)
- ❖ Symphonies No. 35 (*Haffner*); No. 39; No. 40; No. 41 (*Jupiter*)

❖ Franz Schubert (1797–1828); Austrian

Works include:

- ❖ Symphony No. 8 (Unfinished)
- ❖ *Ave Marie* (vocal music)

❖ Igor Stravinsky (1882–1971); Russian

Works include:

- ❖ *The Fire Bird* (ballet)
- ❖ *Petrushka* (ballet)
- ❖ *The Rite of Spring* (ballet)

❖ Peter Ilich Tchaikovsky (1840–93); Russian

Works include:

- ❖ Symphonies No. 4; No. 5; No. 6 (*Pathétique*)
- ❖ Marche Slave
- ❖ 1812 Overture
- ❖ *The Nutcracker* (ballet) (suite)
- ❖ *Swan Lake* (ballet)
- ❖ *Sleeping Beauty* (ballet)

❖ Giuseppe Verdi (1813–1901); Italian

Works include:

- ❖ *Rigoletto* (opera)
- ❖ *Il Trovatore* (opera)
- ❖ *La Traviata* (opera)
- ❖ *Aida* (opera)

OTHER ITEMS OF INTEREST

- ❖ The lines on a G Staff are: e, g, b, d, f.

- ❖ The spaces on a G Staff are: f, a, c, e.

- ❖ Generally considered the classic example of Baroque music, the opera, *Orfeo Favola in Musica* was written by Italian Claudio Monteverdi in 1607.

- ❖ Tchaikovsky's *Swan Lake* debuted at Moscow's Bolshoi Theatre in 1877.

- ❖ Thomas Edison patented his invention, the phonograph, in 1878.

- ❖ In the Roarin' Twenties, Chicago served as home base to such jazz giants as Louis Armstrong and Jelly Roll Morton.

DID YOU KNOW?

In the late nineteenth-century in England, Gilbert and Sullivan created many comic operas that are still popular today, including *H.M.S. Pinafore* (1878), *The Pirates of Penzance* (1879), and *The Mikado* (1885). Of the duo, Sir William S. Gilbert was the lyricist and Sir Arthur Sullivan was the composer. They were introduced by Richard D'Oyly Carte, who went on to produce the operas.

❖ Duke Ellington got a jump on the Swing Era with his 1932 classic, "It Don't Mean A Thing, If It Ain't Got That Swing."

❖ While many may think that Bing Crosby first sang his monster hit "White Christmas" in the 1954 film of the same name, he actually sang it first in *Holiday Inn* in 1942.

❖ While Perry Como was given the first gold record by The Recording Industry Association of America for "Catch a Falling Star" in 1958, RCA Victor had symbolically sprayed Glenn Miller's hit "Chattanooga Choo Choo" with gold paint in 1942 to signify its having sold more than a million copies.

❖ Radio DJ and stage-show host Alan Freed is credited with coining the term *rock and roll* in the early 1950s.

❖ "Rock Around the Clock," by Bill Haley and the Comets, is generally considered the first rock and roll song to reach number 1 (1955).

❖ The *Billboard Chart*'s top five singles on April 4, 1964, were all Beatles' songs: "Can't Buy Me Love," "Twist and Shout," "She Loves You," "I Want To Hold Your Hand," and "Please Please Me."

❖ Only two artists have won Album of the Year Grammy Awards in consecutive years: Frank Sinatra (*September of My Years,* 1966; *Sinatra: A Man and His Music,* 1967) and Stevie Wonder (*Innervisions,* 1974; *Fulfillingness' First Finale,* 1975).

❖ The original Woodstock music festival was held in August 1969 in upstate New York.

❖ MTV began in 1981. The first music video it showed was *Video Killed the Radio Star,* by The Buggles.

❖ In 2002, for the first time since 1980, a musical artist won Grammies in the same year for Single of the Year, Album of the Year, and Best New Artist—Norah Jones.

Resources for Further Exploration

READING

General Resources and Relevant Books

Broughton, Simon, and Mark Ellingham. *World Music, vol. 2, Latin and North America, Caribbean, India, Asia, and Pacific: The Rough Guide*. New York: Rough Guides, 2000.

Cross, Milton John. *The Milton Cross New Encyclopedia of the Great Composers and Their Music*. New York: Bantam Dell, 1969.

Kelly, Thomas Forrest. *First Nights: Five Musical Premiers*. New Haven: Yale University Press, 2001.

Landeck, Beatrice, et al. *Making Music Your Own*. Morristown, New Jersey: Silver Burdett, 2000.

Sandburg, Carl. *The American Songbag*. Fort Washington, Pennsylvania: Harvest Books, 1990.

Theory

Edwards, Bill. *Fretboard Logic SE: The Reasoning Behind the Guitar's Unique Tuning + Chords Scales and Arpeggios Complete (The Fretboard Logic Guitar Method Parts I and II)*. Coeur d'Alene, Idaho: Edwards Music Publishing, 1997.

Green, Barry. *The Mastery of Music: Ten Pathways to True Artistry*. New York: Broadway Books, 2003.

Wyatt, Keith, and Carl Schroeder. *Harmony & Theory: A Comprehensive Source for All Musicians*. Los Angeles: Musicians Institute, 1998.

Rock

Crampton, Luke, and Dafydd Rees. *Rock and Roll Year by Year*. New York: DK Publishing, 2003.

Hal Leonard Publishing Corporation. *The Beatles—Complete Scores*. Milwaukee, Wisconsin: Hal Leonard Corporation, 1993.

Romanowski, Patricia, ed., et al. *Rolling Stone Encyclopedia of Rock and Roll: Revised and Updated for the 21st Century*. New York: Simon & Schuster, 2001.

Instruments
Humphries, Carl. *The Piano Handbook: A Complete Guide for Mastering Piano.* Book & CD edition. San Francisco: Backbeat Books, 2003.
Suzuki, Shinichi. *Suzuki Violin School: Violin Part, vol. 1.* New York: Warner Brothers Publications, 1999.

Classical
Libbey, Theodore. *The NPR Guide to Building a Classical CD Collection : The 350 Essential Works.* New York: Workman Publishing, 1999.

Blues
Murray, Albert, and Dan Morgenstern. *Good Morning Blues: The Autobiography of Count Basie.* New York: Da Capo Press, 2002.

Opera
Plotkin, Fred, and Placido Domingo. *Opera 101: A Complete Guide to Learning and Loving Opera.* New York: Hyperion, 1994.
Tynan, Ronan. *Halfway Home: My Life 'til Now.* New York: Citadel Press, 2003.

Jazz
Schuller, Gunther. *Early Jazz: Its Roots and Musical Development.* New York: Oxford University Press, 1986.
———. *History of Jazz, vol. II: The Swing Era.* New York: Oxford University Press, 1991.
Shapiro, Nat, and Nat Hentoff. *Hear Me Talkin' To Ya: The Story of Jazz as Told by the Men Who Made It.* Mineola, New York: Dover, 1966.
Steinel, Mike. *Building a Jazz Vocabulary.* Milwaukee, Wisconsin: Hal Leonard Corporation, 1995.
Stewart, Rex. *Jazz Masters of the Thirties.* New York: Da Capo Press, 1982.

Latin
Morales, Ed. *The Latin Beat: The Rhythms and Roots of Latin Music, from Bossa Nova to Salsa and Beyond.* New York: Da Capo Press, 2003.

WEB SITES

Libraries
http://www.loc.gov/rr/perform/ihas/ihashome.html—Library of Congress: I Hear America Singing—Music, Theater, Dance Collections.

http://hcl.harvard.edu/loebmusic/online-ir-intro.html—The Loeb Music Library, Harvard University. "Internet resources for music scholars."

http://www.nypl.org/links/index.cfm?Trg=1&d1=141&d3=Music—New York Public Library Directory for Music.

http://www.library.yale.edu/musiclib/webres.htm—Yale University Music Library. Comprehensive directory of Web resources.

http://www.musiclibraryassoc.org/—Music Library Association.

Directories

http://www2.siba.fi/Kulttuuripalvelut/music.html—General directory.

http://library.wustl.edu/subjects/music/—Music directory. Washington University, St. Louis.

http://www.lib.msu.edu/coll/main/finearts/music/websites.htm—Directory hosted by Michigan State University.

http://music.dir.nodeworks.com/—Nodeworks. Music directory.

http://library.usask.ca/resources/display.php?cat=Music—Music directory with a Canadian flavor.

http://www.rochester.edu/Eastman/sibley/—Sibley Music Directory, Eastman School of Music.

General Resources and Relevant Sites

http://www.allmusic.com/—All-Music Guide.

http://www.sun.rhbnc.ac.uk/Music/Links/index.html—"The Golden Pages: Links for Musicians on the WWW."

http://www.library.ucsb.edu/subjects/music/music.html—Music Information Resources. University of California, Santa Barbara.

http://www.lib.utk.edu/music/net/net.html—Music on the Net. University of Tennessee.

http://www.musicsearch.com/—Music Search. Search engine.

http://library.wustl.edu/subjects/music/diss_info.html—Music Dissertation Information.

http://www.music.indiana.edu/music_resources/—Internet Music Resources, Indiana University School of Music.

http://www.sas.upenn.edu/music/ams/musicology_www.html—"Sites of Interest to Musicologists." American Musicological Society.

http://je5qh2yg7p.search.serialssolutions.com/?V=1.0&L=JE5QH2YG7P&N=100 &S=SC&C=FIMUSI—Online Music Journals.

http://www.cd-info.com/—CD Information Center.

http://www.themefinder.org/—Themefinder.

http://www.saintmarys.edu/~jhobgood/Jill/lyrics.html—Lyrics Page. Lyrics to musicals.

http://www.metmuseum.org/Works_Of_Art/department.asp?dep=18—Metropolitan Museum of Art—Musical Instruments.

http://hcl.harvard.edu/loebmusic/online-ir-digital.html—Digital Music Collections.

Music Schools
http://www.music.ua.edu/resources/addresses.html—Music School Address Book.

Sacred Music
http://www.lib.washington.edu/music/sacred.html#Sacred%20Music—Sacred Music. University of Washington.

Concerts and Live Performances
http://www.musi-cal.com/—Search for concert schedules, live performances.

Sheet Music
http://scriptorium.lib.duke.edu/sheetmusic/—Historic American Sheet Music.
http://www.free-scores.com/index_uk.php3—Free Scores. Free Sheet Music Directory.

Classical
http://www.classical.net/—Classical Music—reviews, files, links.
http://www.lib.duke.edu/dw3/—Duke University Library classical music site.
http://www.musiclassical.com/—MUSIClassical. Classical Music Directories.
http://www.gprep.org/classical/—Classical Music Virtual Library.
http://voyager.physics.unlv.edu/webpages2/websyt/archive.html—Classical Composers' Archive. Pictures of composers.

19th Century
http://lcweb2.loc.gov/ammem/amsshtml/—America Singing. Nineteenth-Century Song Sheets.
http://memory.loc.gov/ammem/cwmhtml/cwmhome.html—Band Music from the Civil War Era.

Rock
http://www.rock.com/—"The Official Site of Rock Music." News, videos, posters, etc.
http://www.scaruffi.com/history/—The History of Rock Music. Decade-by-decade descriptions.

Latin
http://www.caravanmusic.com/GuideLatinMusic.htm—Guide to Latin Music. Country-by-country descriptions.

http://www.laritmo.com/—Latin American Rhythm Magazine. Articles, inter-
views, etc.
http://www.music.indiana.edu/som/lamc/—Latin American Music Center.

African American
http://memory.loc.gov/ammem/award97/rpbhtml/aasmhome.html—African
American Sheet Music, 1850–1920.

Jazz
http://www.jazz-clubs-worldwide.com/—Jazz Clubs of the World. Directory.
http://www.jazz-clubs-worldwide.com/docs/festivals.htm—Jazz Festivals Worldwide.
http://www.jazzreview.com/preview.cfm—Jazz Concerts Calendar Schedule.
http://www.jazzvalley.com/—Jazz links (in French and English).

Opera
http://www.operaamerica.org/perfdatabase.asp—Opera America's Season
Schedule of Performances.
*http://directory.google.com/Top/Arts/Music/Styles/Opera/Houses_and_Compa
nies/*—Google Directory—Opera.
http://www.fsz.bme.hu/opera/companies.html—List of Opera Companies on
the Web.
http://operabase.com/en/—Operabase—Database: artists, performances, etc.

Choirs and Orchestras
http://www.choralnet.org/choirs/index.phtml—Directory of Choirs on the
Web.
http://www.jwoollard.freeserve.co.uk/—Orchestra News. Worldwide.

OTHER RESOURCES

Blues Archive, University of Mississippi
Archives and Special Collections
J. D. Williams Library
University, MS 38677
(662) 915–7753
e-mail: *gj1@olemiss.edu*
http://www.olemiss.edu/depts/general_library/files/archives/blues/

Rock and Roll Hall of Fame and Museum
One Key Plaza
751 Erieside Avenue

Cleveland, OH 44114
(216) 781-ROCK
http://www.rockhall.com/

Grand Ole Opry
2802 Opryland Drive
Nashville, TN 37214
(615) 871-OPRY
http://www.opry.com/

American Classical Music Hall of Fame
4 West Fourth Street
Cincinnati, OH 45202
(800) 499-3263 (FAME) or (513) 621-3263 (FAME)
e-mail: *info@classicalhall.org*
http://culture.ohio.gov/project.asp?proj=classical
http://www.americanclassicalmusic.org/

14. Sports

IF YOU DON'T KNOW A FULL COUNT from a fullback, or a double dribble from a double play or a daily double, you'll want to pick up a basic guide to the sport you're interested in, like one of the *Dummies* series: *Baseball for Dummies,* by former pro ballplayer Joe Morgan and Richard Lally (Indianapolis: Wiley, 2000), which has something for everyone, whether you're a longtime fan or new to the national pastime; *Football for Dummies,* by former NFL star Howie Long and John Czarnecki (Indianapolis: Wiley, 2003), which clearly explains terms, positions, rules, penalties, and strategies; or *Basketball for Dummies,* by former Notre Dame coach Digger Phelps, et al. (Indianapolis: Wiley, 2000), which covers the fundamentals of the game, and about which TV analyst Dick Vitale wrote: "Awesome, baby." To get an even more intimate knowledge of the individual games, look at the rules books, such as *Official Rules of the NFL* (New York: Triumph, 2003) or *Official NBA Rules Book* (St. Louis: Sporting News, 2003). There's also a cute book titled *The Cool Chick's Guide to Baseball,* by Lisa Martin (Layton, Utah: Gibbs Smith, 2003); which gives tips not only on the less obvious details (e.g., it's a cap, not a hat) but also on what to wear to the ballpark and how many calories in the hot dog at the concession stand.

If you are beyond the basics, you'll want to have a general reference book at hand to keep track of the individual and team statistics as the season progresses, something like the *ESPN Sports Almanac: The Definitive Sports Reference Book,* by Gerry Brown (New York: Hyperion, 2004), which will serve you well as the ultimate argument-ender.

If you want to learn about thoroughbred horse racing, stick with the Harvard grads, Andy Beyer, a columnist for *The Washington Post,* and Steve Crist, chairman and publisher of *The Daily Racing Form.* Nobody knows the Sport of Kings better than they do. Beyer, in fact, singlehandedly revolutionized the thoroughbred racing industry by creating his own "speed figures," putting an innovative, commonsense slant on how to time horses. For the details, take a look at his book, *Picking Win-ners: A Horseplayer's Guide* (Boston: Houghton Mifflin, 1994). And read Crist's chapter on getting the best value for your betting dollars in *Bet with the Best,* by the editors of *The Daily Racing Form* (New York: Daily Racing Form Press, 2001).

On the Web you really don't have to venture farther than the ESPN site at **http://www.espn.com**, where you'll find news and stats about every sport. If you want alternatives, however, CBS Sportsline is good (**http://www.sportsline.com/**), as is Fox Sports (**http://msn.foxsports .com/**) and USA Today Sports (**http://www.usatoday.com/sports /front.htm**). For a good directory, go the Sports Hot Sheet (**http:// hotsheet.port5.com/sports.htm**), the most comprehensive sports gateway imaginable, with links to everything from sports news sources to home pages for every college and pro team, auto racer, tennis player, and golf pro.

Starting Points and Conversation Pieces

BASKETBALL

❖ Michael Jordan averaged 37 points per game in 1987, but Wilt Chamberlain holds the single-season NBA record: 50.4 points per game (1962).

❖ Wilt Chamberlain is also the all-time career leader in rebounds with 23,924.

❖ Phil Jackson has won NBA Coach of the Year once (1996, Bulls). Pat Riley has won it three times (1990, Lakers; 1993, Knicks; 1997, Heat).

HORSE RACING

❖ Thoroughbred racing's Triple Crown consists of the Kentucky Derby, the Preakness, and the Belmont. All are races for three-year-olds only.

❖ As of 2004, the last horse to win the Triple Crown was Affirmed in 1978.

HOCKEY

* In the NHL, the Detroit Redwings won back-to-back Stanley Cups (championships) in 1997 and 1998.

* Only one NHL player has scored 200 or more points in a single season: Wayne Gretzky, who did it four times and holds the record with 215 points (1986).

FOOTBALL

* The Denver Broncos won back-to-back NFL Super Bowls in 1997 and 1998.

* The first two NFL Super Bowls (1966 and 1967) were won by the Green Bay Packers, coached by Vince Lombardi.

* Dick Vermeil won Coach of the Year honors 21 years apart: in 1978 (Eagles) and in 1999 (Rams).

* The last NFL player to win three MVP Awards, back-to-back-to-back, was Brett Favre (1995, 1996, and 1997).

* In 2003–2004, the New England Patriots set the NFL record for most consecutive wins—18 regular season games, 21 including the playoffs.

BASEBALL

* The all-time pitching leader in strikeouts is Nolan Ryan (5,714).

* The pitcher with the all-time record for wins is Cy Young (511).

* The all-time leader in stolen bases is Rickey Henderson (1,406).

* Babe Ruth set the record for home runs in a season with 60 in 1927. Roger Maris broke that record by hitting 61 in 1961. Mark McGwire hit 70 in 1998, and Barry Bonds hit 73 in 2001.

* Only three players have hit more than 700 home runs in their career: Babe Ruth (714), Hank Aaron (755), and Barry Bonds (still active—broke 700 in 2004).

* In 2004, Ichiro Suzuki broke Hall of Famer George Sisler's 84–year-

old record of most hits in a single season. Sisler had 257 hits in 1920. Suzuki ended his season with 262 hits.

❖ At season's end in 2004, Major League Baseball returned to Washington, D.C., after an absence of 33 years, when the Montreal Expos franchise was moved to the nation's capital and renamed the Washington Nationals. (The Washington Senators moved to Texas in 1971.)

❖ In 2004, the Boston Red Sox won the World Series for the first time in 86 years (1918). They swept the St. Louis Cardinals in four games.

GOLF

❖ The all-time record for Major wins is Jack Nicklaus with 18. (US Open, British Open, PGA, Masters.)

TENNIS

❖ In men's tennis, the player with the most career wins in Grand Slam Singles is American Pete Sampras with 14 (including seven Wimbledon titles). In women's tennis, it's Australian Margaret Court (Smith) with 24 (including 11 Australian Open titles).

COLLEGE

❖ The Big Ten Conference has 11 teams in it.

CYCLING

❖ In 2004, Lance Armstrong won the Tour de France for an unprecedented sixth time.

Resources for Further Exploration

READING

Baseball
Asinof, Eliot. *Eight Men Out: The Black Sox and the 1919 World Series*. New York: Owl Books, 2000.

Halberstam, David. *October 1964*. New York: Ballantine, 1995.

Kahn, Roger. *The Boys of Summer*. New York: Perennial Classics, 2000.

Football

Bissinger, H. G. *Friday Night Lights: A Town, a Team, and a Dream*. Cambridge, Massachusetts: Da Capo Press, 2000.

Running, Hiking, Cycling

Armstrong, Lance, Chris Carmichael, and Peter Joffre Nye. *The Lance Armstrong Performance Program: Seven Weeks to the Perfect Ride*. Emmaus, PA: Rodale, 2000.

Brooks, Christopher, and Catherine Brooks. *60 Hikes within 60 Miles: New York City: With Northern New Jersey, Southwestern Connecticut, and Western Long Island*. Birmingham, AL: Menasha Ridge Press, 2004.

Whitsett, David A., Forrest A. Dolgener, and Tanjala Jo Kole. *The Non-Runner's Marathon Trainer*. New York: McGraw-Hill, 1998.

General References

Editors of Sports Illustrated. *Sports Illustrated Almanac*. New York: Sports Illustrated, 2004.

———. *Sports Illustrated: Fifty Years of Great Writing*. New York: Sports Illustrated, 2003.

Hirshberg, Charles. *ESPN 25: 25 Mind-Bending, Eye-Popping, Culture Morphing Years of Highlights*. New York: Hyperion, 2004.

Jacobs, Timothy, and Russell Roberts. *100 Athletes Who Shaped Sports History*. San Mateo, California: Bluewood Books, 2003.

Mandelbaum, Michael. *The Meaning of Sports: Why Americans Watch Baseball, Football, and Basketball and What They See When They Do*. New York: Public Affairs, 2004.

Golf

Mankoff, Robert. *The New Yorker Book of Golf Cartoons*. New York: Bloomberg Press, 2002.

Parent, Joseph. *Zen Golf: Mastering the Mental Game*. New York: Random House, 2002.

Woods, Tiger. *How I Play Golf*. New York: Warner Books, 2001.

Basketball

Sporting News. *Official NBA Register: Every Player, Every Stat 2004–05 Edition*. St. Louis: Sporting News, 2004.

College Basketball "Legend"
Wooden, John. *Wooden*. New York: McGraw-Hill, 1997.

Fishing
Santella, Chris. *Fifty Places to Fly Fish Before You Die: Fly-Fishing Experts Share the World's Greatest Destinations*. New York: Stewart, Tabori, and Chang, 2004.

Walker, Spike. *Working on the Edge: Surviving in the World's Most Dangerous Profession: King Crab Fishing on Alaska's High Seas*. New York: St. Martin's, 1993.

Tennis
Gallwey, W. Timothy. *The Inner Game of Tennis*. New York: Random House, 1997.

Other Sports
Hillenbrand, Laura. *Seabiscuit: An American Legend*. New York: Ballantine Books, 2001.

Warshaw, Matt. *The Encyclopedia of Surfing*. New York: Harcourt, 2003.

WEB SITES

General Resources and Relevant Sites
http://sportsillustrated.cnn.com/—CNN/Sports Illustrated.
http://www.headlinespot.com/subject/sports/—HeadlineSpot. Sports directory.
http://msnbc.msn.com/id/3032113/?ta=y—MSNBC Sports.
http://sports.yahoo.com/—Yahoo Sports.
http://www.tsn.ca/—TSN—Canada's Sports Leader.
http://www.sportingnews.com/—Sporting News.
http://sports.excite.com/—Excite Sports.
http://www.sportsnetwork.com/home.asp—The Sports Network.

College Sports
http://www2.ncaa.org/—National Collegiate Athletic Association. NCAA.
http://theacc.collegesports.com/—Atlantic Coast Conference. ACC.
http://www.bigeast.org/—Big East Conference.
http://bigten.collegesports.com/—Big Ten Conference.
http://big12sports.collegesports.com/—Big 12 Conference.
http://www.ivyleaguesports.com/—Ivy League.
http://www.pac-10.org/—Pac-10 Conference.

http://www.secsports.com/—Southeast Conference. SEC.
http://www.collegesports.com/—College Sports TV.

Golf
http://www.thegolfchannel.com/core.aspx?—Golf Channel.
http://www.golfdigest.com/—Golf Digest.
http://www.pga.com/home/—Professional Golfer's Association.
http://www.pgatour.com/—PGA Tour.
http://www.lpga.com/—Ladies Professional Golf Association.
http://www.usga.org/home/index.html—United States Golf Association.

Auto Racing
http://www.speedtv.com/—Speed Channel.
http://www.nascar.com/—NASCAR.
http://welcome.to/cartracing—CART Racing Update.
http://www.indyracing.com/—Indy Racing League.
http://racingone.com/—Racing One. Racing news.
http://www.motorsport.com/—Motorsport.

Football
http://www.nfl.com/—National Football League.
http://www.nflpa.org/main/main.asp—NFL Players Association.
http://www.nfleurope.com/—NFL Europe.
http://www.cfl.ca/—Canadian Football League.
http://www.arenafootball.com—Arena Football League.

Baseball
http://mlb.mlb.com/NASApp/mlb/index.jsp—Major League Baseball.
http://www.minorleaguebaseball.com/—Minor League Baseball.

Basketball
http://www.nba.com/—National Basketball Association.
http://www.usbl.com/—United States Basketball League.
http://www.wnba.com/—Women's National Basketball Association.

Hockey
http://www.nhl.com/—National Hockey League.
http://www.thehockeynews.com/—The Hockey News.
http://uscollegehockey.com/—U.S. College Hockey.

Soccer

http://www.mlsnet.com/MLS/index.jsp—Major League Soccer.
http://www.socceramerica.com/—Soccer America magazine.
http://www.soccertimes.com/—Soccer Times.

Tennis

http://www.atptennis.com/en/default.asp—Association of Tennis Professionals.
http://www.usta.com—United States Tennis Association.
http://www.daviscup.com/—Davis Cup Tennis.
http://www.wtatour.com/—Women's Professional Tennis.
http://www.tennis.com/—Tennis Magazine.

Horse Racing

http://www.ntra.com/—National Thoroughbred Racing Association.
http://www.equibase.com/—Equibase. Thoroughbred horseracing site.
http://www.aqha.com/—American Quarter Horse Association.

Dogs

http://www.nationalkennelclub.com/—National Kennel Club.

Cycling

http://www.cyclingnews.com/—Cycling News.
http://www.letour.fr/indexus.html—Tour de France. (In English or French.)
http://www.mountainbike.com/—Mountain Bike Magazine.

Running

http://www.usatf.org/—USA Track and Field.
http://www.runningnetwork.com/—Running Network.

Snow Sports

http://www.usskiteam.com/—U.S. Ski Team and Snowboarding.
http://www.skimag.com/skimag/—Ski Magazine.
http://sports.espn.go.com/espn/wire?sportId=1850—ESPN Figure Skating News
    Wire.

Olympics

http://www.olympic.org/uk/index_uk.asp—Official Olympic Movement site.
http://www.olympic.org/uk/games/beijing/index_uk.asp—2008 Beijing
    Olympics.
http://www.specialolympics.org—Special Olympics. News and schedules.
http://www.olympic.org/uk/games/torino/index_uk.asp—2006 Winter
    Olympics—Turin.

Fishing

http://www.fishing.com/—Fishing. Reports and articles for anglers.
http://www.fishingworld.com/—Fishing World. News and resources.

Sailing

http://www.americascup.com/en/—America's Cup. Sailing.
http://www.ussailing.org/—U.S. Sailing Association.

Other Sports

http://expn.go.com/expn/index—Extreme Sports.
http://www.climbingnews.com/—Climbing News. News, resources, and
    directory.
http://www.outsidemag.com/—Outside Magazine. News about travel, gear,
    and fitness.
http://sports.espn.go.com/sports/boxing/index—ESPN Boxing.
http://sports.espn.go.com/espn/wire?sportId=1550—ESPN Gymnastics News
    Wire.
http://sports.espn.go.com/espn/wire?sportId=300—ESPN Rugby News Wire.
http://www.wrestlingusa.com/—Wrestling USA Magazine.

OTHER RESOURCES

National Baseball Hall of Fame and Museum
25 Main Street
Cooperstown, NY 13326
1–888–HALL-OF-FAME
http://www.baseballhalloffame.org/

Pro Football Hall of Fame
2121 George Halas Drive NW
Canton, OH 44708
(330) 456–8207
http://www.profootballhof.com/

Olympic Museum Lausanne
1, Quai d'Ouchy
CH-1001 Lausanne
Switzerland
telephone (41.21) 621 65 11
http://www.olympic.org/uk/index_uk.asp

International Bowling Museum and Hall of Fame
111 Stadium Plaza

FIVE MUST-SEE SPORTS FILMS

- Rudy
- The Natural
- Field of Dreams
- Caddyshack
- Hoosiers.

St. Louis, MO 63102
(314) 231-6340
http://www.bowlingmuseum.com/

International Swimming Hall of Fame
One Hall of Fame Drive
Ft. Lauderdale, FL 33316
(954) 462-6536
http://www.ishof.org/

15. Gardening / Nature

TO TELL ONE PLANT OR TREE FROM ANOTHER, or one bird or fish from another, you'll want to look at a good field guide, like *National Audubon Society Field Guide to Trees: Eastern or Western* (two volumes), by Elbert Luther Little (New York: Knopf, 1980), more than 1,300 pages of text and photos on more than 600 species of trees, with various identifying categories like bark, color, leaf shape, fruit, and flower—enough information to satisfy any level of tree peeper—or *National Audubon Society Field Guide to Fishes: North America,* by Carter Rowell Gilbert and James D. Williams (New York: Knopf, 2002), a comprehensive volume on both freshwater and saltwater fish, stocked with photos, illustrations, glossary, and maps, or *Peterson Field Guides: Eastern Birds,* by Roger Tory Peterson (Boston: Houghton Mifflin, 2003), a book that instills classic beauty into the science of ornithology with Peterson's world-renowned paintings of birds grouped by related species, their key "field marks" pointed out by arrows.

Gardening books abound, but for an introduction or a refresher in the fundamentals get *Better Homes and Gardens Step-by-step Garden Basics* by Liz Ball (Des Moines, Iowa: Better Homes and Gardens Books, 2000), with 400 color photographs, inspiring ideas for beginners, and a wealth of information on fundamental topics like seeds, diseases, planting, and fertilizing, or *The New Gardener,* by Pippa Greenwood (New York: Dorling Kindersley, 1998), which covers topics like lawns, beds, fencing, and container gardening, and in each chapter lays out fun and useful projects, such as pruning bushes or creating garden paths.

Online, start with GardenWeb, which claims to be the "largest gardening site on the Web" (**http://www.gardenweb.com**). There you'll find articles, directories, and forums. And visit the Internet complement to the Home and Garden television channel (**http://www.hgtv.com/**), a visually appealing, well-designed site with lots of neat information on topics ranging from gardening basics to harvesting root crops to landscaping makeovers.

This is a subject area that calls for outdoor activity. Visit a zoo, nature center, or arboretum. For help in finding the right one, go to **http://www.museumspot.com/categories/zoos.htm**—Directory of Zoos; or **http://www.museumspot.com/categories/naturecenters. htm**—Directory of Nature Centers; or **http://www.museumspot.com/ categories/arboreta.htm**—Directory of Arboreta.

Three Naturalists You Should Know About
A Very Brief Look at the Evolution of Evolution

While Charles Darwin (1809–1882), author of the seminal work *The Origin of Species,* rightfully gets most of the credit for delivering the theory of evolution, two other scientists deserve recognition as well: Jean-Baptiste Lamarck (1744–1829) and Gregor Mendel (1822–84).

Simply stated, Darwin's theory of evolution holds that living organisms change over time, and that "natural selection" governs how they change. In the process of natural selection, characteristics of an organism that foster its survival and reproduction are passed down to succeeding generations. Over time, those characteristics become common in the species. Organisms with characteristics unfavorable to survival have less chance of reproducing, and those unfavorable characteristics will become less common. Many describe this process succinctly as "survival of the fittest." Darwin contended that current living organisms, descended from ancient organisms and influenced by natural selection, had gradually changed through the ages.

Jean-Baptiste Lamarck, though highly criticized in his day, did garner Darwin's praise as a pioneer in the field. Lamarck's theory of "inheritance of acquired traits" contended that the characteristics developed by an organism during its lifetime, those influenced by the environment, could be passed down to generations. This was eventually proven incorrect, but Darwin pointed out Lamarck's significant contribution in getting the scientific world to take note of the probability of changing organisms, a revolutionary concept in the early part of the nineteenth century.

Gregor Mendel, an Austrian monk, conducted experiments with garden peas and discovered the laws of heredity that ultimately discredited

Lamarck's theory. Mendel found that the offspring of the pea plants were not influenced by the environment, but instead inherited parental traits through discrete units—later to be named "genes." This work formed the roots of today's genetics.

Starting Points and Conversation Pieces

❖ The term *deciduous* is used to describe trees and other plants that lose their leaves (usually in autumn).

❖ Most *evergreens* stay green throughout the year (thus, ever green) and do not lose all their leaves at any one time.

❖ Plants/flowers known as *annuals* live for about a year (or less).

❖ *Perennial* plants last several years, usually losing top growth in winter and returning in spring.

❖ A *runner* is a slim, creeping, root-producing stem sent out from a plant.

❖ *Mulch,* like bark or straw, is used to cover soil for any of several reasons, including protection or decoration.

A QUICK WORD ABOUT TAXONOMIC CLASSIFICATION

Scientists identify and classify plants and animals with a system—the Taxonomic Classification System—created by Carl Linnaeus (1707–1778), a Swedish biologist and botanist. Taxonomy is a division of biology. Linnaeus established a hierarchy with seven levels: kingdom, phylum (or division), class, order, family, genus, and species. Each category contains one or more groups from the level below it. (You can remember this hierarchy with the mnemonic device: King Philip Came Over For Good Soup.)

To help understand the hierarchical classification, consider a geographical analogy. Divide the world into continents. The continents are made up of countries. The countries are divided into units such as states (as in the country of the United States of America). The states are broken down into counties, which are broken down into cities, which are divided into streets, which contain numbered units (houses or apartments). With this seven-level hierarchy, you could identify and classify the world's population.

Traditionally, the names used for identification in the biological classification system are taken from the Latin, signifying first the genus and then the species, such as the classification for humans—Homo sapiens.

- *Cuttings* are pieces of a plant's stem or root that may be nurtured to grow new roots, and eventually new plants.

- A *tuber* is a fat, underground stem, like a potato.

- *Compost* is fertilizer made from a mixture of decaying organic matter, like grass clippings, leaves, vegetables, or manure.

- A *defoliant* is a chemical or other substance applied to a plant to cause it to lose its leaves. (Note: Plants may also be *defoliated*—that is, lose their leaves—due to wind, heat, frost, or drought.)

- A *conifer* is a cone-bearing tree or other plant, usually evergreen, such as juniper, pine, spruce, or fir.

- The *rose* was officially proclaimed the "national floral emblem" of the United States in 1986.

- Some grass is well suited to the cool North (e.g., *Kentucky bluegrass, fescue, ryegrass*), while others thrive in the warmth of the South (e.g., *Bermuda, St. Augustine, zoysia*).

- A *raised bed* is a construction using good soil within retaining walls, often implemented to replace or to complement gardens with poor soil.

- The letters *N-P-K* on fertilizer packages stand for the nutrients: nitrogen (N), phosphorous (P), and potassium (K).

- Birdwatchers *identify birds* by noting geographic location, time of year, and specific characteristics, including, but not limited to, size, bill, field marks, voice, actions, and habitats.

- The animal world contains main groups called *phyla,* and each phylum is broken down into *classes.* Classes are broken down into *orders,* orders into *families,* families into *genera,* and each genus into *species.*

- *Arthropods,* which include insects, crustaceans, spiders, and more, make up the largest phylum.

- *Spiders* have eight legs.

- *Insects* have three pairs of legs.

- It is invariably the *female mosquito* that bites you and sucks your blood. Males prefer to suck plants.

- The largest group of insects is composed of *beetles*.

- The four-stage (*metamorphosis*) life cycle of the butterfly: egg, larva, pupa, adult.

- A *marsupial* is a pouched mammal, such as a kangaroo or an opossum, which raises its young in its pouch.

- A *tree* has three main parts: roots, shoot system, and leaves. The shoot system consists of its trunk and branches.

- *Rings* in a tree trunk indicate the age of the tree: one year per ring.

- The trees with the *thickest bark* are redwoods (up to one foot thick) and giant sequoias (up to two feet thick).

- *Fish* are divided into three groups: jawless (e.g., lamprey), cartilaginous (e.g., shark), and bony (e.g., sea bass).

- A *lateral line* is an organ that runs along both sides of the body of a fish and senses movement and temperature.

- The largest order of *amphibians* is composed of *frogs*.

Resources for Further Exploration

READING

Gardening

Allen, Oliver E. *Gardening with the New Small Plants*. Boston: Houghton Mifflin, 1997.

Armitage, Allen M. *Armitage's Garden Perennials*. Portland, Oregon: Timber Press, 2000.

Bender, Steve, ed. *The Southern Living Garden Book*. Birmingham, Alabama: Oxmoor House, 1998.

Brickell, Christopher, and David Joyce. *The American Horticultural Society Pruning and Training*. New York: Dorling Kindersley Publishing, 1996.

Brown, Deni. *Herbal: The Essential Guide to Herbs for Living*. New York: Barnes and Noble Books: 2001.

Buchanan, Rita. *Better Homes and Gardens Step-by-step Vegetables*. Des Moines, Iowa: Better Homes and Gardens Books, 1994.

Cole, Rebecca. *Potted Garden*. New York: Clarkson Potter, 1997.

Crockett, James Underwood. *Crockett's Flower Garden*. Boston: Little, Brown, 1981.

Fell, Derek. *Bulb Gardening with Derek Fell*. New York: Friedman/Fairfax Publishers, 1997.

Gertley, Jan and Michael. *The Family Garden: Clever Things to Do In, Around & Under the Garden*. New York: Sterling Publishing, 1997.

Lanza, Patricia. *Lasagna Gardening: A Layering System for Big Results in Small Gardens and Containers*. Emmaus, Pennsylvania: Rodale, 2002.

Lloyd, Christopher and Richard Bird. *The Cottage Garden*. New York: Dorling Kindersley, 1999.

Oudolf, Piet, and Henk Gerritsen. *Planting the Natural Garden*. Portland, Oregon: Timber Press, 2003.

Pavord, Anna. *The Border Book*. New York: Dorling Kindersley, 2000.

Peel, Lucy. *Family Garden: A Practical Guide to Creating a Fun and Safe Family Garden*. Hauppauge, New York: Barron's, 1999.

Search, Gay. *Gardening Without a Garden*. New York: Dorling Kindersley, 2000.

Smith, P. Allen, and Jane Colclasure. *P. Allen Smith's Garden Home*. New York: Clarkson N. Potter Publishers, 2003.

Verey, Rosemary. *Rosemary Verey's Making of a Garden*. New York: Barnes and Noble Books, 1995.

Von Trapp, Sara Jane. *The Landscape Makeover Book*. Newtown, Connecticut: Taunton Press, 2000.

Nature Guides

Burnett, R. Will, et al. *Zoology: An Introduction to the Animal Kingdom*. New York: Golden Press, 1958.

Cebenko, Jill Jesiolowski and Deborah L. Martin, eds. *Insect, Disease, and Weed I.D. Guide*. Emmaus, Pennsylvania: Rodale, 2001.

Cortright, Sandy. *Birding Basics*. New York: Sterling Publishing, 1995.

Fingerman, Milton. *Animal Diversity*. New York: Holt, Rinehart and Winston, 1969.

Gilkeson, Linda, et al. *Rodale's Pest and Disease Problem Solver*. Emmaus, Pennsylvania: Rodale, 1996.

General Resources and Relevant Books

Canfield, Jack, Mark Victor Hansen, and Steve Zikman. *Chicken Soup for the Nature Lover's Soul: Inspiring Stories of Joy, Insight and Adventure in the Great Outdoors*. Deerfield Beach, Florida: HCI Books, 2004.

Pick, Nancy. *The Rarest of the Rare: Stories behind the Treasures at the Harvard Museum of Natural History*. New York: HarperResource, 2004.

Pollan, Michael. *The Botany of Desire: A Plant's-Eye View of the World*. New York: Random House, 2002.

Rickett. H. W., ed. *The Botanic Manuscript of Jane Colden, 1724–1766: First Woman Botanist of Colonial America.* New York: Chanticleer Press, 1963.

Tompkins, Peter. *The Secret Life of Plants.* New York: Perennial, 1989.

Winchester, Simon. *The Map That Changed the World: William Smith and the Birth of Modern Geology.* New York: HarperCollins, 2001.

WEB SITES

Gardening

http://www.usda.gov/news/garden.htm—U.S. Department of Agriculture home gardening site. Info on gardening, fruit production, landscaping, etc.

http://today.excite.com/tiphome.html—Garden Tips.

http://www.garden.org—National Gardening. Reports, articles, how-to projects, gardening with kids, etc.

http://www.rhs.org.uk—The Royal Horticultural Society—Gateway to Gardening. British.

http://www.bbc.co.uk/gardening—BBC—Gardening. History of gardening, news, etc.

http://www.canadiangardening.com—Canadian Gardening Online. Gardening magazine. Tips on growing, designing, etc. Forums.

http://www.gardenguides.com/—Garden Guides. Information from garden writers, seasonal tips, etc.

http://www.gardening.com—Directory for supplies, seeds, tools, etc.

http://www.greengardening.com—"Earth-friendly solutions to gardening problems."

http://www.gardening.about.com—Info about starting seeds, site design, planting techniques, etc.

http://www.pallensmith.com—P. Allen Smith, TV host and professional garden designer. Tips to better gardening.

http://www.marthastewart.com/—Martha Stewart.

http://www.organicgardening.com—Organic Gardening.

http://www.gardeners.com—Gardener's Supply Co.

http://www.bettersoils.com/—Wallace Labs. Soil testing.

http://www.burpee.com—Burpee Co.—seeds and plants.

Nature News

http://news.bbc.co.uk/1/hi/sci/tech/default.stm—BBC. Science/Nature news.

Museums of Natural History

http://www.amnh.org/museum/?src=toolbar—American Museum of Natural History.

http://www.museumspot.com/categories/naturalhistory.htm—Directory of Museums of Natural History.
http://www.mnh.si.edu/—National Museum of Natural History—Smithsonian.
http://www.sdnhm.org/—San Diego Natural History Museum.
http://www.flmnh.ufl.edu/—Florida Museum of Natural History.
http://www.dmns.org/main/en/—Denver Museum of Nature and Science.
http://www.hmnh.harvard.edu/—Harvard Museum of Natural History.
http://www.carnegiemnh.org/—Carnegie Museum of Natural History. Pittsburgh.
http://www.wmnh.com/wmhome.htm—Worldwide Museum of Natural History. Online museum.
http://www.fieldmuseum.org/—The Field Museum. Chicago.
http://www.nhm.ac.uk/—Natural History Museum—UK. London.
http://www.nhm.org/—Natural History Museum of Los Angeles.
http://www.calacademy.org/naturalhistory/—California Academy of Sciences Natural History Museum.

Animal Planet
http://www.animal.discovery.com/—Animal Planet. Complement to television channel.

Weather
http://www.nhc.noaa.gov/index.shtml—National Hurricane Center.
http://aa.usno.navy.mil/data/docs/MoonPhase.html—Moon Phases.

Botany
http://www.sciencedaily.com/directory/Science/Biology/Botany—Research news in botany.

National Parks
http://www.nps.gov/—National Park Service.
http://www.nps.gov/cave/home.htm—Carlsbad Caverns.
http://www.nps.gov/yell/home.htm—Yellowstone National Park. Old Faithful.
http://www.nps.gov/yose/index.htm—Yosemite National Park.
http://www.nps.gov/acad/home.htm—Acadia National Park.
http://www.nps.gov/grca/home.htm—Grand Canyon National Park.

Nature Centers
http://www.museumspot.com/categories/naturecenters.htm—Great Plains Nature Center.
http://www.nature.ca/nature_e.cfm—Canadian Museum of Nature.
http://www.treehill.org/—Tree Hill Nature Center. Jacksonville, Florida.

Zoos
http://www.sandiegozoo.org/—San Diego Zoo.
http://nationalzoo.si.edu/—National Zoo.

Aquariums
http://www.museumspot.com/categories/aquariums.htm—Directory of
    Aquariums.
http://www.aqua.org/—National Aquarium in Baltimore.
http://waquarium.otted.hawaii.edu/—Waikiki Aquarium.

Arboreta
http://www.bbg.org/—Brooklyn Botanical Garden.
http://www.arboretum.org/—Los Angeles Arboretum.
http://www.chicago-botanic.org/—Chicago Botanic Garden.

Birdwatching
http://www.birdwatchersdigest.com/—Bird Watcher's Digest. Articles and
    photos.
http://www.birdnature.com—The Nutty Birdwatcher. Information on bird-
    watching, Eastern U.S. birds, bird feeders, backyard setups, etc.
http://www.news.nationalgeographic.com/birds.html—National Geographic on
    birds.

Naturalist Intelligence
http://www.lesley.edu/faculty/kholmes/presentations/naturalist.html—About
    naturalist intelligence. Lesley College.
http://www.uwsp.edu/education/lwilson/learning/natintel.htm—The Eighth
    Intelligence. Descriptions and Q & A concerning naturalist intelli-
    gence.
http://www.america-tomorrow.com/ati/mi8.htm—How technology enhances
    naturalist intelligence.

OTHER RESOURCES

San Diego Zoo
Balboa Park
2920 Zoo Drive
San Diego, CA 92101
(619) 234–3153
http://www.sandiegozoo.org/

National Zoo
3001 Connecticut Avenue NW
Washington, D.C. 20008
http://nationalzoo.si.edu/

Waikiki Aquarium
University of Hawaii—Manoa
2777 Kalakaua Avenue
Honolulu, HI 96815
(808) 923–9741
http://waquarium.otted.hawaii.edu/

Carlsbad Caverns National Park
3225 National Parks Highway
Carlsbad, NM 88220
(505) 785-2232
cave_park_information@nps.gov
http://www.nps.gov/cave/home.htm

National Museum of Natural History—Smithsonian
10th Street and
Constitution Avenue NW
Washington, D.C. 20560
202-633-1000
http://www.mnh.si.edu/

American Museum of Natural History
79th Street and Central Park West
New York, NY 10023
(212) 313-7278
http://www.amnh.org/museum/?src=toolbar

Harvard Museum of Natural History
Harvard University
26 Oxford Street
Cambridge, MA 02138
(617) 495-3045
http://www.hmnh.harvard.edu/

Great Plains Nature Center
6232 E. 29th Street North
Wichita, KS 67220-2200
(316) 683-5499
http://www.museumspot.com/categories/naturecenters.htm

Canadian Museum of Nature
Victoria Memorial Museum Building (VMMB)
240 McLeod Street
Ottawa, Ontario, Canada
(613) 566-4700
1-800-263-4433
http://www.nature.ca/nature_e.cfm

Gardener's Supply Co.
128 Intervale Road
Burlington, VT 05401-2850
 1-800-833-1412 or (800) 427-3363
http://www.gardeners.com

Soil Testing:
Wallace Labs
365 Corel Circle
El Segundo, CA 90245
(310) 615-0116
http://www.bettersoils.com/

Seeds and Plants:
W. Atlee Burpee & Co.
300 Park Avenue
Warminster, PA 18974
1-800-333-5808 or (800) 888-1447
http://www.burpee.com

16. Art History

FOR AN INTRODUCTION OR REFRESHER to Art History, you'll want to begin with a classic in the field, *The Story of Art,* by E. H. Gombrich (London: Phaidon Press, 1995). With crisp text and hundreds of images, it runs from prehistoric art to Modernism, emphasizing key figures and movements. Beyond this book, use the Web as a principal resource.

There's no better gateway online than the "Voice of the Shuttle" at **http://vos.ucsb.edu/browse.asp?id=3404**, which offers resources for every area of interest imaginable in Art History. An alternative would be a directory like Yahoo's at **http://dir.yahoo.com/Arts/art_history/** or "Best Sites for Art History" at **http://www.besthistorysites.net/Art History.shtml**, which offers extensive commentary for each site.

Brush up on the Renaissance with the essay below and then with a visit to Annenberg's concise site at **http://www.learner.org/exhibits/ renaissance/**. For a review of ancient art, go to Tufts' Perseus Project (**http://www.perseus.tufts.edu/cgi-bin/perscoll?collection=**), "a digital library of resources for the study of the humanities" that includes an extensive collection of tools, texts, and images on the "Archaic and Classical Greek world," including Greek and Latin translation tools and search engines, plus maps, essays, bibliographies, and invaluable primary sources.

One of the best sites for viewing paintings of the masters is the Web Gallery of Art (**http://www.wga.hu/index.html**), which has a database of more than 12,000 images of European painting and sculpture from 1100 to 1800.

The Renaissance in a Nutshell
Featuring Some of the Greatest Artists and Intellects of the Era

In the 14th century, excited and energized by the work of gifted artists such as **Giotto di Bondone** (c. 1267–1337) and talented writers such as

Dante Alighieri (1265–1321) and **Francesco Petrarch** (1304–1374), Italy felt the beginnings of a rebirth of the arts, the literature, and the intellectual fervor that had marked the Classical Age in ancient Rome and Greece. This new era rivaled the brilliance of the ancient centuries, a period that had produced epic poems like the *Iliad* and the *Odyssey* by Homer (c. eighth century B.C.), inspired work such as Virgil's *Aeneid* (19 B.C.) and Cicero's "On the Republic" (c. 52 B.C.), sculptures like *Venus de Milo* (by an unknown artist, c. 200 B.C.); and pieces depicting Apollo and Aphrodite by Praxiteles (c. 390 B.C.–340 B.C.). Classic architecture as well contributed models and inspiration for the new era, such as the Greek Parthenon (c. 450 B.C.), the Roman Colosseum (c. 80 A.D.), the Pantheon (c. 130 A.D.), and Trajan's Column (c. 114 A.D.).

Perhaps no Italian city generated more passion and commitment during this period than Florence, with its prominently wealthy merchant family, the **Medici**, enthusiastic patrons of the arts. Other Italian cities as well, however, joined in vigorously supporting the creativity of the era, notably Milan, Venice, and Rome (with papal patrons).

Though surfacing first in Italy, this revived artistic and intellectual spirit subsequently manifested itself in countries throughout Europe, including France, England, Germany, Spain, and the Netherlands. The movement eventually flowed into virtually every facet of study and creativity, including art, literature, science, philosophy, and religion, which underwent radical changes in thinking and expression. In addition, the exploration of the world beyond Europe increased dramatically.

The new era dawning in the 14th century, then, was viewed as a time of reawakening, rebirth. Historians have appropriately named it **the Renaissance**, using the French word for *rebirth*.

The intervening years—that is, the middle period between the Classical Age and the Renaissance—understandably came to be known as the Middle Ages, the label that has endured even to today to describe the fifth century through the 14th century. The Renaissance may be said to have closed the Middle Ages with a shifting out of the medieval way of life, and to have given birth to the values of the modern world.

With the extremely important invention of the printing press in 1445 by **Johann Gutenberg** (c. 1397–1468), books became much more accessible. The significance of this invention cannot be overemphasized. Before that moment in history, all surviving literature had been copied by hand and was limited in distribution. Now, however, books could be reproduced quickly and distributed widely to the masses, thus spreading Renaissance thinking quickly and widely as well.

One of the primary philosophies marking the Renaissance, **Humanism** celebrated individual achievement and expression, and looked to the ancient classics for inspiration and models.

The Renaissance produced hundreds of prominent figures, many of whom made contributions in more than one discipline. A few of the more prominent **artists** to emerge during the Renaissance include: **Donatello** (Italian sculptor, 1386–1466); **Sandro Botticelli** (Italian painter, 1445–1510); **Hieronymus Bosch** (Dutch painter, 1450–1516); **Leonardo da Vinci** (Italian painter and inventor, 1452–1519); **Albrecht Dürer** (German painter and engraver, 1471–1528); **Michelangelo Buonarroti** (Italian painter and sculptor, 1475–1564); **Titian** (Italian painter, c. 1477–1576); and **Raphael** (Italian painter, 1483–1520).

Some of the more prominent **writers** of the period include: **Giovanni Boccaccio** (Italian, 1313–75); **Niccolo Machiavelli** (Italian, 1469–1527); **John Colet** (English, c. 1467–1519); **Desiderius Erasmus** (Dutch, 1466–1536); **Sir Thomas More** (English, 1478–1535); **Martin Luther** (German, 1483–1546); **François Rabelais** (French, c. 1495–1553); **Michel de Montaigne** (French, 1533–92); **Francis Bacon** (English, 1561–1626); **William Shakespeare** (English, 1564–1616); and **Edmund Spenser** (English, 1552–99).

Note: Any limited, "nutshell" mention of the artists and intellectuals of the Renaissance will likely omit many who would merit recognition in a longer piece. Please use the resources below and throughout the text for a more in-depth look at the era.

Starting Points and Conversation Pieces

IMPORTANT ARTISTS AND THEIR WORKS

Renaissance

❖ Leonardo da Vinci (Italian, 1452–1519). Works include *The Last Supper*; *Mona Lisa* (*La Joconde*).

❖ Michelangelo Buonarrati (Italian, 1475–1564). Works include Ceiling of the Sistine Chapel; *David* (sculpture).

❖ Sandro Botticelli (Italian, 1445–1510). Works include *The Annunciation*; *The Birth of Venus*.

❖ Albrecht Dürer (German, 1471–1528). Works include *A Young Hare*; *Virgin and Child with St. Anne*; *The Nativity* (engraving); *Adam and Eve* (engraving).

Spanish

❖ Francisco de Goya (1746–1828). Works include *The Clothed Maja*; *The Colossus*; *Group on a Balcony*.

❖ Pablo Picasso (1881–1973). Works include *The Blind Man's Meal*; *Demoiselles d'Avignon*.

❖ Salvador Dali (1904–1989). Works include *Meditative Rose*; *La Persistance de la Memoire*.

Dutch

❖ Rembrandt van Rijn (1606–1669). Works include *The Night Watch*; *Aristotle Contemplating the Bust of Homer*; *The Reconciliation of David and Absolom*; *Self Portrait*.

❖ Vincent van Gogh (1853–90). Works include *Starry Night*; *Sunflowers* (series).

French

❖ Edouard Manet (1832–83). Works include *Olympia*; *Young Girl on the Threshold of the Garden at Bellevue*.

❖ Edgar Degas (1834–1917). Works include *The Rehearsal*; *Little Dancer* (sculpture).

❖ Claude Monet (1840–1926). Works include *Woman with a Parasol*; *Rouen Cathedral*.

❖ Pierre-Auguste Renoir (1841–1919). Works include *The Umbrellas*; *A Girl With a Watering Can*.

❖ Henri Matisse (1869–1954). Works include *La Musique*; *Green Stripe* (Madame Matisse).

American

❖ Winslow Homer (1836–1910). Works include *Crossing the Pasture*; *Boy Fishing*.

❖ John Singer Sargent (1856–1925). Works include *In a Hayloft*; *Mrs. Joshua Montgomery Sears* (portraits).

❖ Edward Hopper (1882–1967). Works include *Nighthawks*; *Cape Cod Evening*.

❖ Georgia O'Keeffe (1887–1986). Works include *Ranchos Church*; *Red Poppy*.

❖ Jackson Pollock (1912–56). Works include *The She-Wolf*; *Lavender Mist*.

Norwegian

❖ Edvard Munch (1863–1944). Works include *The Cry* (or *The Scream*); *The Dance of Life*.

MOVEMENTS

❖ The Impressionism movement in 19th century France took its name from a painting by Monet, *Impression: Sunrise*.

❖ Among the most important artists of the Impressionist movement were: Claude Monet, Pierre-Auguste Renoir, Edouard Manet, Edgar Degas, and Mary Cassatt.

❖ The Hudson River School, a Romantic movement of the mid-1800s, focused on painting images of the Hudson River Valley in upstate New York. Principal artists included Thomas Cole, Frederic Edwin Church, and Albert Bierstadt.

❖ The Bauhaus School of design was centered in pre-Nazi Germany in the 1920s and early 1930s. It was noted for applying concepts of Expressionist art to projects of design and architecture.

❖ An important idea behind Cubism, whose principal artists included Pablo Picasso and Georges Braque, is that one may not see the true nature of an object unless it is presented from many perspectives at once.

❖ Perhaps one of the best known artists of the Art Nouveau movement of the late 19th century and early 20th century was Louis Comfort Tiffany, renowned American glass artist.

❖ The Pop Art movement of the 1950s and 1960s, which geared itself to the common themes of contemporary culture, included such well-known artists as Andy Warhol, Robert Rauschenberg, and Roy Lichtenstein.

Resources for Further Exploration

READING

General Resources and Relevant Books

Atkins, Robert. *ArtSpeak : A Guide to Contemporary Ideas, Movements, and Buzzwords, 1945 to the Present*. New York: Abbeville Press, 1997.

Beckett, Sister Wendy, and Patricia Wright. *Sister Wendy's Story of Painting*. New York: Dorling Kindersley Publishing, 2000.

Cumming, Robert. *Great Artists: The Lives of 50 Painters Explored Through Their Work*. New York: Dorling Kindersley Publishing, 1998.

Dorling Kindersley Publishing. *Art: A World History*. New York: Dorling Kindersley Publishing, 2002.

Harrison, Charles, and Paul Wood. *Art in Theory 1900–2000: An Anthology of Changing Ideas*. Malden, Massachusetts: Blackwell Publishers, 2002.

McInnis, Maurie D., and Angela Mack. *In Pursuit of Refinement: Charlestonians Abroad*. Columbia, South Carolina: University of South Carolina Press, 1999.

Stiles, Kristine, and Peter Howard Selz. *Theories and Documents of Contemporary Art: A Sourcebook of Artists' Writings*. Berkeley, California: University of California Press, 1996.

Stokstad, Marilyn. *Art History Revised*. Upper Saddle River, New Jersey: Prentice Hall, 2004.

Strickland, Carol, and John Boswell. *The Annotated Mona Lisa: A Crash Course in Art History from Prehistoric to Post-Modern*. Kansas City, Missouri: Andrews McMeel Publishing, 1992.

Vasari, Giorgio, et al. *The Lives of the Artists*. New York: Oxford University Press, 1998.

Ancient

Robins, Gay. *The Art of Ancient Egypt*. Cambridge, Massachusetts: Harvard University Press, 2000.

Architecture

Blumenson, John J. G. *Identifying American Architecture: A Pictorial Guide to Styles and Terms, 1600–1945*. Walnut Creek, California: Altamira Press, 1995.

Curtis, William. *Modern Architecture Since 1900*. London: Phaidon Press, 1996.

Glancey, Jonathan. *The Story of Architecture*. New York: Dorling Kindersley Publishing, 2003.

Art Deco

Benton, Tim, et al. *Art Deco: 1910–1939*. New York: Bulfinch, 2003.

Modern

Arnason, H. H. *History of Modern Art*. Upper Saddle River, New Jersey: Prentice Hall, 2003.

Hopkins, David. *After Modern Art, 1945–2000*. New York: Oxford University Press, 2000.

Renaissance

Da Vinci, Leonardo. *The Notebooks of Leonardo Da Vinci, volume 1*. New York: Dover Press, 1970.

Hartt, Frederick, and David G. Wilkins. *History of Italian Renaissance*. Upper Saddle River, New Jersey: Prentice Hall, 2003.

Hibbert, Christopher. *The House of Medici: Its Rise and Fall*. New York: Perennial, 1999.

King, Ross. *Michelangelo and the Pope's Ceiling*. New York: Penguin, 2003.

Seymour, Charles. *Michelangelo: The Sistine Chapel Ceiling*. New York: W. W. Norton, 1972.

Zollner, Frank, and Johannes Nathan. *Leonardo Da Vinci: The Complete Paintings and Drawings*. Los Angeles: Taschen, 2003.

Baroque

Wittkower, Rudolf, et al. *Art and Architecture in Italy 1600–1750, vol. 1: Early Baroque*. New Haven, Connecticut: Yale University Press, 2000.

Blake

Erdman, David V., and William Blake. *The Illuminated Blake: William Blake's Complete Illuminated Works With a Plate-By-Plate Commentary*. New York: Dover Press, 1992.

Hogarth

Shesgreen, Sean, ed. *Engravings by Hogarth*. New York: Dover Press, 1975.

Norman Rockwell
Buechner, Thomas S. *The Norman Rockwell Treasury*. New York: Galahad
    Books, 1979.

Preservation
Tyler, Norman. *Historic Preservation: An Introduction to Its History, Principles,
    and Practice*. New York: W. W. Norton, 1999.

WEB SITES

General Resources and Relevant Sites
http://artcyclopedia.com/—Artcyclopedia—Fine Arts Search Engine.
http://witcombe.sbc.edu/ARTHLinks.html—Art History resources on the Web.
http://history.evansville.net/renaissa.html—Explores history through the arts.
http://art-history.concordia.ca/AHRC/—The Art History Resource Centre.
http://arthistory.about.com/?once=true&—Variety of resources from
    about.com.
http://arthist.cla.umn.edu/aict/html/index.html—Art Images for College
    Teaching.
http://www.artchive.com/—Artchive. More than 2,000 images for educa-
    tional use.
http://www.arthistory.net/index.html—Links, journals, magazines, and gen-
    eral resources.
http://vos.ucsb.edu/browse-netscape.asp?id=2707—Focus on modern and con-
    temporary. Extensive listings of resources, hosted by University of
    California, Santa Barbara.
http://www.chart.ac.uk/vlib/—Link collection, general resource.
http://askart.com/—AskArt—Directories, links, artist info.
http://www.huntfor.com/arthistory/—"Hunt for Art History" profiles, etc.
http://www.art-design.umich.edu/mother/—Gateway to Art History depart-
    ments and other research resources.
http://www.19thc-artworldwide.org/—Focus on 19th-century art.
http://www.brynmawr.edu/Admins/DMVRC/lanterns/—Bryn Mawr collection
    of slides and prints. Wide variety of subjects.
http://www.metmuseum.org/special/Poets_Lovers_Heroes/prints_more.htm—
    Poets, Lovers, and Heroes in Italian Prints.
http://nga.gov/—National Gallery of Art, Washington, D.C.
http://www.unc.edu/depts/wcweb/handouts/arthistory.html—How to write an
    Art History paper.

Ancient
*http://www.metmuseum.org/explore/new_pyramid/pyramids/html/el_pyramid_in
    tro.htm*—Egyptian Art in the Age of the Pyramids from The Met.

http://www.metmuseum.org/explore/First_Cities/firstcities_main.htm—Art of the ancient first cities from The Met.
http://www.metmuseum.org/explore/Greek/Greek1.htm—Greek art from The Met.
http://www.lib.uchicago.edu/e/dl/proj/neh2/—Art from the ancient Near East.
http://www.metmuseum.org/explore/Byzantium/byzhome.html—The Glory of Byzantium.
http://www.artic.edu/cleo/index.html—Cleopatra: Multimedia Guide to the Ancient World.
http://www.mfa.org/egypt/amarna/—Pharaohs of the Sun. MFA in Boston.
http://wings.buffalo.edu/AandL/Maecenas/—Images of Ancient Greece and Rome.
http://museums.ncl.ac.uk/archive/index.html—Museum of Antiquities.

Renaissance
http://www.wsu.edu/~dee/REN/REN.HTM—Early Modern Italian Renaissance.
http://www.mos.org/sln/Leonardo/LeoHomePage.html—"Exploring Leonardo."
http://graphics.stanford.edu/projects/mich/—The Digital Michelangelo Project.
http://www.open2.net/renaissance2/index.html—BBC's "Renaissance Secrets."
http://www.artmuseums.harvard.edu/Renaissance/index.html—Harvard Art Museum. "Investigating the Renaissance."
http://www.pbs.org/empires/medici/—PBS' "Medici—Godfathers of the Renaissance."
http://www.metmuseum.org/special/Leonardo_Master_Draftsman/draftsman_splash.htm—Drawings by Leonardo at the Metropolitan Museum of Art.
http://www.utm.edu/research/iep/r/renaiss.htm—Concise site for Renaissance info.
http://www.arthistory.sbc.edu/artartists/renaissance.html—Art and artists in the Renaissance. Sweet Briar College site.
http://www.artcyclopedia.com/history/high-renaissance.html—Artists and their works—the High Renaissance.
http://www.sc.edu/library/spcoll/sccoll/renprint/renprint.html—Printing: Renaissance and Reformation. Thomas Cooper Library, University of South Carolina.
http://www.ibiblio.org/wm/paint/glo/renaissance—Web Museum. Brief commentary.
http://www.lib.virginia.edu/dic/colls/arh102/index.html—Architectural history, Renaissance and Baroque.
http://www.pbs.org/treasuresoftheworld/a_nav/mona_nav/mnav_level_1/3technique_monafrm.html—PBS on Mona Lisa.
http://michelangelo.com/buon/bio-index2.html?http://www.michelangelo.com/buon/bio-early.html—Michelangelo.

Museums
http://www.getty.edu/—The Getty Museum.
http://www.metmuseum.org/toah/splash.htm—The Metropolitan Museum of
　　Art Timeline of Art History.
http://www.louvre.fr/louvrea.htm—The Louvre.
http://www.americanart.si.edu/index2.cfm—Smithsonian American Art
　　Museum.
http://lcweb2.loc.gov/ammem/ammemhome.html—American Memory Histori-
　　cal Collection from the Library of Congress.
http://www.photo.rmn.fr/us/index.html—Photos in France's National Museum.

Countries and Regions
http://www.nyu.edu/gsas/dept/fineart/html/chinese/index.html—Chinese and
　　Japanese Art History Virtual Library
http://www.artguide.org/uk/—Art Lover's Guide to Britain and Ireland.
http://oi.uchicago.edu/OI/MUS/QTVR96/QTVR96_Tours.html—Oriental Insti-
　　tute Virtual Museum.
http://www.metmuseum.org/special/Genesis/origin_images.htm—Genesis: Ideas
　　of Origin in African Sculpture.

Age of Enlightenment
http://mistral.culture.fr/files/imaginary_exhibition.html—Painters of the Age of
　　Enlightenment from the national museums of France.

Vatican and Churches
http://www.christusrex.org/www1/splendors/splendors.html—Worldwide Tour
　　of Churches, Cathedrals, and Monasteries.
http://mv.vatican.va/3_EN/pages/MV_Home.html—Vatican Museums.

Ottoman
http://www.dia.org/test/ottomantest/index.html—Empire of the Sultans:
　　Ottoman Art.

Islamic
http://www.lacma.org/islamic_art/intro.htm—Islamic Art.

American Photos
http://americanart.si.edu/collections/exhibits/helios/amerphotos.html—Ameri-
　　can photographs, 1839–1939, from the Smithsonian.

Impressionism
http://www.biography.com/impressionists/—The Impressionists.

Rodin
http://www.rodin-web.org/—Devoted to Rodin.

OTHER RESOURCES

The Metropolitan Museum of Art
1000 Fifth Avenue at 82nd Street
New York, NY 10028-0198
General information: 212-535-7710
TTY: 212-570-3828 or 212-650-2551
http://www.metmuseum.org/explore/index.asp

The Getty Center
1200 Getty Center Drive
Los Angeles, CA 90049
 (310) 440-7300
http://www.getty.edu/

The Louvre Museum
Musée du Louvre
F-75058 Paris Cedex 01
France
Tel.: +33 1 40 20 53 17
http://www.louvre.fr/louvrea.htm

National Museum of American Art
Smithsonian Institution
Washington, D.C.
202-275-1500
Main exhibition space closed until July 4, 2006 due to major renovations.
    In the meantime, exhibitions offered at Renwick Gallery near the
    White House, Pennsylvania Avenue and 17th Street NW (202) 633-
    2850
Also, library open at 750 Ninth Street NW (202) 275-1912
http://www.americanart.si.edu/index2.cfm

National Gallery of Art
On the National Mall
Between Third and Seventh Streets at Constitution Avenue NW
Washington, D.C.
(202) 737-4215
http://nga.gov/

17. Psychology

WHETHER REVISITING PSYCHOLOGY after a long layoff, or jumping into the subject for the first time, you'll want a basic text like *Introduction to Psychology: Gateways to Mind and Behavior,* by Dennis Coon (Belmont, California: Wadsworth Publishing, 2003). Coon, a former professor at Santa Barbara City College, discusses a wide range of topics, including behavior, learning, memory, emotion, language, cognition, and conditioning. Or try *Schaum's Outline of Theory and Problems: Introduction to Psychology,* by Arno F. Wittig (New York: McGraw-Hill, 2001), a thin but competent view. To brush up on terms and vocabulary, get the *Penguin Dictionary of Psychology,* by Arthur S. Reber (New York: Penguin, 1995), written for a broad audience.

You'll find ample help online at Galaxy Psychology (**http://www. galaxy.com/galaxy/Social-Sciences/Psychology.html**), a general directory offering hundreds of psychology sites, or at the Psi Café (**http:// www.psy.pdx.edu/PsiCafe/**), a gateway with a search engine, news, and other resources.

For biographies on key players, use the All Psych bio site (**http:// allpsych.com/biographies/index.html**), and for a dictionary and glossary in English and Spanish, go to **http://www.glossarist.com/ glossaries/humanities-social-sciences/psychology.asp**.

For help in finding relevant research on your topic, such as journal articles, try the American Psychological Association's site—Library Research in Psychology—created to help nonpsychologists (**http:// www.apa.org/science/lib.html**).

Starting Points and Conversation Pieces

TERMS

- *Reinforcement:* Stimulation following a response, which increases the likelihood that the same response will be made in the future under similar circumstances.

- *Sublimation:* Using a socially acceptable form of expression for urges that may be unsatisfied or socially unacceptable.

- *Libido:* Freud's term for an innate, pleasure-driven motivation.

- *Phobia:* Irrational fear.

- *Introvert:* One who tends to direct attention inward.

- *Extrovert:* One who tends to direct attention outward.

- *Desensitization:* Therapy designed to relieve anxiety through gradual exposure to the cause.

- *Sensorimotor Stage:* Piaget's first stage of intellectual development (birth to two years) in which the child develops motor actions and reflexes.

- *Preoperational Stage:* Piaget's second stage of intellectual development (two years to seven years), in which the child develops the ability to see objects, images, and words as symbols.

- *Concrete Operational Stage:* Piaget's third stage of intellectual development (seven years to 11 years), in which the child uses logical processes and relational terms.

- *Formal Operational Stage:* Piaget's fourth stage of intellectual development (11 years and beyond) in which the child/adolescent is capable of using abstract thought and adult logic.

- *Cognition* involves the comprehensive process of thinking, including learning, memory, language, problem-solving, and more.

- *REM sleep* refers to a time of *rapid eye movement,* frequently when dreams occur.

- Freud's theory of personality described the *id,* the *ego,* and the *superego.*

NOTED PSYCHOLOGISTS

❖ *Sigmund Freud:* Austrian psychologist known for creating "psycho-analysis," a therapy that emphasizes the connection between human behavior and unconscious drives and motivations.

❖ *Carl Jung:* Proponent of the "self-actualization" theory (which emphasizes the connection between human behavior and self-created goals and aspirations) and originator of the concept of the "collective unconscious"—that is, innate feelings and attitudes humans universally derive from ancestral roots.

❖ *B. F. Skinner:* Proponent of "behavior modification," which seeks to change behavior through learning techniques.

❖ *Carl Rogers:* Created "client-centered" therapy, which emphasizes "unconditional positive regard" for the client. Though behavior may be criticized, the client is not.

❖ *Jean Piaget:* Formulated four stages of intellectual development: sensorimotor; preoperational; concrete operational; formal operational.

PHILOSOPHY

❖ Greek philosopher *Aristotle* (384–322 B.C.) was a student of Plato (428–348 B.C.), who was a student of Socrates (470–399 B.C.).

HISTORY

❖ The history of psychology may be traced back to the fourth century B.C. when Plato spoke of the connection between the brain and mental processes.

❖ In 1878, G. Stanley Hall was the first to earn a Ph.D. in psychology in America, and in 1892 he founded the American Psychological Association.

❖ An early classic, *Principles of Psychology,* was written by William James in 1890.

❖ One of the earliest intelligence tests was created by Alfred Binet in 1905 in France.

MORE PSYCHOLOGISTS

❖ Connect Ivan Pavlov with "classical conditioning," Max
Wertheimer with "Gestalt psychology," and John Watson with
"behavioral psychology."

❖ Abraham Maslow, a "Humanistic" psychologist, developed a theory that said humans had a "Hierarchy of Needs"—physiological,
safety, love, esteem, and self-actualization.

ARTIFICIAL INTELLIGENCE

❖ Supporters of "artificial intelligence" beamed when "Deep Blue," a
supercomputer, defeated a world-class chess champion (Kasparov)
in 1997.

Resources for Further Exploration

READING

Publications and Resources

American Psychological Association. *Publication Manual of the American
Psychological Association*. Washington, D.C.: American Psychological
Association, 2001.

Baxter, Pam. *Psychology: A Guide to Reference and Information Sources*. Englewood, Colorado: Libraries Unlimited, 1993.

Caton, Hiram. *Bibliography of Human Behavior*. Westport, Connecticut:
Greenwood Press, 1993.

Qualitative Methods

Bannister, Peter. *Qualitative Methods in Psychology*. Philadelphia: Open University Press, 1994.

Manual

American Psychiatric Association. *Diagnostic and Statistical Manual of Mental Disorders DSM-IV-TR*. Arlington, Virginia: American Psychiatric
Association, 2000.

Classics by Dewey and Erikson

Dewey, John. *Experience and Education*. New York: Free Press, 1997.

Erikson, Erik H. *Childhood and Society*. New York: W. W. Norton, 1993.

Freud

Freud, Sigmund. *Freud: Dictionary of Psychoanalysis*. Edited by Frank Gaynor. New York: Fawcett Books, 2000.

———. *Interpretation of Dreams*. Translated and edited by James Strachey. New York: Avon, 1980.

———. *New Introductory Lectures on Psychoanalysis*. Translated and edited by James Strachey. New York: W. W. Norton, 1965.

———. *An Outline of Psychoanalysis*. Translated and edited by James Strachey. New York: W. W. Norton, 1995.

Child Development

Ginsburg, Herbert, and Sylvia Opper. *Piaget's Theory of Intellectual Development*. Englewood Cliffs, New Jersey: Prentice Hall, 1987.

Popular Studies in Psychology

Greenberg, Joanne. *I Never Promised You a Rose Garden*. New York: Signet, 1984.

Kaysen, Susanna. *Girl, Interrupted*. New York: Vintage, 1994.

Plath, Sylvia. *The Bell Jar: A Novel*. New York: Perennial Books, 2000.

Schreiber, Flora Rheta. *Sybil*. New York: Warner Books, 1989.

History of Psychology

Lawry, John D. *Guide to the History of Psychology*. Totowa, New Jersey: Littlefield, Adams, 1981.

Leahy, Thomas Hardy. *A History of Psychology: Main Currents in Psychological Thought*. Upper Saddle River, New Jersey: Prentice Hall, 1997.

Viney, Wayne. *History of Psychology: A Guide to Information Sources*. Detroit: Gale Research, 1979.

Guides

Loke, Wing Hong. *Guide to Journals in Psychology and Education*. Metuchen, New Jersey: Scarecrow Press, 1990.

Martin, Paul R. *Measuring Behavior: An Introductory Guide*. New York: Cambridge University Press, 1993.

Intelligence

Gardner, Howard. *Changing Minds: The Art and Science of Changing Our Own and Other People's Minds*. Boston: Harvard Business School Press, 2004.

———. *Frames of Mind: The Theory of Multiple Intelligences*. New York: Basic Books, 1983.

———. *Intelligence Reframed*. New York: Basic Books, 2000.

————. *Multiple Intelligences: The Theory in Practice*. New York: Basic Books, 1993.

Goleman, Daniel. *Emotional Intelligence: Why It Can Matter More Than IQ*. New York: Bantam, 1995.

————. *Working With Emotional Intelligence*. New York: Bantam, 1998.

Salovey, P., and J.D. Mayer, (1990). "Emotional intelligence." *Imagination, Cognition, and Personality* 9, 185–211.

WILLIAM JAMES BOOK AWARD 1995–2004
AMERICAN PSYCHOLOGICAL ASSOCIATION

For books that "serve to integrate material across psychological subfields or to provide coherence to the diverse subject matter of psychology."

1995 *Images of Mind*, by Posner, Michael, and Marcus E. Raichle (Scientific American Library, 1994).

1996 *Will We Be Smart Enough?* by Hunt Earl (Russell Sage Foundation Publications, 1995).

1996 *Memory in Oral Traditions*, by Rubin, David C. (Oxford University Press, 1995).

1997 No award.

1998 *Searching for Memory*, by Schacter, Daniel L. (Basic Books, 1997).

1998 *Practicing Feminism: Reconstructing Psychotherapy*. by Morawski, Jill G. (University of Michigan Press, 1994).

1999 *How the Mind Works* by Pinker, Steven (W.W. Norton & Company, 1999).

1999 *Believing in Magic: The Psychology of Superstition*, by Vyse, Stuart A. (Oxford University Press, 1997).

2000 *The Origins of Genius: Darwinian Perspectives on Creativity*, by Simonton, Dean Keith (Oxford University Press, 1999).

2000 *Jeopardy in the Courtroom: A Scientific Analysis of Children's Testimony*, by Ceci, Steven, and Maggie Bruck (American Psychological Association, 1999).

2001 *The Cultural Origins of Human Cognition*, by Tomasello, Michael (Harvard University Press, 2001).

2002 *The New Cognitive Neurosciences*, by Gazzaniga, Michael (Bradford Books, 1999).

2003 *The Blank Slate: The Modern Denial of Human Nature*, by Pinker, Stephen (Penguin Putnam, 2002).

2004 *The Geography of Thought: How Asians and Westerners Think Differently . . . and Why*, by Nisbett, Richard (Free Press, 2003)

Sternberg, Robert J. *Successful Intelligence: How Practical and Creative Intelligence Determine Success in Life.* New York: Plume, 1997.
Sternberg, Robert J., et al. *Practical Intelligence in Everyday Life.* New York: Cambridge University Press, 2000.
Sternberg, Robert J. *The Triarchic Mind: A New Theory of Intelligence.* New York: Viking, 1988.

General Resources and Relevant Books
Gregory, R. L. *Eye and Brain: The Psychology of Seeing.* New York: McGraw-Hill, 1973.
Kubler-Ross, Elisabeth. *On Death and Dying.* New York: Scribner, 1997.
Mussen, Paul, et al. *Psychology: An Introduction.* Lexington, Massachusetts: D. C. Heath, 1973.
Rosenzweig, Mark R., et al. *Biological Psychology: An Introduction to Behavioral and Cognitive Neuroscience.* Sunderland, Massachusetts: Sinauer Associates Inc., 2004.
Stanovich, Keith E. *How to Think Straight About Psychology.* Boston: Allyn & Bacon, 2001.
Wurtzel, Elizabeth. *Prozac Nation: Young and Depressed in America: A Memoir.* New York: Riverhead Books, 1997.

WEB SITES

General Resources and Relevant Sites
http://www.fenichel.com/Current.shtml—Current Topics in Psychology.
http://www.purgatory.net/merits/index.htm—A Beginner's Guide to Abnormal Psychology.
http://www.psych-central.com/—Psychology Online Resource Central.
http://psych.athabascau.ca/html/aupr/psycres.shtml—Athabasca University Center for Psychology Resources.
http://www.brainnet.org/—Brain Disorders Network.
http://mentalhealth.miningco.com/—Mental Health Resources.
http://www.nimh.nih.gov/—National Institute of Mental Health.
http://www.psychometrics.co.uk/test.htm—Psychometric Assessment.
http://www.rider.edu/~suler/gradschl.html—Graduate School and Careers in Psychology.
http://www.pbs.org/wnet/brain/—The Secret Life of the Brain.
http://www.utm.edu/research/iep/—Internet Encyclopedia of Philosophy.
http://plato.stanford.edu/contents.html—Stanford Encyclopedia of Philosophy.
http://www.lib.utexas.edu/subject/ss/psyc/—Research Guide. University of Texas.

http://www.sosig.ac.uk/psychology/—Social Science Information Gateway.
http://www.mentalhealth.org/cmhs/MentalHealthStatistics/default.asp—Mental Health Statistics. U.S. Department of Health and Human Services.

Dictionaries
http://allpsych.com/dictionary/—Online Psychology Dictionary.
http://www.artsci.wustl.edu/~philos/MindDict/—Dictionary of Philosophy of Mind.
http://human-nature.com/odmh/—Online Dictionary of Mental Health. (Hosted by Human Nature).
http://www.shef.ac.uk/~psysc/psychotherapy/—Online Dictionary of Mental Health. (British version.)
http://www.glossarist.com/glossaries/humanities-social-sciences/psychology.asp—Psychology Dictionary, Glossary, and Terms Directory.

Associations
http://www.cwu.edu/~warren/today.html—The American Psychological Association Historical Database.
http://www.alcoholics-anonymous.org/—Alcoholics Anonymous.
http://www.counseling.org//AM/Template.cfm?Section=Home—American Counseling Association.
http://www.aabt.org/—Association for the Advancement of Behavior Therapy.
http://www.nysamp.org/—New York State Association of Masters in Psychology.

Journals
http://www.apa.org/journals/amp.html—American Psychologist. Journal.
http://www.apa.org/journals/psp.html—Journal of Personality and Social Psychology.
http://192.152.249.232/uhtbin/cgisirsi/jGHtI4LeBh/216750119/58—Adolescence. Journal.
http://www.blackwellpublishing.com/journal.asp?ref=0009-3920—Child Development. Journal.
http://www3.interscience.wiley.com/cgi-bin/jhome/4438—Applied Cognitive Psychology. Journal.
http://www.press.uillinois.edu/journals/ajp.html—American Journal of Psychology.
http://www.blackwellpublishing.com/journal.asp?ref=0022-3506—Journal of Personality.
http://www.uiowa.edu/~grpproc/crisp/crisp.html—Current research in social psychology.
http://www.psycline.org/journals/psycline.html—Psycline Article and Journal Locator.
http://www.human-nature.com/—The Human Nature Review.

Intelligence

http://www.pz.harvard.edu/PIs/HGpubs.htm—Howard Gardner's principal publications.

http://www.pz.harvard.edu/PIs/HG.htm —Howard Gardner's Web site.

http://www.igs.net/~cmorris/sternberg_ref.html—List of published works by Sternberg.

http://www.yale.edu/rjsternberg/—Robert Sternberg's home page.

http://eqi.org/mayer.htm—List of works by John Mayer, Peter Salovey, and David Caruso, psychologists whose early work set the foundation for studies in Emotional Intelligence.

Disorders

http://www.caringonline.com/—Caring Online. Eating Disorders.

http://www.allaboutdepression.com/—All About Depression.

http://www.suicidology.org/—Understanding and Preventing Suicide.

http://www.psycom.net/depression.central.bipolar.html—Bipolar disorder.

http://www.athealth.com/Consumer/disorders/Agoraphobia.html—Agoraphobia.

http://www.nimh.nih.gov/publicat/ocdsoms.cfm—Obsessive Compulsive Disorder (OCD).

http://www.schizophrenia.com/—Schizophrenia.

http://www.addictionsearch.com/addictionsearch/—Addictions. Search feature.

http://www.campusblues.com/—Campus Blues. Issues faced by college students.

Directories

http://www.psych-central.com/megasite.htm—Psych Central Mega-sites Directory.

http://www.umsl.edu/~mgriffin/genpsych/PsychWebsites.html—Directory of Psych Web sites. Comprehensive.

Libraries

http://www.library.yale.edu/socsci/subjguides/psychology/psychology.html—Yale University Library—Psychology Subject Guide.

http://www.clas.ufl.edu/users/gthursby/psi/—Psychology Virtual Library.

http://healthpsych.com/index.shtml—Health Psychology Library.

18. Religion

BEGIN YOUR REVIEW IN THIS SUBJECT with a survey of religions, such as found in *The World's Religions: Our Great Wisdom Traditions*, by Huston Smith (San Francisco: HarperSanFrancisco, 1991), for decades an acclaimed introduction to the subject, or *Religions in America*, by Leo Rosten (New York: Simon & Schuster, 1975), which includes statistics on virtually every religion and articles by recognized authorities in each denomination.

For a capsule view of the Bible, read the essay below, "A Brief History of the Bible: With Major Figures, Favorite Stories, and Familiar Quotations."

You'll want to have a commentary at hand if you read the Bible at length. *Matthew Henry's Concise Commentary on the Whole Bible*, by Matthew Henry, (Nashville: Thomas Nelson, 1997) offers insight into each book and chapter.

The best concordance available is *Strong's Exhaustive Concordance of the Bible*, by James Strong (Nashville: Thomas Nelson, 1990).

You can conduct a survey on the Web as well. Start with a wide-angle view at **http://www.letusreason.org/Cult11.htm**—History Timeline of World Religions. Then visit World Religion Resources (**http://www.refdesk.com/factrel.html**), which offers links to more than a hundred sites, and Overview of World Religions (**http://philtar.ucsm.ac.uk/encyclopedia/index.html**), which categorizes by region and by name of religion, from Buddhism to Zoroastrianism.

You can read the Bible, Koran, Book of Morman, or other religious texts online. Check the Web resource guide on page 270 for the specific sites.

A Brief History of the Bible
With Major Figures, Favorite Stories, and Familiar Quotations

No other book in human history has captured the world's attention like the **Bible**. With a story stretching from Creation in the Book of Genesis to the end of the world as we know it in the Book of Revelation, the Bible consists of nearly 1,200 chapters, 32,000 verses, and 800,000 words.

While the identities of some Bible writers are clear, questions remain about who specifically wrote much of it, owing to its having been created and pieced together over a period of 1,200 years, from c. 1000 B.C. to c. A.D. 200. The authors wrote in different styles and formats, including poetry, stories, history, law, philosophy, prophesy, songs, sermons, lists, and letters, and they wrote in different languages—Hebrew, Aramaic, and Greek. They didn't know that their writings would be collected and connected into a single entity that would eventually become the number-one best-selling book of all time. Binding these writers together, however, was the shared understanding—by those who read, admired, and honored their work—that what they wrote was inspired by God, thus meriting the label of "Sacred Scriptures."

The word *bible* means "the books," deriving from the Greek word *biblos*. Exactly which books, and how many books, comprise the Bible varies from religion to religion, tradition to tradition. The Hebrew Bible, for example, consists of the 39 books that Christians call the Old Testament. They include the books of the Law (Torah), the Prophets (Nevi'im), and the Writings (Kethuvim), collectively represented in the acronym Tanakh.

The five books of the Torah (also known as the Books of Moses, or the Pentateuch) are Genesis, Exodus, Leviticus, Numbers, and Deuteronomy. The 21 books of the Prophets, which other religions may order differently, include Joshua, Judges, First Samuel, Second Samuel, First Kings, Second Kings, Isaiah, Jeremiah, Ezekiel, Hosea, Joel, Amos, Obadiah, Jonah, Micah, Nahum, Habakkuk, Zephaniah, Haggai, Zechariah, and Malachi. And the 13 books of the Writings consist of Psalms, Proverbs, Job, Song of Solomon, Ruth, Lamentations, Ecclesiastes, Esther, Daniel, Ezra, Nehemiah, First Chronicles, and Second Chronicles.

The Christian Bible adds 27 books of the New Testament to the 39 of the Old Testament to arrive at a total of 66 books in the complete text. The New Testament is composed of the four Gospels—Matthew, Mark, Luke, and John—plus Acts, Romans, 1 Corinthians, 2 Corinthians,

Galatians, Ephesians, Philippians, Colossians, 1 Thessalonians, 2 Thessalonians, 1 Timothy, 2 Timothy, Titus, Philemon, Hebrews, James, 1 Peter, 2 Peter, 1 John, 2 John, 3 John, Jude, and Revelation.

The Roman Catholic Church recognizes seven additional Old Testament books, which it refers to as "deuterocanonical books," a "second canon." The Protestant tradition refers to these and other books as the Apocrypha, which they do not sanction but generally do include between the Old Testament and the New Testament. The Catholic deuterocanonical books include 1 and 2 Maccabees, Tobit, Judith, Wisdom of Solomon, Sirach (also known as Ecclesiasticus), and Baruch.

Many traditions place the Old Testament's books into four categories: Law, History, Wisdom, and Prophesy. Law is composed of the first five books, Genesis, Exodus, Leviticus, Numbers, and Deuteronomy. The History books include Joshua, Judges, Ruth, 1 and 2 Samuel, 1 and 2 Kings, 1 and 2 Chronicles, Ezra, Nehemiah, and Esther. The Wisdom books are Job, Psalms, Proverbs, Ecclesiastes, and Song of Solomon. Prophesy is made up of two subcategories, Major Prophets (i.e., the longer books) and Minor Prophets. The books of the Major Prophets are Isaiah, Jeremiah, Lamentations, Ezekiel, and Daniel. The books of the Minor Prophets include Hosea, Joel, Amos, Obadiah, Jonah, Micah, Nahum, Habakkuk, Zephaniah, Haggai, Zechariah, and Malachi.

The Bible has been translated into numerous languages and versions. The Old Testament was written originally in Hebrew and Aramaic, and the New Testament in Greek. The Septuagint was the first Greek translation of the Old Testament (third century B.C.). It derived its title from having had 72 translators, and it added books to the original compilation. The first Latin translation of the Bible developed as early as the second century A.D. , but historians credit St. Jerome's fourth-century version, known as the Vulgate, as most instrumental in bringing the Scriptures to the common people. Before the 15th century, translations and copies were produced painstakingly by hand, but with Gutenberg's development of the printing press in 1445, reproductions were turned out in a fraction of the time. In fact, Gutenberg's first project was to print a copy of the Bible.

Among the most popular English versions of the Bible are:

King James Version (KJV—1611): Classic, poetic, with "thee" and "thou."

Revised Standard Version (RSV—1973): Attempts to be both classical and contemporary in style.

New King James Version (NKJV—1982): Changes the "thee" and "thou" language.

New International Version (NIV—1984): Includes gender-neutral language.

New American Bible (NAB—1989): Preferred by the Roman Catholic Church.

New Revised Standard Version (NRSV—1989): Conspicuous for its politically correct language.

New American Standard Bible (NASB—1995): Written in response to the New Revised Standard Version, which the NASB translators perceived as too liberal. (For example, in Isaiah, the NRSV changes "virgin" to "young woman." The NASB retains the original translation.)

New Living Translation (NLT—1997): Thought-for-thought, not word-for-word; paraphrases.

The Message (TM—2002): While the above versions derive from committees and panels of numerous scholars, this version has only one translator, who uses intensely colloquial, conversational language and eliminates verse numbers.

The Bible begins with God's creation of the world, and with His offering paradise to its first human inhabitants, Adam and Eve. He asks for love and obedience in return. Adam and Eve's disobedience triggers a life of challenges for them and their descendants. Down through the ages, humanity struggles to show love for God, but fails consistently. Time after time God forgives the sins of His people and offers further opportunities for redemption.

The Old Testament tells the story of the Jews, God's chosen people of Israel. From their captivity in Egypt to their escape and wandering, searching for the "promised land," to the settlement and maintenance of that land. It is the story of their covenant with God, their history, their laws, their wisdom, their failures, and their prophesies. God promises a Messiah, a Savior.

The New Testament, beginning with the Gospels, tells of the humble life and world-changing ministry of Jesus Christ, son of God, the Messiah sent to redeem His people, as prophesied in the Old Testament. It follows Him from His birth in a manger to His death on a cross to His resurrection after three days. The Acts of the Apostles and the epistles describe the subsequent organization of His church, and the development of the faith of His people. The last book, Revelation, tells of visions of the future.

The Bible is filled with memorable stories and figures. What follows are some of the most prominent. (The King James Version is used, unless otherwise noted.)

Old Testament

Creation: "In the beginning God created the heaven and the earth." (Genesis 1:1) In the first five days God created light, sky, waters, land, day, night, and animals. On the sixth day, "God created man in His own image . . . male and female created he them. And God blessed them, and God said unto them, 'Be fruitful and multiply . . .'" (Genesis 1:27) And God "rested on the seventh day from all his work which he had made." (Genesis 2:2)

Adam and Eve: God put Adam and Eve in the Garden of Eden and told them, "Of every tree of the garden thou mayest freely eat; But of the tree of the knowledge of good and evil, thou shalt not eat of it, for in the day that thou eatest thereof thou shalt surely die." (Genesis 2:16) Tempted by the serpent, Eve ate the fruit of the tree and gave it to Adam, who also ate it. God drove them from the garden.

Noah: God saw the wickedness of humanity and grieved. God told Noah that He had determined to destroy the earth and all flesh; "for the earth is filled with violence through them." (Genesis 6:13) God instructed Noah to make an ark and "of every living thing of all flesh, two of every sort thou bring into the ark." (Genesis 6:19) Noah obeyed. God told Noah to go into the ark, for in seven days "I will cause it to rain upon the earth forty days and forty nights; and every living substance that I have made will I destroy from off the face of the earth." (Genesis 7:4) God flooded the earth and, after the rain, the waters receded. God told Noah, "Be fruitful and multiply, and replenish the earth." (Genesis 9:1)

Abraham: The Lord said to Abram, "I will make of thee a great nation, and I will bless thee, and make thy name great." (Genesis 12:2) God promised Abram that he would have as many children as there were stars in the sky. When Abram was 99 years old, God said to him that his name would no longer be Abram, "but thy name shall be Abraham; for a father of many nations have I made thee." (Genesis 17:5)

Joseph: Joseph dreamed that his brothers would one day bow down to him. This upset them. The brothers envied Joseph and plotted against him. They threw him into a pit and sold him to merchants, who took him to Egypt. Joseph was made a slave, and was cast into prison, but eventually won favor with the Pharaoh when he interpreted his dreams. When Joseph told the Pharaoh to gather and store food in preparation for a famine, the Pharaoh put him in charge of all the land. The famine came and people from every country traveled to Egypt to buy food, including Joseph's brothers. They did not recognize Joseph, who eventually revealed himself to them and told them to return home to bring back their father and younger brother, both of whom Joseph missed. Joseph's father, having believed his son dead for years, was overjoyed at the news and went to him. All were reunited and Joseph provided for his family. When his father died, his brothers came before him and bowed, saying that they were his servants. Thus, the dream that Joseph had had as a youth came to pass. Joseph said to them, "I will nourish you, and your little ones. And he comforted them." (Genesis 50:21)

Moses: When the Pharaoh ordered that male children be killed, Moses' mother put him in a basket and sent him down the river. The Pharaoh's daughter found him and raised him. "She called his name Moses: and she said, Because I drew him out of the water." (Exodus 2:10)

While tending sheep one day, Moses saw a burning bush and God spoke to him. "Come, I will send thee unto Pharaoh, that thou mayest bring forth my people the children of Israel out of Egypt." (Exodus 3:10)

Passover: Moses told the elders of Israel to kill a lamb and smear its blood on their doors. "For the Lord will pass through to smite the Egyptians; and when he seeth the blood upon the lintel, and on the two side posts, the Lord will pass over the door, and will not suffer the destroyer to come in unto your houses to smite you." (Exodus 12:23)

Red Sea: As Moses led the people of Israel out of Egypt, Pharaoh and his army chased after them. At the banks of the Red Sea, "Then Moses stretched out his hand over the sea; and the Lord caused the sea to go back by a strong east wind all that night, and made the sea dry land, and the waters were divided." (Exodus 14:21) The people of Israel crossed through the walls of water. The Egyptian soldiers followed. The Lord told Moses to stretch out his hand over the sea. "The waters returned and covered the chariots and the horsemen, and all the host of Pharaoh that came into the sea after them; there remained not so much as one of them." (Exodus 14:28) "Thus the Lord saved Israel that day out of the hand of the Egyptians." (Exodus 14:30)

Ten Commandments: After leaving Egypt, the people of Israel were camped in the wilderness and Moses went up to the top of Mount Sinai to speak with the Lord. God gave Moses the Ten Commandments, beginning with "I am the Lord thy God, which have brought thee out of the land of Egypt, out of the house of bondage. Thou shalt have no other gods before me. Thou shalt not make unto thee any graven image." (Exodus 20:2) God said you shall not take the name of the Lord in vain; remember to keep holy the Sabbath day; honor your father and mother; you shall not kill; you shall not commit adultery; you shall not steal; you shall not bear false witness against your neighbor; you shall not covet your neighbor's house; you shall not covet your neighbor's wife, "nor anything that is thy neighbor's." (Exodus 20:17)

Joshua and the Battle of Jericho: The Lord said to Joshua, "This day will I begin to magnify thee in the sight of all Israel, that they may know that, as I was with Moses, so I will be with thee." (Joshua 3:7) Joshua approached the walled city of Jericho, and the Lord instructed him to have seven trumpet-blaring priests join all the armed men in marching around the city for six days. On the seventh day, he was to have the seven priests with seven trumpets march around the city seven times, blowing their trumpets, and when they did, all the people were to shout. Joshua obeyed, and on the seventh day, when the people heard the sound of the trumpets, they shouted and "the wall fell down flat, so that the people went up into the city, every man straight before him, and they took the city." (Joshua 6:20)

Samson and Delilah: The Philistines wanted to know the source of Samson's great strength so that they could defeat him. They bribed the woman he loved, Delilah, to get the information for them. Several times she asked Samson, but he refrained from revealing the secret. "And it came to pass, when she pressed him daily with her words, and urged him, so that his soul was vexed unto death. That he told her all his heart, and said unto her, There hath not come a razor upon my head . . . If I be shaven, then my strength will go from me, and I shall become weak, and be like any other man." (Judges 16:16) Later, when Samson was asleep, she had his hair cut, enabling the Philistines to capture him.

David: When the high priest Samuel was to select the successor for King Saul, he went to Jesse in Bethlehem to see his sons. One by one, seven passed before him, but all were rejected. Samuel asked if there were any more. Jesse said that David, the last one, was tending the sheep. Samuel sent for him, and he was brought in. "And the Lord said, Arise, anoint him; for this is he." (1 Samuel 16:12)

When the evil spirit came upon Saul, David played a harp and Saul was refreshed.

David and Goliath: The Philistines and the Israelites were poised for battle. A Philistine champion named Goliath, a giant of a man, called to the Israelites to send a warrior out to fight him, one on one, to decide the entire battle's victor. David wanted to go, but Saul said to him, "Thou art but a youth, and he a man of war from his youth." (1 Samuel 17:33) But David convinced Saul to let him fight. He did not wear armor. Sling in hand, he put five stones into his shepherd's bag. Goliath taunted him, but David replied, "Thou comest to me with a sword, and with a spear, and with a shield; but I come to thee in the name of the Lord." (1 Samuel 17:45) "And David put his hand in his bag and took thence a stone, and slang it, and smote the Philistine in his forehead, that the stone sunk into his forehead; and he fell upon his face to the earth." (1 Samuel 17:49) With no sword of his own, David ran to Goliath, drew the giant's sword, and killed him. When the Philistines saw that their champion had been killed, they fled.

Solomon: God said to Solomon, son of David, "I have given thee a wise and an understanding heart; so that there was none like thee before thee, neither after thee shall any arise like unto thee." (1 Kings 3:12) "And God gave Solomon wisdom and understanding exceeding much, and largeness of heart, even as the sand that is on the seashore." (1 Kings 4:29)

Psalm 23 (KJV)

The Lord is my Shepherd; I shall not want.
He maketh me to lie down in green pastures:

He leadeth me beside the still waters.
He restoreth my soul:
He leadeth me in the paths of righteousness for his name's sake.
Yea, though I walk through the valley of the shadow of death,
I will fear no evil: for thou art with me;
Thy rod and thy staff, they comfort me.
Thou preparest a table before me in the presence of mine enemies:
Thou anointest my head with oil;
My cup runneth over.
Surely goodness and mercy shall follow me all the days of my life:
And I will dwell in the house of the Lord for ever.

Isaiah (7:14): "Behold, a virgin shall conceive, and bear a son, and shall call his name Immanuel."

Jonah: God told Jonah to go to Nineveh, for He was unhappy with its wickedness, but Jonah set out by ship in the opposite direction. God sent a great storm to the ship and the sailors feared for their lives. When Jonah confessed that he was fleeing from God, the crew threw him overboard. A great fish swallowed Jonah and he was in its belly for three days and three nights. He prayed from the belly of the fish. "And the Lord spake unto the fish, and it vomited out Jonah upon the dry land." (Jonah 2:10)

New Testament

John (3:16): "For God so loved the world, that he gave his only begotten Son, that whosoever believeth in him should not perish, but have everlasting life."

Matthew (1:23): "Behold, a virgin shall be with child, and shall bring forth a son, and they shall call his name Emmanuel, which being interpreted is, God with us."

The Annunciation: The angel Gabriel appeared to Mary and said, "And behold, thou shalt conceive in thy womb, and bring forth a son, and shall call his name Jesus." (Luke 1:31) "The Holy Ghost shall come upon thee, and the power of the Highest shall overshadow thee: therefore also that holy thing which shall be born of thee shall be called the Son of God." (Luke 1:35) "And Mary said, 'Behold the handmaid of the Lord; be it unto me according to thy word.'" (Luke 1:38)

Magnificat (beginning): When visiting her cousin, Elizabeth, Mary said: "My soul doth magnify the Lord, and my spirit hath rejoiced in God my Savior, for he hath regarded the low estate of his handmaiden: for, behold, from henceforth all generations shall call me blessed. For he that is mighty hath done to me great things; and holy is his name." (Luke 1:46)

John the Baptist: "Now Elisabeth's full time came that she should be delivered; and she brought forth a son." (Luke 1:57) Some wanted to name him Zechariah after his father, but his mother said, "Not so; but he shall be called John." (Luke 1:60) Unable to speak, Zechariah asked for a writing tablet and wrote: "His name is John." (Luke 1:63) "And his mouth was opened immediately, and his tongue loosed, and he spake, and praised God." (Luke 1:64)

Birth of Jesus: In response to a decree from Caesar Augustus, Mary and Joseph traveled from Nazareth to Bethlehem for taxing. "And while they were there, the days were accomplished that she should be delivered. And she brought forth her firstborn son, and wrapped him in swaddling clothes, and laid him in a manger; because there was no room for them in the inn." (Luke 2:6)

There were shepherds in the nearby fields and an angel appeared to them and said, "Fear not: for, behold, I bring you good tidings of great joy, which shall be to all people; for unto you is born this day in the city of David a Savior, which is Christ the Lord. And this shall be a sign unto you; Ye shall find the babe wrapped in swaddling clothes, lying in a manger." (Luke 2:10)

Wise men from the East came to look, saying, "Where is he that is born King of the Jews? for we have seen his star in the east, and are come to worship him." (Matthew 2:2) "And when they were come into the house, they saw the young child with Mary his mother, and fell down, and worshipped him: and when they had opened their treasures, they presented unto him gifts; gold, and frankincense, and myrrh." (Matthew 2:11)

Jesus among the Teachers: When Jesus was 12 years old, his parents took him to Jerusalem for Passover. Mary and Joseph lost track of him, but found him in the temple, sitting with the teachers, listening to them and asking them questions. When his parents told him that they had worried, he said, "How is it that ye sought me? Wist ye not that I must be about my Father's business?" (Luke 2:49)

John Baptizes Jesus: John baptized the people of Jerusalem and Judea. He said, "I indeed baptize you with water unto repentance; but he that cometh after me is mightier than I, whose shoes I am not worthy to bear: he shall baptize you with the Holy Ghost, and with fire." (Matthew 3:11) When Jesus came to the Jordan to John to be baptized, John said, "I have need to be baptized of thee, and comest thou to me?" (Matthew 3:14) After Jesus was baptized, "the heavens were opened unto him and he saw the Spirit of God descending like a dove, and lighting upon him: and lo, a voice from heaven, saying, This is my beloved Son, in whom I am well pleased." (Matthew 3:16)

The Apostles: Walking by the Sea of Galilee, Jesus saw two brothers, Simon and Andrew, fishing. Jesus said to them, "Follow me, and I will make you fishers of men. And they straightway left their nets and followed him." (Matthew 4:19) "The names of the twelve apostles are these: The first, Simon, who is called Peter, and Andrew his brother; James the son of Zebedee, and John his brother; Philip and Bartholomew; Thomas and Matthew the publican; James the son of Alphaeus, and Lebbaeus, whose surname was Thaddaeus; Simon the Cananaean, and Judas Iscariot, who also betrayed him." (Matthew 10:2)

First Miracle: The Marriage in Cana: Jesus, his mother, Mary, and his disciples were invited to a wedding. When it was reported that the wine had run out, Mary turned to the servants and said, "Whatsoever he saith unto you, do it." (John 2:5) Jesus told them to fill six stone jars with water and take some to the steward of the feast. When the steward tasted it, he said to the bridegroom, "'Every man at the beginning doth set forth good wine; and when men have well drunk, then that which is worse: but thou hast kept the good wine until now.' This beginning of miracles did Jesus in Cana of Galilee, and manifested forth his glory; and his disciples believed on him." (John 2:10)

Sermon on the Mount: Seeing the crowds, Jesus went up on the mountain. He taught his disciples: "Blessed are the poor in spirit: for theirs is the kingdom of heaven. Blessed are they that mourn: for they shall be comforted. Blessed are the meek: for they shall inherit the earth. Blessed are they which do hunger and thirst after righteousness: for they shall be filled. Blessed are the merciful: for they shall obtain mercy. Blessed are the pure in heart: for they shall see God. Blessed are the peacemakers: for they shall be called the children of God. Blessed are they which are persecuted for righteousness' sake: for theirs is the kingdom of heaven. Blessed are ye, when men shall revile you, and persecute you and shall say all manner of evil against you falsely, for my sake. Rejoice, and be exceedingly glad: for great is your reward in heaven, for so persecuted they the prophets which were before you." (Matthew 5:3)

Jesus on Forgiveness: The scribes and the Pharisees brought to Jesus a woman who had been caught in adultery, and said that the law demanded that she be stoned. They asked him his opinion. Jesus bent and wrote something on the ground with his finger, and said, "He that is without sin among you, let him first cast a stone at her." (John 8:7) One by one, they walked away, until Jesus was alone with the woman. He said, "Hath no man condemned thee? She said, No man, Lord. And Jesus said, Neither do I condemn thee: go, and sin no more." (John 8:10)

Jesus Calms the Sea: Jesus was on a boat with his disciples when a great storm arose suddenly. The disciples were afraid for their lives. Jesus "rebuked the wind and the raging of the water; and they ceased, and there was a calm." (Luke 8:24) The disciples marveled, saying "What manner of man is this, for he commandeth even the winds and water, and they obey him?" (Luke 8:25)

The Good Samaritan: A lawyer asked Jesus what to do to inherit the earth, and Jesus told him a story of a man who was attacked by thieves and left for dead on a road. A priest came along, saw him, yet passed him by. So too did others see him and pass him by, until a Samaritan came by and had compassion for him, tending to his wounds and taking him to an inn for care. Jesus asked the lawyer, "Which now of these three, thinkest thou, was neighbor unto him that fell among the thieves? And he said, He that shewed mercy on him. Then Jesus said unto him, Go, and do thou likewise." (Luke 10:36)

Jesus Raises Lazarus from the Dead: When Jesus heard that Lazarus had died, he went to him. Upon arrival, he learned that Lazarus had lain in the tomb for four days. Martha, sister of Lazarus, asked Jesus for help. Jesus directed that the stone be removed from the tomb, and said, "Lazarus, come forth. And he that was dead came forth, bound hand and foot with graveclothes."(John 11:43)

The Last Supper: At Passover, Jesus sat at table with his disciples. "And he took bread, and gave thanks, and brake it, and gave unto them, saying, This is my body which is given for you: this do in remembrance of me. Likewise also the cup after supper, saying, This cup is the new testament in my blood, which is shed for you." (Luke 22:19)

Judas: For thirty pieces of silver, Judas agreed to betray Jesus, and he led the crowd and the chief priests to the Garden of Gethsemane. When he drew near to Jesus to identify him with a kiss, Jesus said, "Judas, betrayest thou the Son of Man with a kiss?" (Luke 22:48)

Pontius Pilate: Jesus was brought before Pontius Pilate, the Roman governor, who questioned Jesus but found no fault with him. When the chief priests and the crowd insisted that he prosecute Jesus, he gave them a choice of releasing either Jesus or Barabbas, a murderer. They chose Barabbas to be released, and called for Jesus to be crucified. "When Pilate saw that he could prevail nothing, but that rather a tumult was made, he took water, and washed his hands before the multitude, saying, I am innocent of the blood of this just person: see ye to it." (Matthew 27:24)

Death of Jesus: Jesus was tortured, mocked, and nailed to a cross. After a while, "with a loud voice, he said, Father, into thy hands I commend my spirit: and having said thus he gave up the ghost." (Luke 23:46) A nearby centurion said, "Truly this was the Son of God." (Matthew 27:54)

Resurrection of Jesus: On the third day after Jesus was buried, Mary Magdalene and Mary the wife of Cleophas went to his tomb. An angel appeared to them, rolled back the tomb's stone, and said, "Fear not ye: for I know that ye seek Jesus, which was crucified. He is not here: for he is risen, as he said." (Matthew 28:5)

Jesus Appears to the Apostles: The apostles were gathered and Jesus appeared to them, saying, "These are the words which I spake unto you, while I was yet with you, that all things must be fulfilled, which were written in the law of Moses and in the prophets and in the psalms, concerning me . . . Thus it is written, and thus it behoved Christ to suffer, and to rise from the dead the third day: and that repentance and remission of sins should be preached in his name among all nations." (Luke 24:44) "While he blessed them, he was parted from them, and carried up into heaven." (Luke 24:51)

Paul: Saul, a persecutor of the disciples and the church, approached Damascus, "and suddenly there shined round about him a light from heaven. And he fell to the earth, and heard a voice saying unto him, Saul, Saul, why persecutest thou me? And he said, Who art thou, Lord? And the Lord said, I am Jesus, whom thou persecutest . . . And the Lord said unto him, Arise, and go into the city, and it shall be told thee what thou must do." (Acts 9:3)

The Lord appeared to Ananias and said of Saul, who was also to be known as Paul, "for he is a chosen vessel unto me, to bear my name before the Gentiles, and kings, and the children of Israel." (Acts 9:15) Paul gradually regained his strength "And straightaway he preached Christ in the synagogues, that he is the Son of God." (Acts 9:20)

Revelation: "And I heard a great voice out of heaven saying, Behold, the tabernacle of God is with men, and he will dwell with them, and they shall be his people, and God himself shall be with them, and be their God. And God shall wipe away all tears from their eyes, and there shall be no more death, neither sorrow, nor crying, neither shall there be any more pain: for the former things are passed away." (Revelation 21:3)

> But be ye doers of the word, and not hearers only,
> deceiving your own selves.
>
> JAMES 1:22

Starting Points and Conversation Pieces

THE FIVE LARGEST RELIGIONS

The following are approximate numbers, as estimates vary periodically and from source to source.

❖ Christianity: 2 billion

FAMILIAR BIBLICAL PHRASES

Apple of the eye (Psalm 17:8); Eat, drink, and be merry (Luke 12:19); Holier than thou (Isaiah 65:5); Man after mine own heart (Acts 13:22); Man shall not live by bread alone (Matthew 4:4); Many are called, but few are chosen (Matthew 22:14); More blessed to give than to receive (Acts 20:35); Out of the mouth of babes (Psalm 8:2); Pride goeth before destruction (Proverbs 16:18).

- Islam: 1.3 billion

- Hinduism: 900 million

- Buddhism: 360 million

- Chinese Traditional (combination of Taoism, Confucianism, Buddhism): 225 million

OTHER SELECTED RELIGIONS

- Sikhism: 23 million

- Judaism: 14 million

- Jainism: 4 million

- Shintoism: 3 million

- There are an estimated 225 million Christians in the United States, approximately 80 percent of the country's total population at the turn of the millennium.

- The two largest branches of Islam are Sunni and Shi'ite.

- The largest Hindu population is in India (approximately 750 million).

- The largest Buddhist population is in China (approximately 102 million), followed by Japan (approximately 90 million).

- Punjab, India is home to approximately 80 percent of the Sikhs in the world.

- The Jewish population in the United States is larger than in Israel (approximately 5.6 million versus approximately 4.4 million).

- In the United States, two of the largest "megachurches" (2,000 or more in average weekly attendance) are Willow Creek Community Church in Chicago (average weekly attendance of 14,000+) and the First Baptist Church of Hammond, Indiana (12,000+).

PRESIDENTS

❖ More U.S. presidents have been Episcopalian (12) than any other religion. In second place: Presbyterian (nine).

❖ John F. Kennedy was the only Catholic president.

TERMS

❖ An *agnostic* is one who believes that it is not possible to prove or to disprove the existence of God.

❖ The *Koran* (often spelled Quo'ran or Quran) is the sacred text of Islam.

❖ In Judaism, *Yom Kippur* is a high holy day of atonement characterized by prayer and fasting.

❖ *Revelation* is the last book of the Christian Bible.

OTHER NOTES

❖ The opening of the *Book of Mormon*—"The First Book of Nephi, His Reign and Ministry"—begins: "An account of Lehi and his wife Sariah and his four sons . . ."

❖ Peter is considered to have been the first pope. Linus was the second.

❖ In the Great Schism (1378–1415), the Catholic papacy was split, with one pope in Rome and one in Avignon, France.

❖ Hinduism, the oldest major religion, traces its roots back 3,000 years to Vedism, the religion of the ancient people of India.

❖ Three important Hindu deities: Brahma, Vishnu, and Shiva.

❖ In the Catholic Church, cardinals rank just below the Pope and make up the administration, called the Roman Curia.

❖ In the Church of England, the Archbishop of Canterbury serves as the Metropolitan for the Southern Province and as the Primate of All England.

Resources for Further Exploration

READING

Dictionaries

Achtemeier, Paul J. *HarperCollins Bible Dictionary*. San Francisco: Harper-SanFrancisco, 1996.

Rahner, Karl, and Herbert Vorgrimler. *Dictionary of Theology*. New York: Crossroad, 1988.

Bible Commentaries and Guides

Boadt, Lawrence. *Reading the Old Testament: An Introduction*. New York: Paulist Press, 1984.

Gabel, John B., et al. *The Bible As Literature: An Introduction*. New York: Oxford University Press, 1999.

Perkins, Pheme. *Reading the New Testament*. New York: Paulist Press, 1978.

Classics

Aquinas, Thomas. *On Law, Morality, and Politics*. Indianapolis: Hackett Publishing, 1988.

Augustine. *Confessions*. New York: Oxford University Press, 1998.

Lucretius. *The Nature of Things*. New York: W. W. Norton, 1977.

Bible

May, Herbert Gordon, and Bruce Manning Metzger. *The New Oxford Annotated Bible with the Apocrypha*. New York: Oxford University Press, 1977.

Thomas Nelson Publishers. *The Holy Bible: Containing the Old and New Testaments in the King James Version*. Nashville: Thomas Nelson Publishers, 1984.

History of the Bible

Blair, Edward P. *The Illustrated Bible Handbook*. Nashville: Abingdon Press, 1987.

Davis, Kenneth C. *Don't Know Much About the Bible*. New York: Eagle Brook/William Morrow, 1998.

Miller, Stephen M., and Robert V. Huber. *The Bible: A History: The Making and Impact of the Bible*. Intercourse, Pennsylvania: Good Books, 2003.

Reader's Digest Association. *The Bible Through the Ages*. Pleasantville, New York: Reader's Digest , 1996

Best-sellers

Strobel, Lee. *The Case for Christ*. Grand Rapids, Michigan: Zondervan, 2001.

Walsch, Neale Donald. *Conversations with God*. New York: Putnam's, 1996.

Warren, Rick. *The Purpose Driven Life*. Grand Rapids, Michigan: Zondervan, 2002.

Wilkinson, Bruce. *The Prayer of Jabez*. Sisters, Oregon: Multnomah Publishers, 2000.

General Resources and Relevant Books

Berg, Michael. *Becoming Like God*. Los Angeles: Kabbalah Publishing, 2004.

Fromm, Erich. *Psychoanalysis and Religion*. New York: Bantam, 1972.

Hahn, Scott. *Hail, Holy Queen: The Mother of God in the Word of God*. New York: Doubleday, 2001.

Hume, David, and J. C. A. Gaskin. *Dialogues and Natural History of Religion*. New York: Oxford University Press, 1998.

Kant, Immanuel. *Religion Within the Limits of Reason Alone*. Translated and edited by Theodore M. Greene and Hoyt H. Hudson. New York: Perennial, 1958.

Kushner, Harold S. *When Bad Things Happen to Good People*. New York: Avon, 1983.

Lewis, C. S. *The Screwtape Letters*. San Francisco: HarperSanFrancisco, 2001.

Lucado, Max. *It's Not About Me: Rescue from the Life We Thought Would Make Us Happy*. Brentwood, Tennessee: Integrity Publishers, 2004.

Mogel, Wendy. *The Blessing of a Skinned Knee: Using Jewish Teachings to Raise Self-Reliant Children*. New York: Penguin, 2001.

Szulc, Tad. *Pope John Paul II: The Biography*. New York: Scribner, 1995.

Telushkin, Joseph. *Jewish Literacy: The Most Important Things to Know About the Jewish Religion, Its People and Its History*. New York: William Morrow, 1991.

U.S. Catholic Church. *Catechism of the Catholic Church*. New York: Doubleday, 1995.

WEB SITES

General Resources and Relevant Sites

http://www.religion-online.org/—Religion Online. In-depth resource.

http://www.religiousresources.org/—Directory of Religious Resources on the Internet.

http://www.worldprayers.org/—World Prayers. Multicultural.

http://religion.rutgers.edu/vri/index.html—Virtual Religion Index. Hosted by Rutgers University. Lots of links.

http://www.facetsofreligion.com/—Facets of Religion. Study resources.
http://www.beliefnet.com/—Beliefnet. Wide-ranging religious resource.
http://www.religioustolerance.org/var_rel.htm—Religious Tolerance.
http://www.aril.org/World.html—World Religion Resources.
http://www.adherents.com/index.html—Religion Statistics and Geography.
http://www.wabashcenter.wabash.edu/Internet/front.htm—Wabash Center, Theology and Religion.
http://www.aarweb.org/—American Academy of Religion.
http://www.hirr.hartsem.edu/org/faith_denominations_homepages.html—Hartford Institute for Religion Research. Denominational directory.
http://www.thearda.com/—American Religion Data Archive.
http://www.nypl.org/links/index.cfm?Trg=1&d1=95&d3=Religion%20and%20Theology—New York Public Library Religion and Theology Directory.
http://www.uni-marburg.de/religionswissenschaft/journal/sor/—Science of Religion. Abstract and Index of Articles.

Journals
http://www.jcrt.org/—Journal for Cultural and Religious Theory.
http://theologytoday.ptsem.edu/—Theology Today. Journal.

Early Modern Europe
http://www.mhs.ox.ac.uk/gatt/—The role of biblical interpretation in early modern Europe. Hosted by Oxford University.
http://www.folger.edu/institute/sacred/index.html—16 college teachers connect religion and literature via "Redefining the Sacred in Early Modern England."

Churches
http://www.christusrex.org/www1/splendors/splendors.html—Worldwide Tour of Churches, Cathedrals, and Monasteries.

Museums and Libraries
http://mv.vatican.va/3_EN/pages/MV_Home.html—Vatican Museums.
http://www.ccel.org/—Christian Classics Ethereal Library.

Bible and Religious Texts
http://www.hti.umich.edu/k/kjv/—King James Bible.
http://www.biblegateway.com/cgi-bin/bible—Bible Gateway.
http://www.bible.com—Bible.com. General resources relating to the Bible.
http://davidwiley.com/religion.html—Religious and Sacred Texts.
http://www.hti.umich.edu/k/koran/—The Koran.
http://unbound.biola.edu/—Twenty-four versions of the Bible.

http://scriptures.lds.org/bm/contents—Book of Mormon.
http://www.bible.org—Bible.org. Bible resources.
http://www.talkingbible.com/—Talking Bible.
http://ntgateway.com/multibib/—All-in-One Biblical Resource.

Bible History
http://www.bible-history.com—History of the Bible.

Bible Study
http://www.biblenotes.net/—Bible Notes. Bible summaries, notes, and key-points.
http://www.biblestudytools.net/—Bible Study Tools.
http://www.bsw.org/—Biblical Studies on the Web.

Jewish
http://www.chabad.org/holidays/chanukah/default.asp—Virtual Hanukkah. Information about Hanukkah.
http://pinenet.com/~rooster/hasid1.html—FAQs on Hasidic Culture.
http://www.jewishnet.net/—Global Jewish Network.
http://www.jewishnet.net/subjects/food.html—Jewish Food.

Christian
http://www.christianmusic.org/cmp/artists/—Christian Music Place.
http://www.christianitytoday.com/—Articles, links, and resources.

Catholic
http://www.newadvent.org/cathen/—Catholic Encyclopedia.
http://www.vatican.va/—Vatican: The Holy See.
http://www.newadvent.org/—Catholic Resources.
http://www.newadvent.org/cathen/12272b.htm—List of Popes.

The Passion of the Christ
http://info.alexa.com/data/details?newadventcatholi&url=thepassionofthechrist.com—Information on the film, *The Passion of the Christ.*

The Reformation
http://www.bbc.co.uk/history/state/church_reformation/index.shtml—BBC on "Church and Reformation."
http://www.bbc.co.uk/radio4/history/voices/voices_reformation.shtml—BBC audio focus on the Reformation.
http://www.educ.msu.edu/homepages/laurence/reformation/index.htm—The Reformation Guide.
http://www.pbs.org/empires/martinluther/—PBS on Martin Luther.

http://www.iclnet.org/pub/resources/text/wittenberg/wittenberg-home.html—
Works by and about Martin Luther and Lutherans.
http://www.ccel.org/c/calvin/—Bio on John Calvin.
http://homepage.mac.com/shanerosenthal/reformationink/index.html—Primary
source for Reformation documents.

Baptist
http://www.abc-usa.org/—American Baptist Churches.
http://www.sbc.net/—Southern Baptist Convention.

Lutheran
http://www.elca.org/—Evangelical Lutheran Church in America.

Episcopal
http://www.ecusa.anglican.org/index_flash.htm—Episcopal Church, USA.

Presbyterian
http://www.pcusa.org/—Presbyterian Church, USA.

Methodist
http://www.umc.org/index.asp—United Methodist Church.

Mormon
http://www.lds.org/—Church of Jesus Christ of Latter Day Saints home page.

Jehovah's Witness
http://www.watchtower.org/—Jehovah's Witness: Watchtower Society official
Web site.

Christian Science
http://www.tfccs.com/index.jhtml;jsessionid=ADBT4JMRTUVJPKGL4L2SFEQ—
Church of Christ, Scientist.

Scientology
http://www.scientology.org/—Scientology home page.

Amish
http://www.holycrosslivonia.org/amish/—Amish history, culture, politics.

Baha'i
http://www.bcca.org/bahaivision/—A Baha'i Faith Page.

Muslim
http://www.pbs.org/wgbh/pages/frontline/shows/muslims/—Muslims. PBS site.

Islamic Art
http://www.lacma.org/islamic_art/intro.htm—Islamic art.

Hindu
http://www.hindunet.org/—The Hindu Universe.

Hare Krishna
http://webcom.com/~ara/—Hare Krishna home page.

Zen Buddhism
http://www.ciolek.com/WWWVL-Zen.html—Zen Buddhism Virtual Library.

Buddha
http://www.buddhanet.net/—Buddhanet. Buddhism. Directory and resources.

Taoism
https://maxvps001.maximumasp.com/v001u23zac/Tao/Index2.asp—Taoism. Center of Traditional Taoist Studies.

Dalai Lama
http://www.tibet.com/—Dalai Lama home page.

Sikhism
http://www.sikhs.org/—Sikhism. History, philosophy, resources.

Jainism
http://www.jainism.org/—Jainism. Resource center.

Confucianism
http://www.askasia.org/frclasrm/readings/r000004.htm—Article on Confucianism.

OTHER RESOURCES

Notre Dame Cathedral
Place du parvis de Notre Dame
75004 Paris, France
1-800-645-6140
http://www.paris.org/Monuments/NDame/

The Israel Museum, Jerusalem
POB 71117
Jerusalem 91710, Israel
Tel: 972-2-6708811
http://www.imj.org.il/eng/about/

Mormon Tabernacle Choir
50 East North Temple, 20th Floor
Salt Lake City, UT 84150
(801) 240-4150
http://www.mormontabernaclechoir.org/

Crystal Cathedral Ministries
13280 Chapman Avenue
Garden Grove, CA 92840
(714) 971-4000
http://www.crystalcathedral.org/

19. Quotations

HERE YOU WON'T NEED MUCH MORE in the way of a general reference book than *Bartlett's Familiar Quotations,* by John Bartlett (Boston: Little, Brown, 2002), the "canonical reference work," according to *Publishers Weekly,* with an easily accessible index and more than 1,400 pages and 5,000 years of timeless treasures in chronological order.

When Bartlett's doesn't satisfy completely, try *The Oxford Dictionary of Quotations,* by Elizabeth Knowles (New York: Oxford University Press, 1999), which the editors at Amazon.com call "erudite, enjoyable, and educational," though it does lean to favoring British authors, or an offering from the creator of Hooked on Phonics, John M. Shanahan, *The Most Brilliant Thoughts of All Time in Two Lines or Less* (New York: HarperResource, 1999), which contains witty and wise morsels from such notables as Oscar Wilde, Winston Churchill, and Aesop.

Turn to *Reader's Digest's Quotable Quotes: Wit and Wisdom for All Occasions from America's Most Popular Magazine* (Pleasantville, New York: Reader's Digest, 1997) for a wide assortment of authors on a wide variety of topics, collected from the magazine's popular feature.

On the Web, start with the quotations directory at refdesk.com (**http://www.refdesk.com/factquot.html**), which offers dozens of sites, in alphabetical order, opening the door to thousands of quotations by thousands of authors on thousands of topics.

Bartlett's is online at **http://www.bartleby.com/100/**, and other "general" sites worth visiting include The Quotations Page (**http://www.quotationspage.com/**), which claims to be the oldest quotations site on the Web (1994), and which has forums and more than 20,000 entries and 2,500 authors, QuoteLand (**http://www.quoteland.com/**), which has popular forums for the quotations buff, and ThinkExist.com (**http://www.thinkexist.com/**), which has more than 120,000 quotations by more than 11,000 authors, and which also has forums and a keyword-search feature.

For more specific topics, see the Web section at the end of this chapter, where you will find sites on such subjects as math (**http://www. mathacademy.com/pr/quotes/**—Math Quotes), biting humor (**http:// www.curmudgeon-online.com/**—Curmudgeon-Online), and wisdom (**http://www.wiseoldsayings.com/**—Wise Old Sayings).

Who Are Today's Heroes?

At a recent dinner party, the host asked his guests to name a hero. The responses varied, from ancient warriors to superheroes to those who died in the tragedy of September 11, 2001. Interestingly, everyone could name a few legendary ancient warriors—Agamemnon and Odysseus, Hector and Achilles—and more than a few superheroes— including Superman, Batman, and Spider-Man—but no one could come up with the name of a 9/11 hero.

On the surface, perhaps, all who were mentioned fit neatly into the concept of the term *hero,* but upon closer review it becomes clear that there is a marked difference among heroes. The heroes of yesterday are very different from the heroes of today.

Ancient warriors fought in accord with the Heroic Code, which prompted them to seek honor and immortality. How others viewed them was of utmost importance. The glory of battle, especially of victory, would bring them fame, and with fame came immortality—their names would live forever. In light of the responses at the dinner party, many succeeded in their quest. The glory won by Agamemnon and Achilles and the other classic heroes, vividly depicted in stories of action and daring, has lived for more than a thousand years and shows no sign of ever dying. Indeed, the Heroic Code of the day encouraged them to gain honor and glory enough to warrant inclusion in the epics of the poets. Homer, for one, sang of heroes in the *Iliad* and the *Odyssey.* How pleased the warriors would have been to know that their names would live on to the 21st century.

Worth noting about ancient, Heroic Code warriors, however, is that their deeds focused on self-advancement. They did not seek to help others. They sought to kill others, conquer their lands, enjoy their spoils. They fought with premeditated determination to gain praise and respect from their peers and their communities. This self-centered approach differs dramatically from the selfless approach of superheroes and of true heroes of today. While, of course, superheroes are melodramatic fabrications, they embody to a large degree the ideals of the true hero concept. Not to consider what they represent would be unwise. Clearly, they matter to us. We follow their exploits. We want to be them, to walk in their footsteps, to lead their lives. We know them. And we remember their names.

Superheroes, too, gain fame in their world, but not of their choosing. Bigger-than-life characters that they are, their deeds are bigger-than-life as well, and garner mass attention from media and community. Most superheroes, however, focus on others, not self, which separates them from Heroic Code warriors. They are heroes because they help the needy, the afflicted, and the victimized. They seek to safeguard and rescue, not conquer and kill. And, looking through a certain lens, their fame seems ironic, in that they devote themselves to anonymity in their life outside of costumes and weapons and supernatural powers.

True heroes of today differ in yet another way. Like superheroes, these people do not seek fame. They do not seek to place themselves before others. In most cases, they are thrown into danger without notice, and they respond with courage, vigor, and selflessness. They, too, seek to safeguard and rescue, not to conquer and kill. But while superheroes gain fame, the true heroes of today gain anonymity.

The name Rodger L. Parker probably does not sound familiar. A mailman in Germantown, Tennessee, he was driving home one afternoon in September 2003, when he witnessed an accident that sent a pickup truck into a river. A man and a woman were trapped inside and the truck was sinking fast. Without hesitation, Rodger ran from his vehicle and dove into the water. At the side of the truck, he pulled the woman free and hoisted her onto his back. The suction of the sinking pickup began to draw him under, but he fought against it and pulled the struggling man out as well, only seconds before the truck submerged completely. Rodger brought the couple to shore. Emergency crews arrived and, after assuring himself that the victims were safe, Rodger quietly returned to his vehicle and went home. He had not even left his name. It wasn't until the next day that his identity was discovered.

Likewise, the names Gary and Mary Jane Chauncey may not ring a bell, but that does not make them any less the heroes. Their story, like so many others, is noted for its bravery and selflessness. In 1993, they and their 11-year-old daughter, Andrea, wheelchair-bound with cerebral palsy, were involved in an Amtrak wreck in Louisiana. The train ended up in a river. As it was sinking, Gary and Mary Jane managed to squeeze their daughter out a narrow window to nearby rescuers. She was barely out when the train slipped into the depths of the water. Saving Andrea's life was their last act on this Earth.

The name Rick Rescorla, too, may not register. After the planes hit the World Trade Center in the tragedy of 9/11, Rick, a senior employee with Morgan Stanley, guided his colleagues out of the company's forty-fourth floor office in the south tower and helped to evacuate them from the building. With utter selflessness, he stayed poised and positive, committed to the safety of others. In the end, he sacrificed his own life. He might have made it out himself except that he stayed behind to look for three employees who were still unaccounted for. He wanted to be certain that all had escaped. The building collapsed around him. The

OTHER RECOGNIZABLE HEROES

Hector, Achilles, Odysseus, and Agamemnon are but four of thousands of recognizable heroes. Here are a few more who have carved their deeds into the minds of Americans and the world, with collective titles for some:

- European Explorers of the Renaissance: Including Ferdinand Magellan (Portuguese, sailed also for Spain), the first to circumnavigate the globe; Vasco da Gama (Portuguese), established the first trade route between Europe and India; Christopher Columbus (Italian, sailed for Spain and other countries), most notable (and perhaps most controversial) explorer to reach the Americas; Ponce DeLeon (Spanish), explored Florida and discovered the Gulf Stream; John Cabot (born in Italy, sailed for England), explored the North American continent; Marco Polo (Italian—pre-Renaissance), established routes and trade with China.

- Meriwether Lewis and William Clark: They forged a path across America.

- American Patriots: America has been blessed with heroes who have worked to establish and maintain a free country. To name just a few: Presidents George Washington, Thomas Jefferson, and Abraham Lincoln; Patrick Henry ("Give me liberty or give me death."); Nathan Hale ("I only regret that I have but one life to lose for my country.").

- Space Explorers: Those who have dared to investigate "the final frontier."

- G.I. Joe and G.I. Jane: The men and women of the U.S. armed forces who have fought for our country since its inception.

- Mother Teresa: With boundless energy and courage, single-handedly won the world's heart and showed how powerful an individual effort could be in fighting for the dignity of the disadvantaged.

company said later that all but six of 3,700 employees made it out that day. They credited Rick with saving their lives.

So, who are today's heroes? You may not recognize their names. But that is understandable, as anonymity helps to define the concept of hero in these best-of-times, worst-of-times days. Selfless, courageous, committed to helping others at a moment's notice, today's heroes do not seek fame. Perhaps their deeds are noted, but inevitably they face the challenge of fading memories. Perhaps they come from the ranks of the men and women of the armed forces, fighting to keep us free. Perhaps they rise from the battery of police officers and firemen and other emergency workers who serve as our last line of defense. But, most assuredly, they also emerge from the blunted background of our daily lives. They are the people next door, the men and women in line with us at the supermarket, the everyday neighbors at the bank and in the school pickup line, who blend into the landscape of the community. They are those who do not hesitate to risk their lives for others. At the next dinner party, we may not know their names when the question is asked. But we know who they are.

Starting Points and Conversation Pieces

- ❖ "What does it profit a man if he gains the whole world but loses his soul?" (Bible, Matthew 16:26.)

- ❖ "Do not use a cannon to kill a mosquito." (Confucius, 551–479 B.C.)

- ❖ "All the world's a stage, And all the men and women merely players." (William Shakespeare, *As You Like It,* II, vii.)

- ❖ "I think, therefore I am." (René Descartes, *Le Discourse de la Methode,* 1637.)

- ❖ "Don't one of you fire until you see the whites of their eyes." (William Prescott, at Bunker Hill, 1775.) (Also attributed to John Paul Jones.)

- ❖ "These are the times that try men's souls." (Thomas Paine, *The American Crisis,* 1776.)

- ❖ "I find that the harder I work, the more luck I seem to have." (Thomas Jefferson, 1743–1826.)

❖ "Glory is fleeting, but obscurity is forever." (Napoleon Bonaparte, 1769–1821.)

❖ "The reports of my death are greatly exaggerated." (Mark Twain, cable to the Associated Press, 1857.)

❖ "Of course America had often been discovered before Columbus, but it had always been hushed up." (Oscar Wilde, 1854–1900.)

❖ "I have nothing to offer but blood, toil, tears, and sweat." (Winston Churchill, 1940.)

❖ "Nuts." (U.S. General Anthony Clement McAuliffe, 101st Airborne Division, reply to German demand to surrender at Bastogne, Battle of the Bulge, 1944.)

❖ "Not everything that can be counted counts, and not everything that counts can be counted." (Albert Einstein, 1879–1955.)

❖ "You can lead a man to Congress, but you can't make him think." (Milton Berle, 1908–2002.)

❖ "The medium is the message." (Marshall McLuhan, *Understanding Media*, 1964.)

❖ "When you come to a fork in the road, take it." (Yogi Berra, 1925–).

❖ "I love you not only for what you are, but for what I am when I am with you. I love you not only for what you have made of yourself, but for what you are making of me." (Elizabeth Barrett Browning, 1806–1861.)

❖ "There are no facts, only interpretations." (Friedrich Nietzsche, 1844–1900.)

❖ "If you can dream it, you can do it." (Walt Disney, 1901–1966.)

❖ "A little learning is a dangerous thing." (Alexander Pope, "An Essay on Criticism.")

❖ "Because I could not stop for death, he kindly stopped for me." (Emily Dickinson, "The Chariot.")

❖ "I celebrate myself, and sing myself." (Walt Whitman, *Leaves of Grass*.)

❖ "Those who cannot remember the past are condemned to repeat it." (George Santayana, *The Life of Reason*.)

Resources for Further Exploration

READING

Quotations—General

Anderson, Peggy, and Michael McKee. *Great Quotes from Great Leaders*. Independence, Kentucky: Career Press—Thomson Learning, 1997.

Byrne, Robert. *The 2,548 Best Things Anybody Ever Said*. New York: Fireside, 2002.

Phrases and Clichés

Ammer, Christine. *Have a Nice Day—No Problem: A Dictionary of Clichés*. New York: Dutton, 1992.

Evans, Ivor H. *Brewer's Dictionary of Phrase and Fable*. New York: Harper-Collins, 1989.

Kipfer, Barbara Ann. *Roget's Thesaurus of Phrases*. New York: MJF Books, 2001.

Humor

Berra, Yogi. *The Yogi Book: "I Really Didn't Say Everything I Said."* New York: Workman, 1993.

Phillips, Bob. *Phillips' Book of Great Thoughts, Funny Sayings: A Stupendous Collection of Quotes, Quips, Epigrams, Witticisms, and Humorous Comments.* Carol Stream, Illinois: Tyndale House Publishers, 1993.

Sherrin, Ned. *The Oxford Dictionary of Humorous Quotations*. New York: Oxford University Press, 1995.

Wit and Wisdom

Grothe, Mardy. *Oxymoronica: Paradoxical Wit & Wisdom From History's Greatest Wordsmiths*. New York: HarperResource, 2004.

Reagan, Michael. *In The Words of Ronald Reagan: The Wit, Wisdom, and Eternal Optimism of America's 40th President*. Nashville: Nelson Books, 2004.

Wilde, Oscar. *Oscar Wilde's Wit and Wisdom: A Book of Quotations*. Mineola, New York: Dover, 1998.

Proverbs

Manser, Martin H., and Rosalind Fergusson. *The Facts on File Dictionary of Proverbs*. New York: Facts on File, 2002.

Titelman, Gregory Y. *Popular Proverbs and Sayings*. New York: Gramercy Books, 1996.

Mark Twain
Baetzhold, Howard G., and Joseph B. McCullough. *The Bible According to Mark Twain*. New York: Touchstone, 1996.
Twain, Mark. *Wit and Wisdom of Mark Twain: A Book of Quotations*. Mineola, New York: Dover, 1999.

Bible
Miner, Margaret, and Hugh Rawson. *A Dictionary of Quotations from the Bible*. New York: Penguin Meridian, 1988.

Chiasmus (Reversing Words in Parallel Phrases)
Grothe, Mardy. *Never Let a Fool Kiss You or a Kiss Fool You*. New York: Penguin, 2002.

Shakespeare
Schmidt, Alexander. *Shakespeare Lexicon and Quotation Dictionary: A Complete Dictionary of All the English Words, Phrases, and Constructions in the Works of the Poet*. Mineola, New York: Dover, 1971.

WEB SITES

Directories
http://dir.yahoo.com/Reference/quotations/—Yahoo Directory of Quotations.
http://www.bartleby.com/quotations/—Bartleby.com. Directory.

Quotations—General
http://www.bartleby.com/66/—The Columbia World of Quotations.
http://www.bartleby.com/63/—Simpson's Contemporary Quotations.
http://www.bartleby.com/73/—Respectfully Quoted. A Dictionary of Quotations.
http://quotations.about.com/?once=true&—About.com. Quotations.
http://www.cs.virginia.edu/~robins/quotes.html—Good Quotations by Famous People.
http://www.quoteworld.org/—QuoteWorld.
http://www.annabelle.net/—Annabelle's Quotation Guide.
http://www.geocities.com/SouthBeach/Tidepool/7853/quote.html—Mary's Favorite Quotes.
http://www.geocities.com/TimesSquare/Bridge/7796/—Gabrielle's Collected Quotes.

http://www.allthingswilliam.com/—Quotations by people named William.
http://www.creativequotations.com/—Creative Quotations.
http://scv.bu.edu/~aarondf/quotes.html—Aaron Fuegi's Collected Quotations.
http://www.quotations.usagreetings.com/cgi-bin/quote_index.cgi—USA Greetings Quotations Collection.
http://www.quoteshead.com/—QuoteHead.
http://www.great-quotes.com/— Great-Quotes.com.
http://www.cute-quote.com/—Cute-Quote.com.
http://www.memorablequotations.com/—Memorable Quotations.
http://www.coolquotescollection.com/—Cool Quotes Collection.
http://www.worldofquotes.com/—World of Quotes.
http://www.goodquotes.com/—GoodQuotes.com.
http://www.indianchild.com/QUOTATIONS%20PAGE.htm—Variety of quotations.
http://www.quotableonline.com/—Quotable Online.
http://www.famousquotes.com/—Famous Quotes.
http://www.aphids.com/quotes/—Quotations Archive.
http://www.quotegeek.com/—Quote Geek.
http://www.quotationscentral.com/—Quotations Central.
http://www.quotes-r-us.org/—Quotes R Us.
http://www.geocities.com/Athens/Oracle/6517/—Quotez 1.
http://www.quotations.co.uk/—Quotez 2 (British version).
http://www.quotemeonit.com/—Quote Me On It.
http://www.quoteslist.net/—QuotesList.

Math
http://math.furman.edu/~mwoodard/mquot.html—Mathematical Quotation Server.

Science
http://naturalscience.com/dsqhome.html/—Dictionary of Scientific Quotations.

Women
http://womenshistory.about.com/library/qu/blqulist.htm—Quotations by Notable Women.

Aphorisms
http://www.ag.wastholm.net/—Aphorisms Galore.

Wit, Wisdom, Humor
http://www.geocities.com/Heartland/Valley/3130/index.html—Wisdom Quotes.
http://www.brainyquote.com/—BrainyQuote.

http://www.tk421.net/quotes/—Witty, Thought-Provoking, and the Humorous.
http://www.boardofwisdom.com/—Board of Wisdom.
http://www.ari.net/cw/cw.html—Conventional Wisdom.
http://www.yuni.com/—Yuni Words of Wisdom.

Proverbs and Poems
http://www.cj.5c.com/—Gem of Proverbs and Poems.
http://www.oneliners-and-proverbs.com/—One-liners and Proverbs.

Friendship and Love
http://www.friendship.com.au/quotes/—Friendship Quotes.
http://www.cute-quotes-love-quotes-famous-quotes.com/—Cute Quotes, Love Quotes, Famous Quotes.

Advertising
http://advertising.utexas.edu/research/quotes/—Advertising Quotations.

Music
http://www.alphamedly.com/—Quotations: Finding the Music in Words.

Aviation
http://www.skygod.com/quotes/—Great Aviation Quotes.

Chiasmus
http://www.chiasmus.com/—Chiasmus. Reversal of words in parallel phrases.

Movies
http://us.imdb.com/Sections/Quotes/—Internet Movie Database—Movie quotes.

Literature
http://www.litquotes.com/—Quotations from literature.

Inspiration
http://www.toinspire.com/—Meant to inspire.

Quiz Answers

ANSWERS TO QUIZ #1 (P. 11)

1. b
2. c
3. d
4. d
5. b
6. a
7. c
8. c. (as of 2004, shares it with Red Auerbach—nine wins)

9. a
10. b. (Note: *La Joconde* is the French name of the painting *Mona Lisa*)
11. a
12. c
13. b

ANSWERS TO QUIZ #2 (P. 22)

1. "Separate but equal" laws
2. Sumerians (or Babylonians)
3. False. It should be "its."
4. Samuel Langhorne Clemens
5. ½ of the base × the height ($A = \frac{1}{2}bh$)
6. Darwin
7. Beethoven

8. The Preakness
9. False
10. Botticelli
11. Libido
12. Christianity
13. a mosquito

ANSWERS TO QUIZ #3 (P. 28)

1. *Brown v. Board of Education*
2. Alexander the Great
3. Spelling should be: stationery
4. Robert Frost
5. 180
6. (a)
7. Beethoven
8. Wilt Chamberlain
9. True
10. Michelangelo
11. Sublimation
12. (a)
13. soul

ANSWERS TO QUIZ #4 (P. 38)

1. State and federal governments
2. Constantine
3. Spelling should be: dessert
4. Walt Whitman
5. A right triangle
6. Medicine
7. Mozart
8. No thoroughbred horse won the Triple Crown in the 1980s.
9. (c)
10. Leonardo da Vinci
11. Freud
12. Islam
13. Thomas Paine

ANSWERS TO QUIZ #5 (P. 48)

1. The Civil War
2. Charlemagne
3. It should be "led" instead of "lead."
4. Emily Dickinson
5. Hypotenuse
6. Isaac Newton
7. e, g, b, d, f and f, a, c, e
8. Wayne Gretzky
9. Grass
10. Vincent van Gogh
11. Formal Operational Stage
12. India
13. Mark Twain

ANSWERS TO QUIZ #6 (P. 73)

1. 1929
2. Feudalism
3. (b)
4. Jane Austen
5. A triangle with at least two equal sides
6. Polio
7. Beethoven
8. Brett Favre
9. Nitrogen (N), Phosphorus (P), Potassium (K)
10. Renoir
11. Carl Jung
12. China
13. Winston Churchill

ANSWERS TO QUIZ #7 (P. 78)

1. U.S. Constitution
2. Hannibal
3. (c)
4. (b)
5. A triangle with no sides equal
6. The sun is the center of the universe.
7. Tchaikovsky
8. Nolan Ryan
9. (c)
10. Edvard Munch
11. Introvert
12. Sikhism
13. Albert Einstein

ANSWERS TO QUIZ #8 (P. 101)

1. The Bill of Rights
2. Pax Romana
3. (a)
4. Miguel de Cervantes
5. A=lw (length x width)
6. Johannes Kepler
7. Mozart
8. Cy Young
9. (b)
10. (d)
11. Desensitization
12. True
13. Marshall McLuhan

FIRST COLLEGES AND UNIVERSITIES

• The first college founded in America: Harvard College, Cambridge, Massachusetts, 1636.

• The first city college: College of Charleston, Charleston, South Carolina, 1770.

• The first state university (chartered): University of Georgia, Athens, Georgia, 1785 (did not open until 1801).

• The first state university (opened): University of North Carolina, Chapel Hill, North Carolina, 1795.

• The first land-grant university: Ohio University, Athens, Ohio, 1804.

• The first women's college: Mount Holyoke College, South Hadley, Massachusetts, 1836.

ANSWERS TO QUIZ #9 (P. 114)

1. On December 7, 1941, Japan bombed the U.S. base at Pearl Harbor, triggering U.S. entry into WW II.

2. Istanbul

3. "Irregardless" should be "Regardless," and "amount" should be "number."

4. (d) (Macbeth was a Scottish general.)

5. (b)

6. The Earth is the center of the universe.

7. Gilbert and Sullivan

8. Pete Sampras

9. (d)

10. Spain

11. Reinforcement

12. John F. Kennedy

13. Yogi Berra

ANSWERS TO QUIZ #10 (P. 118)

1. *Marbury v. Madison* (1803)

2. Athens and Sparta

3. Should be "a lot" not "alot"

4. Edgar Allen Poe

5. Archimedes

6. The structure of DNA

7. Norah Jones

8. Lance Armstrong

9. (b)

10. Impressionism

11. Maslow

12. Archbishop of Canterbury

13. Alexander Pope

Index

About the Author

Before entering the field of Education, Edward F. Droge, Jr., Ed.D., was a police officer in New York City. He earned his B.A. in English at Yale, graduated cum laude, and earned his master's and doctorate degrees at Harvard. He taught Expository Writing at Harvard and helped to launch three teacher education programs there. His academic articles have appeared in national and regional newspapers and journals. He has worked for 25 years as headmaster, teacher, and consultant at independent schools with programs ranging from Pre-Kindergarten to 12th grade. His national honors and distinctions include induction into the Cum Laude Society. Visit him at www.drdroge.com.